ArtsMoney

ArtsMoney

RAISING IT, SAVING IT, AND EARNING IT

Joan Jeffri

University of Minnesota Press · Minneapolis

First University of Minnesota Press printing, 1989

Published by the University of Minnesota Press
2037 University Avenue Southeast, Minneapolis, MN 55414.
Published simultaneously in Canada
by Fitzhenry & Whiteside Limited, Markham.
Printed in the United States of America.

Library of Congress Cataloging-in-Publication Data

Jeffri, Joan.
   Arts money : raising it, saving it, and earning it / Joan Jeffri.
     p. cm.
   Bibliography: p.
   Includes index.
   ISBN 0-8166-1798-8. 0-8166-1794-5 (pbk.)
    1. Arts fund raising. 2. Arts – Finance. 3. Arts – Management.
I. Title.
NX700.J4   1989   89-4805
700'.68'1 – dc19   CIP

For David Mathias, Joshua Hillel, and Anna Miriam

TABLE OF CONTENTS

PREFACE

Stretched between the eternal verities of art and money, arts groups — especially small and medium-sized ones, and those run close to the heartbeat of the artists themselves — often resemble the runner-in-place, trying desperately to learn savvy management techniques only to find them outmoded, no longer a draw for substantial funding, or simply the straw that breaks the manager's spirit as well as his or her back. This book, written for those managers and artists, and their companies, groups, collectives, cooperatives, and institutions, is about money. First, it is about what to do before money: how to consider and choose an organizational format that best suits the mission and purposes of the artists involved, and that allows money to be made and distributed in different ways. Thereafter, it is about obtaining money — raising it through traditional forms of grantsmanship in the private, public, and corporate sectors, making it through earned income activities including back interest and real estate, saving it by sharing costs and activities with other organizations, and understanding its potential in terms of the new technology. It is also a testimony to invention, to perseverance, and to the incredible amount of sweat equity of all those who labor in a field which, fortunately, exists because of the very personal contributions of its servants.

What have we learned in the last few years since this book was first published, years of scarcity in many ways for the arts and culture? We have learned that artists have a viable voice; we have seen them coalesce around rulings on expense deductions spelled out in the 1986 Tax Reform Act and, in concert with others, force the system to change. We have learned that while earned-income activities can help an organization gain greater control of its own destiny, they must be entered into judiciously, lest the institution earn income at the expense of its central mission, to serve the public. In rare cases, like those of the artists' space *and/or* in Seattle, we have learned that the bigger-is-better syndrome perpetuated by funding and other organizations can be eschewed by a group that has fulfilled its mission and chooses to close up shop and gently push its babes out of the nest to grow on their own. And we have learned, in a backhanded way, through concern by small businesses over non-profits' unrelated business income, that we have made a place for ourselves squarely between the profit and nonprofit sectors.

This book could not have been written without the faith and generosity of a number of artists and managers from both those sectors, who continually allow me to share their insights, their triumphs, and their difficulties in founding, managing, and perfecting their organizations. First, I would like to thank them. In Chapter Two I am especially indebted to the guidance and assistance of David White, Anne Focke, and Ted Crawford, who provided me a fuller picture of the organizations than I would have had alone.

I would also like to thank my colleagues at Columbia University, in particular Peter Smith, Dean of the School of the Arts, and Stephen Benedict, and my students, who never cease to be a source of challenge and healthy argument. Last, I would like to thank my family, both past and present, for their aid — my husband, for his continued encouragement, and my children, for their patience.

J. J.
January 1989

CHAPTER ONE

BEFORE MONEY

Management and Organization for Small Arts Groups

BACKGROUND

The American counterpart to European government subsidy of the arts is not, as many think, the National Endowment for the Arts plus a collective body of state and local arts councils. It is the tax law. Since the early part of the century United States tax law has provided certain kinds of institutions, and the people and agencies that offer contributions and donations to these institutions, with a set of incentives for giving to the arts. The most usual mechanism for capitalizing on these incentives is organization of the arts institution as a not-for-profit corporation.[1] While this mechanism, particularly when coupled with the sanction of tax exempt status by the federal government, has allowed arts groups to receive a substantial portion of their income from government, corporate and private sources, it has not been without its price.

With the proliferation of small arts institutions beginning in the 1950s, nonprofit incorporation became synonymous with a set of values and procedures that were decidedly non-commercial: experimentation, creative risk taking, the creation of an atmosphere where artists and institutions had the "right to fail," and support of artists whose work could not necessarily compete in the commercial marketplace. The growth of regional and local organizations, an increase in audiences, the labor-intensive nature of these groups, and constant increases in costs gave rise to operations that were run with larger and larger deficit budgets. A steady maturation process where creative concerns took precedence over financial ones was influenced both by economics and by new audiences. On the one hand, in some organizations costs simply got out of hand; organizations were no longer made suddenly solvent by a board member with a personal check. On the other hand, so much time had been spent cultivating

---

[1]Throughout this book, the terms not-for-profit and nonprofit are used interchangeably.

3

new audiences for the arts it was often difficult, if not impossible, not to pay some heed to their tastes. Problems of facility maintenance made survival even more difficult for arts institutions that had been the recipients of popular donations for bricks and mortar in the 1960s; by the 1980s, many had difficulty paying for oil and electricity. As for the work created, in many cases the "products" of the not-for-profit arts institutions looked perilously like the products of the commercial marketplace. In fact, many nonprofit products ended up in commercial terrain and some nonprofit groups were even accused of starting out with a commercial market in mind.

While nonprofit arts institutions have been reassessing their goals and, in some cases, changing the emphases of their activities, donors have also been undergoing a change. Philanthropy has moved from contribution to investment, and donors want involvement in any number of ways in the direction their money takes. While the bulk of donative responsibility in this country rests with individuals, who still account for over 80 percent of the contributions to not-for-profit institutions, one result of the 1981 Economic Recovery Tax Act may be that those individuals will come from a different economic sector.*

While the intention of the 1981 ERTA was to stimulate private institutions to take more responsibility for nonprofit organizations than they have done in the past, the Act may be doing just the reverse. It has been projected by the Urban Institute in Washington, D.C. that, while charitable giving will continue to increase in absolute terms simply because personal income will continue to increase, it will be reduced by $10 billion in constant dollar terms and $18 billion in actual dollar terms between 1981 and 1984 (as compared with what would have happened if the 1981 Tax Act had not been enacted). At the same time, the Act will help to shift the distribution of contributions from higher income to lower and middle income donors. The nonprofit world is also bound to suffer from the significant federal budget cuts of the Reagan Administration. The Urban Institute study suggests a decline of nonprofit revenues from federal sources of $27.3 billion in current dollars over the 1981–84 period.[2] Corporate, foundation, and

---

*While seeking contributions from individual donors is eminently important to the health of most arts organizations, a description of such practices and strategies would require another book. Therefore, such subjects as bequests, estate gifts, and deferred giving are not within the scope of this book.

[2]Charles T. Clotfelter and Lester M. Salamon, *The Federal Government and the Nonprofit Sector: The Impact of the 1981 Tax Act on Individual Charitable Giving* (Washington, D. C.: The Urban Institute, 1981), pp. 26–27.

estate contributions may also be reduced, even with such incentives as a change in the amount of money corporations may deduct from profits for charitable donations—from 5 percent to 10 percent. (It is well known that corporate money to the arts comes from a small number of corporations and that most corporations in the past have not neared even the previous 5 percent level.)

Institutions may not even be able to maintain existing activity levels, particularly if reduction or withdrawal of foundation and corporate monies accompanies the federal cuts. According to Charles T. Clotfelter and Lester M. Salamon, two sets of factors have yet to show how severely nonprofit organizations will be affected:

> The first set of factors concerns the way nonprofit organizations themselves respond. At a minimum, these organizations will have to renew their attention to careful management and efficient operations, though the savings available from this quarter are far from clear. Beyond this, changes will be needed in basic fund-raising techniques to adjust to the decline in available federal resources and the projected increase in the share of individual giving to be borne by lower- and middle-income persons.[3]

The second set of factors will depend on the reaction of the "public at large." If certain past behavioral patterns of giving can be changed in these new economically stringent circumstances, the struggle for survival might not be quite as difficult as projected. Nevertheless, the difficulty will be, as always, what kind of a struggle it is. ". . . [C]are must be taken to make sure that the struggle for survival does not undermine the very qualities that make the nonprofit sector so important and unique."[4]

Other effects, such as the impending change in postal rates for nonprofit organizations are still to be determined.[5] The total impact of the 1981 Economic Recovery Tax Act has yet to be assessed.

Whatever stringencies are ascribed to arts organizations in general can be magnified ten- or twenty-fold for small and emerging arts groups. Even with the best of public intentions such as those expressed in the Spring of 1982 by National Endowment for the Arts Chairman Frank Hodsoll about the Endowment's general commitment to small organizations, it is questionable how much support

---

[3]Ibid., p. 31.

[4]Ibid., p. 32.

[5]Several tax recommendations made by the Presidential Task Force on the Arts and Humanities in October 1981 have been largely ignored.

those groups will really get, particularly if they seek money singly and not in consortia. Nevertheless, the responsiveness to individual artistic needs and disciplines that has characterized the National Endowment for the Arts and many state art councils will still make public money attractive, both for its cash value and for the accompanying validation.

While the corporate sector is not taking the place of decreasing public support, arts groups are getting more sophisticated in approaching business for gifts in cash and in kind. Loans and donations include executives' expertise, photocopying machines and old furniture as well as money, space, and publicity. Neither are private foundations filling the gap. Many have already curtailed their involvement in the arts. And the ones that have continued support, such as some of the smaller, family-run foundations, frequently have specific arts interests.

In the 1980s distinctions between the profit and nonprofit sectors are harder to recognize than ever before. Inflation, a new administration, and the realization by many groups that the not-for-profit mechanism has its own set of rules, restrictions, and punishments have served to stir up the entrepreneurial blood of many artists and managers. The old prerequisites of artistic control at the possible expense of financial solvency have given way to a desire for self-sufficiency—a break-even budget *and* artistic control. The commercial marketplace is no longer necessarily the villain in the plot; for some, the marketplace both validates the group wishing to obtain a wider audience and provides income necessary for survival. The creation of for-profit subsidiary corporations by nonprofit arts groups, the sale of an institution's air rights, and the development and sale of work for the new technological marketplace are all examples of this development in the arts. The focus on raising money has begun to shift toward a concentration on making money. The words "for profit" have crept back into the arts vocabulary in places other than the Broadway theatre, network television, the blockbuster novel, and the Hollywood movie, as groups of all sizes and all disciplines search for more flexible structures of organization and support.

Some argue that experimental and avant-garde groups could not survive in the profit arena, that they simply could not get an audience to pay the necessary ticket price to view work that is as yet unvalidated and on the cutting edge of society and of art. Nevertheless, some avant-garde groups are amassing income through various subsidiary corporations they have created to provide services that relate to their function and mission.

Whether these groups could have survived until now as profit corporations is questionable; part of the reason they have been able to "sell" these new services is due to the reputation they have built up over the last five, ten, or fifteen years. Their entry into the profit arena has given many of them pause—it has created a great deal of ambivalence that has at its root the basic fact that this country does not value or support art to any meaningful degree when compared with the subsidized systems of Europe. This sad but true fact is not likely to change within the foreseeable future. Entry into the "marketplace" has given other groups a real taste for survival; it has seemed "cleaner" than bending their purposes to fit the requirements of a funding agency and less complex than the whole procedure of grantsmanship.

In some instances, arts groups are turning to each other in lieu of alliances with the world of commerce and trade. The sharing of materials, production facilities, financing schemes, and information is providing them with some tactics for dealing with a loss of traditional sources of funding. Besides providing financial help, such sharing may also provide them with psychological and emotional support; it reminds them that their problems do not exist in a vacuum and it reaffirms their artistic struggle. While many art forms are collaborative, their collaboration does not extend beyond rehearsal, performance, or exhibition. Companies often hold their individuality and their poverty with the same hands. Collaborative management across companies, when many groups have just discovered formal management in the first place, is a new idea. While some groups do not embrace it willingly, others recognize its potential for helping them survive.

The 1960s was an era of largesse—money for buildings, programming, educational activities, pilot projects. It gave way to the 1970s, a decade of expansion—through audience development, marketing strategies, fund-raising sophistication, and geographic dissemination of programs through touring, residencies, local support, minority group work, and grassroots offerings. The largesse and expansion of the last two decades has come to an abrupt halt in the 1980s—a time that promises retrenchment, reevaluation, and new survival strategies. Any study that attempts to address those strategies would be an irresponsible one were it not to issue at the very outset a kind of warning: many schemes that are developed to save our companies and institutions in the arts have nothing to do with art at all. Their concerns may be urban revitalization, product use and development, the lessening of bureaucratic overhead, investment returns, or loan packages, but their primary purposes are not art, culture, or even those other areas such as social services, human resources, advocacy, education, or the quality of life which several decades of public funding have conditioned us to associate with the arts. Their primary purpose is money. Making it, saving it, raising it, and using it. The examples in this book are to be looked at, then, for their money potential; the kind of "art" they produce is not at issue here.

With this warning in mind, arts groups will be able to better negotiate their futures. If they can survive the transition this decade will require—and many will not—it is possible that they will be more financially independent than ever before and much better prepared to define their artistic priorities in financial, as well as creative, terms.

FROM PERSONALITIES TO INSTITUTIONS

People who create arts institutions usually care profoundly about their work, and whatever our consumer-oriented society might view as their "product" is something they may regard as an extension of themselves. Indeed, the founders of such groups are often artists who agree to take on administrative responsibilities in order to get the group off the ground and into some viable organizational form. Such founders possess a tenacity, perseverance, strength of purpose and commitment that sustain them at the group's inception—indeed, are the very reasons for the group's creation—but frequently are resented later on. Business managers are fond of saying that arts groups must learn to move from "personalities to institutions"; most often they mean that the founder has to be able to let go of the institution, to delegate responsibility to others, even if it means training them to assume these responsibilities. Too often the institution resides in his or her brain alone and its future may depend on the fate or whim of this singular individual.

For the founder/artistic director who recognizes only too well the perils of not "letting go" of the institution so that a business manager can share the burdens, there is the opposite danger of a complete "hands-off" policy. In this case, the founder/artistic director stays so far away from the business manager that the latter is asked to manage what amounts to chaos, a situation in which no artistic goals have been articulated and no framework provided within which anyone can work.

Single leadership, often by the organization's founder, is common to small arts groups. In dance, this phenomenon is evidenced by the fact that the names of many companies are the names of their founder/directors—Jose Limon Dance Company, Pearl Lang and Dancers, Lar Lubovitch Dance Company. When such groups begin, most consist of a founder/director and a few dancers. As they expand their repertoires to include works by other choreographers, some members form profound and lasting attachments to their charismatic leader. Such attachments can cause company members to treat that leader as a parent figure, confidant, guru, and therapist, as well as an artistic director. For an artistic director who encourages this, the organizational format that may best suit his or her purposes will be the one that allows for the greatest autonomy—in programming, decision-making, financing, and creative time. As the institution becomes more complex, the founder may relinquish some autonomy over business matters in order to retain it in artistic matters. Leadership then becomes shared.

Shared leadership implies company rule by two (or occasionally more than two) people, one of whom is responsible for artistic decisions, the other for business matters. Although these positions may exist eventually on an equal basis, in the early stages of small arts groups the business manager's function is to make it possible for the artistic director to do his or her work by creating a sound support structure. In certain institutions—some artists spaces, for example—it is common to have an administrator at the helm providing a base for a number of program people or "curators" who function as ad hoc artistic directors.

Some small groups appear to be "board directed" since the members of the board are artist members of the group and the board functions as the main decision-making unit. Chamber music groups frequently have a board composed of players; when the group is a corporation, players sometimes function as corporate officers as well. While such boards may encourage some narrowness of perspective and lack of objectivity about the group, they provide the group with tremendous artistic freedom. In a group where the artistic director is also the founder and cannot find the finances or does not wish to share leadership with a business manager, the development of the board is one alternative to ease the artistic director's load. Nevertheless, fear of a board that can hire and fire managerial personnel—specifically the artistic director—has often forced arts groups to make organizational choices to avoid board domination.

Artistic control is of paramount importance to the emerging arts group, particularly in the formative stages. It is likely that the original intent of the group grew out of the artists' helplessness in trying to work within already established systems, institutions, and markets.

Artistic control and the resultant artistic satisfaction artist members get from having a definite say in organizational, financial, managerial, and artistic matters are important enough to make many group members forego decent salaries, benefits, and even personal comforts.

The type of shared management that perhaps best expresses this desire for artistic control and individual fulfillment is the cooperative. The cooperative, sometimes called the self-governed arts organization, is based on the one-vote one-person concept where all major decisions are subject to a majority vote of the artist members. In the 1950s some theatre groups formed cooperatives (at least in spirit) that were extremely communal in nature, where the work itself grew out of a constant joint exploration of material, where the life style of the participants was often closely tied to the process of development. The Living Theatre, Judith Malina and Julian Beck's theatre, began as early as 1947, Joseph Chaikin's Open Theatre and Richard Schechner's Performance Group came later.

At the same time, a group of cooperative galleries was formed on Tenth Street between Third and Fourth Avenues in Manhattan where gallery maintenance and show-sitting were shared and artists paid fees from their own pockets to keep the organizations solvent. In the 1970s a resurgence of cooperatives in the visual arts evolved and new galleries sprang up around the country, in Europe, Canada, Australia, and Israel. They were joined by a number of media collectives including the Videofreex and Global Village in New York, and Johnny Videotape in California.

Among music cooperatives were the London Symphony Orchestra, the American Symphony Orchestra (which was reorganized as a cooperative after Leopold Stokowski's departure in 1972), the Atlanta Chamber Orchestra, and the Orpheus Chamber Ensemble. In the 1970s, English theatre saw the formation of the short-lived cooperative, the Actors' Company, with actor Ian McKellan as a major participant.

The cooperative is not limited by art form, but a sampling of the kinds of issues over which artists have control should indicate the boundaries by which they previously felt restricted. For performers there are concerns of repertoire, personnel (including conductors and directors), programming, salaries, rehearsal time and pay, publicity, and scheduling. In an effort to ensure truly fair representation by each member, burdensome voting procedures often ensue. In some music groups there is a core group of musicians for every piece to be played. This core group is responsible for pre-rehearsing a specific piece of music, looking over the scores, delineating general questions of interpretation, and proposing a concert master for the piece who generally stays with that piece throughout its life in the group's repertoire. Final choice of the concert master for a specific piece may result from a full membership vote or the piece may remain "conductor-less."

To avoid the often painful and impersonal audition process of establishment institutions, some cooperative music groups require a potential player to play with the group for a number of months before becoming a member. Musicianship is not the only issue in this arrangement; how well a particular player integrates with the group as a member of the cooperative is also important.

In theatre, sometimes it is the making of the work itself that is cooperative. In the case of the Actors' Company in England, attempts were made to be "cooperative" in the one-person one-vote sense and to recreate the Elizabethan atmosphere of a true repertory company where an actor played the lead one night and a servant the next.

In the visual arts, cooperative galleries have tried to avoid resemblances to the commercial gallery where decisions of hanging, lighting, scheduling, exhibition, publicity, and the selection, placement, and price of a work are determined by the dealer. There is a major concern with showing rather than selling. Indeed, there is constant debate over whether it is legal to sell work on the premises if the group is organized as a not-for-profit corporation (general practice has it that it is illegal).

While written rules and by-laws of cooperatives usually provide detailed instructions for the acceptance of new members, the removal of a member is always a difficult matter, particularly due to the democratic nature of the organization. Additionally, if members share administrative and maintenance duties of the organization, one criterion for selection may be their geographic proximity to the actual home base, or, in the case of groups that tour and perform or exhibit in a variety of spaces, a criterion may be the artist's ability to travel over extended periods of time.

While many cooperatives are "manager-run" in the sense that they hire a manager from outside or from within the group, it is clear from the start that the manager works for the group. In no way are artists "employees" of the manager and when the manager is a group member as well, he or she shares artistic concerns.

The choice of management is also, quite realistically, an economic one. When a group is small and just starting out, the person who agrees to organize, finance, and manage the operation is often the same one who sweeps the floor and sends out announcements for the next event, all the while subsidizing the organization through personal funds. As the organization grows, the founder deserves at least a living wage, enough so that the "other" job that has been sustaining the organization since its inception can be given up. As the organization continues to grow and the first real money for salaries comes in, a conflict may arise between paying those artists who have stuck with the founder from the start, working for nothing, supporting and maintaining the organization, or paying someone to become "management," who will try to bring in more money for greater salaries all round.

Of course, it is often several years before an organization can afford the luxury to take stock of its activities and make a management choice. Nonetheless, the search to be better managed is a mandate propounded by funding sources as well as the groups themselves. This process of making a management choice can also aid in revitalizing a group. It can help the group to rearticulate its artistic policies to its board members, its managers, and its publics; to reinvest the rhetoric of its early enthusiasm with the wisdom of its painful adolescence; to measure how far it can go by how far it has come; and to choose—more selectively than it chose when the organization was founded—to make management work for it, not as medicine for the future, but as strategy for survival.

METHODS OF ORGANIZATION

Whether an arts group is managed by one or several leaders, by its board, or by its artist members, it must choose a form of organization if it wishes to operate as a business on the simplest level—for example, to open a bank account. No one form is better than any other in and of itself, but certain forms are more appropriate for certain kinds of activities and if a beginning group can determine at least some of those activities through setting down its goals and objectives, it may be better able to evaluate which organizational format to choose.

It should be remembered, too, that while forms of organization do not necessarily reflect anything about the work an organization produces, there are those who believe the contrary. Zelda Fichandler, founder and producing director of the Arena Stage, can say ". . . being nonprofit does not really define us—our goals, our aims, our aesthetic, our achievements. What defines us, measures us, is our capacity to produce art."[6] Nevertheless, there are those who believe that nonprofit incorporation and/or the acquisition of federal tax exempt status legitimizes an institution in the same way federal and state grants have done in the past, and that an institution's "capacity to produce art" is very definitely connected to its capacity to obtain what it interprets as state and federal sanction. Similarly, certain banks are loath to enter into agreements with groups that are not incorporated.

While the generally accepted method of organization for emerging arts groups has been not-for-profit incorporation, there are other possibilities that may better allow a group time to develop its artistic products without the legal and administrative burdens that form requires. Indeed, the whole not-for-profit mechanism is currently under question by certain arts groups that now face dissolution and need some instruction in dissolution procedures.

An emerging group should carefully consider not only the purposes of its organization, but the best possible ways for it to financially sustain and fulfill those purposes. Not-for-profit does not mean a group makes no money; it simply means that any profit (or surplus, in nonprofit parlance) goes back into the operation of the organization. In this sense, most emerging groups are not-for-profit in intent whether or not they are formally incorporated.[7] But there are other organizational options available to them.[8]

---

[6]Zelda Fichandler, "The Long Revolution," in *1978 TCG Conference Report*, ed. Arthur Ballet and Lindy Zesch (New York: Theatre Communications Group, 1978), p. 16.

[7]Some funding agencies, like the New York State Council on the Arts, do not require not-for-profit incorporation as an eligibility requirement for grants. Groups with not-for-profit intent can file the Charities Registration form with the state instead.

[8]Since rules and regulations for the following organizational forms may vary from state to state, it is wise to check on a case-by-case basis. For those interested in further information, three publications in the bibliography address subjects in greater detail: *An Organizational Manual for Chamber Ensembles, The New York Not-for-Profit Organization Manual,* and *Non-Profit Corporations, Organizations, and Associations.* All three publications provided valuable information for this chapter. Unless otherwise stated, examples in this chapter pertain to the laws in New York State.

Sole Proprietorship

The most common form of organization for the artist who works mostly on an erratic, free-lance basis is the sole proprietorship. In certain disciplines, like modern dance, economic realities have contributed to a tremendous rise in solo repertory and work that is modular and easy to travel—solos, duets with a partner, and workshops. If an artist does business under his or her own name, there is no documentation required to become a sole proprietor; however, when the artist acts on behalf of his or her business, all personal assets are at risk—in other words, the artist has unlimited liability whereby business assets and personal assets are not distinguished.

Small groups that give occasional performances are often organized on this basis. Profits are simply divided up among performers and should be reported as income on individual federal tax return forms. Depending on the state, unincorporated business income tax may be imposed on the sole proprietor. Since sole proprietors are self-employed, they can establish personal Keogh or HR-10 retirement plans in which they put away up to 15 percent of their annual income up to $10,000, tax-free, until retirement. Individual Retirement Accounts are also available to any individual with deposits of up to $2,000 annually, tax-free, until retirement.[9]

Individual artistic control is at a maximum in the sole proprietorship, and documentation at a minimum. This is particularly useful for the young artist who does not yet understand the implications and requirements of other kinds of organization.

Unincorporated Association

Unincorporated association is a form of organization that many small arts groups should consider before they explore not-for-profit incorporation. It is, unfortunately, a form that too many groups know too little about, having grown up with the rhetoric of the 1960s when many groups incorporated as nonprofit organizations without knowing why. Rhoda Grauer, Director of Media Development for the

---

[9]While retirement plans are mentioned throughout this chapter, it is merely as an indication that retirement provisions can be made under any of these organizational formats. A more thorough, personalized exploration would be in order for any individual or group adopting one of these methods of organization.

American Ballet Theatre and former director of the Dance Program at the National Endowment for the Arts, parodies this rather sad situation:

> I used to do a little routine about a dancer coming to New York City and saying, "Hello, I'm here. For two days I've been a dancer—I'd like to be a choreographer now." And the reply to the dancer was, "Well, let me take you to Volunteer Lawyers for the Arts. They'll write up your not-for-profit tax-exempt status papers; we'll then take you to the New York State Council on the Arts, you'll get that application. Borrow $50 from your mother, fly to Washington, D.C., get your application from the National Endowment for the Arts."[10]

An unincorporated association may develop a set of rules, regulations, by-laws, articles of association, and oral or written agreements without any government or other approval. Membership may change without the group dissolving, and the group may be affiliated with an umbrella organization or a sponsoring institution which may serve as a conduit for funds. No statutory rules apply to the formation or operation of an unincorporated association, but there are restrictions on holding property, and on suing and being sued. Since it is not recognized as a legal entity its individual members are liable for actions that are taken by the group. Although such groups can be taxed as corporations or partnerships, often individual members declare their income from the association as self-employed income on their individual tax returns.

An unincorprated association can receive donations. It can also apply for federal tax-exempt status under the Internal Revenue Service Code section 501 (c) (3). (This may, however, be more difficult to obtain than for a not-for-profit corporation.) One advantage of this tax-exempt status is that organizations that have it are immediately recognized by donors to have proven they are organized for religious, charitable, educational, scientific, or literary purposes, and donations are deductible from the donor's taxes.[11] If an organization does not have federal tax-exempt status under IRS Code section 501 (c) (3), the "burden of proof" rests with the donor.

It should be noted that here rests an enormous possibility for

[10]Joan Jeffri, *The Emerging Arts: Management, Survival, and Growth* (New York: Praeger, 1980), p. 136.

[11]For further discussion of federal tax exemption, see the last part of this chapter.

change. It might be possible for a small arts group to exist as an unincorporated association, to receive donations, and to print in its programs of public events something like this: "We are registered with the state Charities Registration Bureau. You may obtain copies of our tax returns from that organization or from our offices and all contributions will be gratefully accepted." Donors might then take personal deductions for such a contribution off their income tax as they would with a donation to a 501 (c) (3) organization, and use the printed program as proof.[12]

The advantages of organizing as an unincorporated association, especially at the beginning stages of a small group, are many. First, it remains unincorporated. Once a group has become incorporated it becomes an entity that has, in a sense, a life of its own, a legal life that becomes difficult and sometimes cumbersome to change or abolish. Second, the unincorporated association offers a large degree of flexibility of operation, particularly important to a group of people with a strong commitment to work together but whose specific purposes have not been well defined or tested. Third, the time-consuming, sometimes expensive process of incorporation may not provide the benefits the group thinks it needs.

For example, an unincorporated association has the ability to enter into agreements on leases or contracts just as a nonprofit corporation does and there is little reason to think that a landlord will look more kindly on a newly organized nonprofit corporation than on an unincorporated association. The limited liability that a nonprofit corporation would provide is worthless in this case since the corporation is so new there are probably no assets. Additionally, being not-for-profit does not automatically bring with it the federal tax-exempt status that many mistakenly think it does. Federal tax-exempt status is a separate procedure and, as previously stated, can be obtained by an unincorporated association as well as a nonprofit corporation. Third and last, the dissolution procedure of an unincorporated association depends on the original contractual relationship—a more flexible procedure than that used for not-for-profit corporations. Termination is usually through the consent of the membership when its purposes have been "achieved or abandoned."[13]

---

[12]Discussion with Leonard Easter, Volunteer Lawyers for the Arts, 16 June 1981.

[13]Harry G. Henn and Michael George Pfeifer, "Nonprofit Groups: Factors Influencing Choice of Form," *Wake Forest Law Review*, 11 (June 1975): 194.

As in the sole proprietorship, the unincorporated association may be responsible for state unincorporated business income tax and, if individuals consider themselves self-employed, they are eligible for the same retirement plans as the sole proprietor.

While artistic control rests solely with the members of an unincorporated association, this organizational form is as important for what it does *not* do as for what it does: it does *not* lock the arts group into a set of restrictive, specific, operational, legally binding prerequisites in its early stages of development.

Partnerships

Unlike the previous modes of organization, a partnership is a legal entity even though a written agreement is not always required. While they may need to file a certificate of doing business if using a name for the business other than their own, partners are not considered employees of any organization since they are supposed to be paid through profits accrued.

GENERAL PARTNERSHIP A general partnership is the joining together of two or more people in a business where the profits will be equally shared among the partners, unless otherwise specified. Profits are shared, however, only after expenses have been paid. Partnership income must be reported to the federal government and declared as income on individual returns, but the partnership itself pays no federal taxes; it may, however, be subject to state unincorporated business income tax, franchise and other state taxes. The for-profit organization of the business allows partners the distinct advantage of deducting from their tax returns any losses incurred by the business.

If partnership members are self-employed, they can establish Keogh, HR-10, or IRA retirement plans. Each partner is personally liable and if any one of them dies or leaves the group, the partnership automatically dissolves. To avoid constant reorganization, written agreements can be drawn up to ensure continuity; in performing groups where members regularly leave and are replaced, this is particularly important.

Small music ensembles that play together and evenly split the profits after expenses are paid may find they are general partners should they wish to open a bank account in the name of the ensemble. They may treat the fees of guest artists, even if equal in amount to each partner's share, as an expense to be deducted before profits are paid out.

LIMITED PARTNERSHIP   A limited partnership is a partnership with one or more general partners who manage the business and may invest in the enterprise, and one or more limited partners who usually provide most if not all of the capital. All the partners own the business and profits are shared according to the limited partnership agreement which also describes "the character of the business, the amount of the investors' contributions, the names and addresses of the limited partners, and the name and location of the business."[14] While the *general* partners in this agreement are liable for their investment and their personal assets, the *limited* partners are liable only up to the amount of their investment. This, and the possibility of deducting any losses from personal income tax, make the limited partnership an attractive investment. While used routinely for mounting Broadway productions, the limited partnership is just beginning to be explored by emerging arts groups.

The limited partnership has many advantages of the corporation but without certain of the administrative difficulties. For example, while the limited partnership is formed by agreement and requires the group to file and publish notice through the state, it does not require a long approval process by various state agencies. More important is the potential for making money. The not-for-profit corporation, as its name implies, cannot pass any corporate surplus not spent on that year's operation to anything except the continuing operation of the organization. While this may be a system that all members are happy with, it means that the only remuneration members or employees can get is in the form of salaries and wages, and payment for services rendered.

Without being taxed, a limited partnership is able to pass on the profits of a successful venture (a record, for a small music group, for example) to individual members. If the organization becomes very successful in a short period of time and reaches another level of operation, the surplus from its activities will not be restricted on a contractual basis as is the case in the not-for-profit corporation, but can be passed on to the individual members/participants/artists. The limited partnership also might be a good tool for an emerging organization

---

[14]Lillian Helman, *An Organizational Manual for Chamber Ensembles* (New York: Chamber Music America, 1981), p. 7.

that has been unsuccessful at the start but is willing to try to be commercially successful and hopes to take the surplus for individual purposes.

Not-for-profit off-off-Broadway theatres transferring plays to Broadway have entered into the limited partnership agreement in the following way: the off-off-Broadway theatre has the rights to a particular play which it then licenses to a limited partnership. In exchange for that licensing, the off-off Broadway theatre gets an up front fee and a percentage of the gross. These terms are negotiable and there are those in off-off Broadway theatre who feel sorely disadvantaged in such negotiations since it is the Broadway producer, as general partner, who usually determines what the off-off Broadway theatres will get (sometimes called their "fair share"). On the other hand, the boards of directors of some off-off-Broadway theatres are loath to let their theatres actually invest in the limited partnership because their assets are liable and they might jeopardize their not-for-profit tax exempt status.

Obviously, there are exceptions. The Plumstead Theatre Company, originating in California, was recently general partner in a production with the Kennedy Center in Washington, D.C. While state laws differ in terms of what is legally allowable in such arrangements, the fact that the Plumstead Theatre Company was in league with a large and impressive cultural center allowed it to set such a precedent.[15] Another exception is Joseph Papp who frequently can mobilize enough private capital to allow the New York Shakespeare Festival to produce on Broadway. (LuEsther T. Mertz's $500,000 contribution helped underwrite *A Chorus Line*.) Papp's uncanny business acumen has thus far allowed him to operate without the kind of intervention by the Internal Revenue Service that other nonprofit theatres might be subject to were they to try the same activities.

The most apparent incentive for the limited partnership is the potential for profit for private individuals—a possibility that not-for-profit incorporation does not allow.

Umbrellas, Conduits, Host Institutions, Sponsors

Organizations that agree to legally take on a sponsorship role for arts groups may do so in several ways, but the categories of umbrella, con-

---

[15]See Chapter III for further discussion of this particular area.

duit, host institution, and sponsor are not legal forms of organization. Each of these will be organized formally and legally in some way—as a not-for-profit corporation, for example. These categories are included as another option for small arts groups that wish to organize under some other organization's structure. One advantage of doing this, particularly in the early stages of a group's development, is that it may avoid duplication of services and may prevent setting in motion more legal entities than are really necessary for the accomplishment of the group's goals.

UMBRELLAS   An umbrella organization is one that offers a kind of protection to groups by taking over certain administrative and production duties. The groups themselves are often organized as separate entities (many as not-for-profit corporations) while the umbrella organization is organized as a separate entity as well. The Public Theatre in New York has been an umbrella for experimental writing and music groups, for avant-garde companies like Mabou Mines; it has provided space, administrative time and help, production facilities, and even more. Dance Umbrella, a not-for-profit production organization begun in 1975, sponsored performances by a number of companies (usually ten) in a New York theatre each season. Not only did it aid in mounting the productions but it provided the companies with a collective auspice, helpful to them in visibility, publicity, fund-raising and audience development.[16] An artists space in Seattle, *and/or*, acts as an umbrella for projects that often develop in response to needs and ideas of the artist community; it tries to nurture these projects through their developmental stages until they can become independent entities.[17]

CONDUITS   A conduit is an organization that agrees to accept (and sometimes apply for) funds for another organization or individual. The usual reason for using a conduit is that the conduit possesses the federal tax-exempt status that many funding sources require when donating money to arts groups or individuals. Conduit organizations sometimes provide financial and management services. The Cultural

---

[16]The lack of a permanent performance space for Dance Umbrella has given it a very perilous existence over the last few years and, at the time of this writing, activities have been suspended.

[17]One grant proposal in Chapter II is from *and/or* and illustrates this point. The name of the group is italicized to provide easier reading.

Council Foundation in New York City has been a conduit for organizations that agree to avail themselves of its management services for a small fee.

Universities and colleges can act as conduits, sometimes when a group member is also on the school faculty, sometimes when the university itself is a host institution. If the conduit is attempting to obtain grants and contributions from the same sources as the arts group, such a sponsoring relationship may be short-lived.

Individual artists have an additional problem. Certain funding agencies require individuals to have tax-exempt status under the IRS Code Section 501 (c) (3) so that the donor can deduct the contribution from his or her taxes. Individuals cannot obtain such status on their own, so they must ally themselves with some organization in order to obtain contributions of this nature. Dance Theater Workshop in New York City will accept contributions for member artists as a "member project fee"; it then acknowledges the donor's contribution as a "restricted contribution" and takes a four percent service charge from the artist. It will not perform this service, however, for state or federal grant monies since it does not wish to accept responsibility for the money and its dispersal, only to act as a conduit for the artists involved. In 1980–1981 DTW passed through $50,000 worth of these gifts.[18]

HOSTS A host institution is one which, in exchange for allowing an arts group to be in residence for a certain period of time (from a few days to time over several years), benefits from a variety of group services—performances, exhibitions, workshops, classes, lectures, even tours. The host may sponsor one, none, or all of the above kinds of activities, but will usually provide in-kind support in the form of space for rehearsal and performance or exhibition, administrative and public relations help, publicity, mailing lists, and an audience. Host institutions vary from colleges and universities to "museums, churches, shopping centers, radio stations, banks, theaters, retirement communities,"[19] artists spaces and community groups.

SPONSORS A sponsor is an entity created by an arts group to allow it to sponsor a variety of activities and sometimes to obtain funding

---

[18]Discussion with David White, Executive Director, Dance Theater Workshop, 4 June 1981.

[19]Helman, *An Organizational Manual for Chamber Ensemble*, p. 26.

from both commercial and non-commercial sectors. A sponsor, sometimes called a "presenting organization," is a federally tax-exempt,
not-for-profit corporation that can receive grants and contributions for
the nonprofit activities it sponsors and can sponsor the non-commercial activities of a commercially viable group. It has been used to good
effect in chamber music where an "ensemble sponsor" essentially
hires a chamber ensemble, receives tax-exempt funds for that ensemble, and engages in other activities as well.[20]

Many of the sponsoring organizations mentioned above receive a
portion of the income—whether contributed or earned—of the groups
they sponsor, to cover "overhead" expenses such as heat, electricity,
and maintenance of the spaces used.

Corporations

The corporate form, while it has the advantage of limiting the personal liability of its directors, officers and members, also limits an organization's method of operation. A corporation is required by law to
have a board of directors (most states require at least three directors),
officers (president, treasurer and secretary), and members (shareholders) who, for the most part, are not responsible for corporate actions. The corporation is thus a separate legal entity that can hold
property in the corporate name and enter into lawsuits and contracts.
As a separate legal entity, the corporation exists even if individual
members, directors, or shareholders leave the corporation—in this respect, the corporation is said to have a "perpetual existence." [21]

In a small arts group, the board members who set policy and the
officers who implement policy may be the same people; indeed, they
may also own stock in the corporation and, thus, may be shareholders
as well. In addition, these people may be artists in the group or
friends of artists.

As a legal entity, the corporation must adopt written by-laws or
rules that delineate each person's responsibilities and powers, and
that serve to regulate the internal operations of the organization.
These legally binding by-laws state the general purposes and scope of

---

[20]Ibid., p. 15.

[21]The Council of N.Y. Law Associates, Volunteer Lawyers for the Arts, Community Law Offices, *The New York Not-for Profit Organization Manual* (New
York: Volunteer Lawyers for the Arts, 1978), p. 3.

corporate activity as well as specifics about the organization such as terms, responsibilities, and frequency of meetings of board members.

There are organizations—some banks and funding agencies, for example, that think a corporate structure reflects some sort of state sanction, as well as "serious dedication to the objectives of the group"[22] and internal regulatory procedures.

The documents required to incorporate include those that state the corporation's purpose, the number of shares that are authorized (in a for-profit corporation), and the corporate name, either in a certificate of incorporation, articles of organization, or a corporate charter. (These vary from state to state.)

To make any changes in the structure or purposes of a corporation, a group must file a certificate amending the corporation's certificate of incorporation. A certificate must also be filed to terminate the corporation. In the case of dissolution, the corporation must pay all unpaid state corporate taxes. For not-for-profit corporation, certain judicial and state approval may be required.[23]

For-Profit Corporations

The major difference between the for-profit and the not-for-profit corporation has nothing to do with profit: it has to do with purpose. Profit corporations are specifically set up to benefit private, individual members or shareholders, not-for-profit organizations are not.

The tax law is extremely strict with corporations. Generally, corporate income is doubly taxed—individual shareholders pay tax on distributions, and earnings fall under the corporate income tax of 17 percent on the first $25,000 which is graduated up to 46 percent on income over $100,000. There are ways this double taxation can be avoided. If shareholders are also employees of the corporation, income can be distributed as salaries rather than as dividends (salaries are deductible as expenses before taxes). Another possibility is the formation of a sub-chapter S corporation, with 15 or fewer shareholders (including no resident-aliens) and with one class of stock offered. Shareholders in a subchapter S corporation can deduct corporate losses from their personal income taxes. Furthermore, the corporate

---

[22]Ibid., p. 4.

[23]*Should You Incorporate?* (New York: The Council of New York Law Associates, 1977), p. 7.

income tax is not imposed, provided the group's passive income—
from "rents, investments, royalties, dividends, annuities, and sales
and exchanges of stock or securities—is not greater than 20 percent of
total receipts."[24]

A small incorporated arts group might easily fall under the category of a personal holding company—five or fewer individuals who
own over 50 percent of the stock at any time during the tax year, and
"at least 60 percent of the adjusted gross income is personal holding
company income"[25] such as royalties or personal service contracts.
Should a group fall within the personal holding company guidelines,
its undistributed income would be taxed not only under guidelines for
regular corporate income tax, but also under a 70 percent personal
holding company tax provision. Additional state franchise and other
taxes may be imposed on the for-profit corporation depending on the
state.

If the arts group has artists who operate as employees (as opposed
to artists who act as independent contractors), withholding taxes
must be taken and employees may be eligible for unemployment
benefits—a widespread form of arts subsidy in this country. If the artists are also corporate officers, however, it is possible that the State
Department of Labor will have difficulty accepting their claims of
unemployment when they are not working.[26]

There are several kinds of tax-shelter benefits provided by retirement plans for corporate employees. These include the tax-deferred
individual retirement plans, profit-sharing and money-purchase pension plans, and tax deductible insurance benefits.[27]

Since the corporation is created for the private benefit of its individual members or shareholders, its sale or dissolution requires a dispersal of its assets to those individuals.

The difficulty in obtaining grants as well as the amount of time and
effort expended in researching and writing them, the scramble for
money in the nonprofit sector with more and more groups approaching many of the same sources, and the development of strategies and
schemes by many nonprofit arts groups of profit-generating subsidiaries have enhanced the attractiveness of the for-profit corporation as
a method of organization. Besides, the possibility of making a living

---

[24]Helman, p. 19.

[25]Ibid.

[26]Ibid., p. 22.

[27]Ibid., p. 23.

from the artist's work has become more of a reality due to a number of factors, not the least of which is the manipulation and "hype" by people and organizations with commercial interests (such as art dealers or Broadway producers). Some feel that if money is to be made from an artist or an institution, the artist or institution should not be the last one to receive remuneration. A desire to bring the artist into contact with an audience and into competition in the marketplace, to provide entry into the "real world" symbolized by those who operate for private rather than public benefit, and to succeed there offers an artistic as well as a financial challenge.

Not-For-Profit Corporations

Each state has a system of classification for nonprofit organizations but they differ greatly in specificity and value. Many state statutes have been partially or completely revised since their creation and it is wise for an organization that plans to incorporate as a nonprofit corporation to consult the current Not-For-Profit Corporations Law in the appropriate state for such revisions. California divides nonprofit organizations into nonprofit corporations and corporations for specific purposes. Wisconsin's nonprofit law falls under its Non-Stock Corporations Law and provides information that is old-fashioned and difficult to use. New York's Not-For-Profit Corporations Law, effective since September 1970, is considered new and different.[28]

In New York State, all the descriptive material on corporations applies equally to not-for-profit corporations—limited liability, boards of directors, officers—except the material delineating private benefit. In New York State there are two basic requirements an organization must meet to qualify as a not-for-profit corporation:

1. Its primary purposes must be non-pecuniary (although the organization may engage in profit-making activities to further that purpose),
2. Except for salaries, fees and wages—"compensation for services rendered"—none of the organization's income, assets, or

---

[28]Howard L. Oleck, *Nonprofit Corporations, Organizations, and Associations*, 3rd ed. (Englewood Cliffs, New Jersey: Prentice-Hall, 1974), pp. 25–45.

profit is to be for private benefit (to the members, officers, directors).[29]

To avoid further confusion, it should be restated that not-for-profit
incorporation and tax-exempt status are not the same thing. Not-for-
profit incorporation is a procedure that goes through the state (just as
for-profit incorporation does); tax-exempt status is a federal procedure. While not-for-profit incorporation may help a group obtain federal tax-exempt status, it is possible for an unincorporated association
to receive tax exemption.

There are four basic types of not-for-profit corporations in New
York State.[30] Type A are corporations that are formed for any nonbusiness purpose and usually include membership organizations
(trade organizations, labor unions) "where the activities by or for the
members predominate."[31]

Type B is the category under which most arts organizations fall. A
Type B not-for-profit corporation does not have to have membership,
but must be organized for "charitable educational, religious, scientific,
literary or cultural purposes or for the prevention of cruelty to animals."[32] Not-for-profit "education corporations" that include libraries,
academic institutions, museums, teacher associations, associations of
students that promote a department of knowledge or education such as
art, history, literature, science, and whose approved purposes are of cultural or educational value are also Type B corporations.

Type C corporations can be organized for any legal business purpose so long as their main objectives are not for profit. Type D covers
those not-for-profit corporations "whose formation is authorized by
any other corporate law of the state for any business or nonbusiness
purpose specified in that law, whether or not such purpose is also
within Types A, B, or C."[33]

----

[29]Council of N.Y. Law Associates, Volunteer Lawyers for the Arts, *The New
York Not-For-Profit Organization Manual*, p. 7.

[30]On page 45 of his 1974 edition of *Nonprofit Corporations, Organizations and Associations,* Howard Oleck refers to the four categories A, B, C, and D as
"purely charitable, merely non-profit, mixed non-profit, *and* profit in nature."

[31]Council of New York Law Associates, Volunteer Lawyers for the Arts, *The
New York Not-For-Profit Manual*, p. 9.

[32]Ibid., p. 10.

[33]Ibid.

The not-for-profit corporation has the following advantages for an arts group:

1. it is a separate legal entity whose directors, officers and members cannot usually be held responsible for corporate actions;
2. it can receive grants, donations and contributions;
3. its existence continues even if a member, director or officer leaves the organization or dies;
4. its very form may convince other organizations with which it deals that it is more responsible and internally regulated than a less formally organized group;
5. it may be an aid in obtaining tax-exempt status from the federal government.

In New York State, the procedure for obtaining not-for-profit incorporation includes the selection of a legally appropriate corporate name, preparation of a certificate of incorporation, obtaining approvals from necessary administrative and judicial state officials, and filing the certificate and supporting documents with the Secretary of State.

In the area of the corporate name, some arts groups unintentionally have created a certain confusion. In the past, some groups planning to apply for tax-exempt status from the Internal Revenue Service found it detrimental to have their group named for an artist/performer. Their use of the artist/performer's name created confusion for the IRS since it appeared that the organization was created for the private benefit of that artist. Originally, the IRS denied certain arts groups tax-exempt status because they appeared to be too small to benefit anyone, publicly or privately. In partial response to this, certain companies added the word "foundation" to their name to make them appear larger and more organized than they were and to avoid the "private benefit" stigma. The "foundation" then appeared to be a conduit and often was refused funding by legitimate foundations on the legal grounds that private foundations cannot fund other foundations.

The not-for-profit corporation is allowed certain legal powers permitting it to enter into lawsuits and contracts, to borrow and lend money, to hold property as security for loans, to buy, lease, receive, deal with, sell, transfer, mortgage, or create a security interest in any of its property, to issue bonds and create security interests, and to invest funds. Any profit accrued from such activities or on its products or services must be put back into the operation of the corporation and not distributed for private benefit. No stock or shares in the corporation may be issued, and no dividends distributed. As stated earlier, compensation for services rendered, salaries, and wages are all permissible.

There are specific legal procedures for the acquisition, transfer, and sale of property. Nonprofit groups entering into real estate transactions should familiarize themselves with the laws of their state, especially as they relate to ownership and title of property, approval and responsibility of the board of directors for transactions, and approval by county and state courts.

As with the for-profit corporations, by-laws must be adopted that include responsibilities and disciplinary actions for members, directors, and officers. These documents must be carefully drawn since they clearly spell out the practices of the corporation and are legally binding. They set forth the operational procedures of the corporation including information on memberships. A not-for-profit corporation may have one or more classes of members that can include corporations, partnerships, and unincorporated associations as well as individuals. (Type B is the only type of nonprofit corporation that can choose not to have members.) It may issue membership cards or certificates to them, may levy dues, fees and penalties (although members are not personally liable for corporate actions), must hold certain annual and special meetings, give proper notice regarding them, and have certain voting procedures. The not-for-profit corporate law of New York State was amended in 1971 to include the one-person, one-vote concept,[34] particularly valuable for certain cooperative organizations (cooperative galleries, orchestras, etc.) whose very structure is based on equal representation.

If a not-for-profit corporation does not intend to seek tax exemption, its members are required to make capital contributions or subventions to the corporation. The certificate of incorporation specifies a certain amount of money (property, labor, or services can be given instead) for which a capital certificate is issued, and which is nontransferrable except in certain instances. Upon redemption of the certificate or dissolution of the corporation, the capital contribution may be redeemed. Instead of a capital contribution, the subvention (or subsidy) may be obtained from members and non-members if the certificate of incorporation so provides. Corporate creditors, however,

---

[34]Ibid., p. 39.

always take precedence over holders of subvention certificates which can be repaid periodically or upon dissolution of the corporation. If there is any suspicion by members or creditors that the Type B or Type C corporation is engaging in activities besides those originally stated in its certificate of incorporation, or tampering with funds or property, a representative of the state Supreme Court may investigate the corporation.[35]

Some of the standard ways in which not-for-profit corporations raise money include membership dues, fees and assessments, donations and bequests, capital contributions and the subventions mentioned above, contributions, and foundation and government grants as well as certain earned income activities.[36]

It is permissible for two or more nonprofit corporations to merge, and even for a nonprofit corporation to merge with a profit corporation, after certain approvals and consents.

The subject of dissolution of the not-for-profit corporation is being discussed more and more frequently as arts institutions begin to find they can no longer survive. When many of these groups were incorporated, they paid little attention to rules and regulations governing dissolution and distribution of assets; groups incorporating as not-for-profit today are better apprised of such procedures.

Normally, a not-for-profit corporation is dissolved when the board of directors puts together a plan for dissolution and the distribution of corporate assets. If the corporation is Type B or Type C and there are no assets, a statement is included to that effect and in New York State it is filed with the Attorney General within ten days of adoption. The members must approve the dissolution plan by a ⅔ vote and it must be submitted to any official or government agency that originally approved the corporation's formation. Judicial approval is required, consent of the State Tax Commission, and filing of a certificate of dissolution by the Secretary of New York State. After this, the corporation may carry on activity only in order to complete its affairs and, finally, the nonprofit corporation must distribute its assets. In Type B corporations, assets must go to organizations involved in similar activities. If the organization is tax exempt under IRS Code Section 501 (c) (3), it must distribute its assets to another exempt organization. All remaining assets are distributed according to the plan of dissolution

---

[35]Ibid., pp. 46–49.

[36]Henn and Pfeifer, "Nonprofit Groups: Factors Influencing Choice of Form," p. 185, n. 10.

or the original certificate of incorporation.[37] At this point fee- and dues-paying members of some types of corporations "may receive distributive rights in the corporate assets."[38] The above procedure is called non-judicial dissolution.

Judicial dissolution usually occurs when there is suspicion of foul play. The Attorney General accuses a corporation of fraud, illegal activity, abuse of power, or a majority of the directors or a statutory majority of members institute judicial dissolution if they feel that corporate assets will not meet corporate liabilities or that dissolution would be beneficial to the members. Additionally, any director or 10 percent of the total membership may institute a petition for judicial dissolution on other grounds, for example, fraud or internal dissolution.[39]

Many arts organizations follow neither plan. Instead, they opt for involuntary bankruptcy and let the already overburdened courts take over the dissolution procedure. Although non-judicial dissolution is time-consuming and bureaucratic, it does allow an arts organization to have some influence over where its assets will be utilized, which involuntary bankruptcy does not.

Although much has been said in the previous pages to educate artists and managers in the organizational options available to them, the fact remains that a good majority of small arts groups are now or will become not-for-profit corporations. Of those that incorporate in this fashion, most will apply for federal tax-exempt status, and most of those under IRS Code Section 501 (c) (3). It is this exemption that will allow them to receive donations and contributions from a variety of donors, all of whom will be able to deduct the donations from their income tax. The remainder of this chapter is devoted to an examination of the qualifications needed to obtain and maintain this exempt status, with particular attention to the specific area of "unrelated business income" that should be kept in mind by arts groups entering into earned income activities.

---

[37]Ibid., pp. 51–53.

[38]Ibid., p. 36.

[39]Ibid., pp. 52–53.

FEDERAL TAX EXEMPTION
FOR ARTS GROUPS

In all nonprofit organizations the bargain struck between charities and the English Crown centuries ago—relief from taxation and other prerogatives of the Crown in exchange for attending to the public welfare—still holds.[40]

The practice of exemption from federal income tax of charitable and religious organizations, mutual benefit groups, and other nonprofit associations has its origin in the British Statute of Charitable Uses of 1601, but the tax law concerning such organizations, groups, and associations has had no systematic development in this country since charitable organizations were exempted from federal income tax in 1894. Since 1894, every revenue act has included a provision for charitable, religious, and educational groups to receive exemption and in 1913 Section 501 (c) (3) of the Internal Revenue Code was created.

Clearly, Congressional interest has focused on "profitmaking organizations, investors, and wage earners, not on charities, churches, fraternal societies, labor unions, and other nonprofit groups which could be, at most, marginal targets for the tax collector."[41] Additionally, some tax attorneys feel that nonprofit organizations should not be taxed because it is difficult, if not impossible, to measure the actual income of organizations in the business of performing public services. Indeed, there are those who believe that activities deemed "charitable" cannot at the same time be called "business" activities—that the two contradict each other. They argue that whatever business activities such a group engages in are entered into for the sole purpose of financing the organization's exempt purposes.

While museums and symphony orchestras have always operated and received federal tax exemption under the allowance for "educational" organizations, the legal form of the not-for-profit corporation with federal tax exemption was embraced by arts groups in great numbers only since the early 1950s. At that time the formula for legally creating a new arts organization became not-for-profit state incorporation and federal tax exemption, usually under Internal Reve-

---

[40]Alan D. Ullberg and Patricia Ullberg, *Museum Trusteeship* (Washington, D. C.: American Association of Museums, 1981), p. 6.

[41]Brotis I. Bittker and George K. Rahdert, "The Exemption of Nonprofit Organizations from Federal Income Taxation," *The Yale Law Journal* 85 (January 1976):304.

nue Service Code Section 501 (c) (3). Some arts groups—particularly emerging ones—have no clear idea what these procedures mean, except that they will enable their organizations to receive gifts, grants, and contributions that their donors can claim as tax deductions. In some cases, other tax benefits, including "corresponding exemption from state and local income, property, sales, or use taxation" and "the privilege of mailing at preferred postal rates"[42] as well as their potential revenue from earned income activities related to their institution's purposes and functions may be as important to an arts group as contributions and donations.

In light of the changing financial situation of most arts groups in this country, it is imperative that such groups gain at least some elementary knowledge of how the tax law can help and hurt their institutions, so that they are better prepared to make informed choices in the future.

The two basic types of tax exempt organizations under the Internal Revenue Code section 501 include a) a wide range of not-for-profit organizations including labor groups, credit unions, business leagues, teachers' retirement fund associations, and chambers of commerce, created to benefit their members or the community and b) under section 501 (c) (3), not-for-profit corporations or organizations that are operated for "religious, charitable, scientific, . . . literary, or educational purposes"[43] that are not organized for private benefit, and do not participate in or try to influence legislation or political candidates.[44]

For organizations of the first type, while income is exempt from taxes, contributions or dues to these organizations are usually not exempt. For organizations of the second type, income is exempt from taxation, and contributions and membership fees are deductible as charitable contributions by the giver. The deductibility is limited, however: an individual may deduct up to 50 percent of his or her contribution base (contribution base is usually the same as one's adjusted

---

[42]James J. McGovern, "The Exemption Provisions of Subchapter F," *Tax Lawyer*, 29 (Spring 1976): 528.

[43]Additional purposes not usually applicable to arts groups are involved with public safety, sports competition, and the prevention of cruelty to children and animals.

[44]Since the Tax Reform Act of 1976, a certain amount of lobbying has been permitted to organizations with 501 (c) (3) tax exemption. Some nonprofit groups have formed affiliate 501 (c) (4) corporations in order to lobby more extensively.

gross income) for contributions to 501 (c) (3) organizations that are not private foundations;[45] a corporation may deduct up to 10 percent of its taxable income. Gifts to 501 (c) (3) organizations from private foundations allow the foundations to avoid federal tax.[46] Additionally, income from investments, interest on bank accounts, fees for services, grants, social security, unemployment, and some earned income are all exempt from taxation, and the exempt organization is eligible for preferred (usually second or third class) postal rates.

The basic rationale behind the provisions for such contributions, deductions, and exemptions is one of public service; both the decentralized choice-making of private individual philanthropists and the public services rendered by such organizations allow for more flexible response to public needs, and a less cumbersome allocation process than that effected by government administration.[47]

Of the legal forms an organization may take to obtain 501 (c) (3) tax exemption, not-for-profit corporations and unincorporated associations are the ones most commonly used by arts groups. Unincorporated associations are considered corporations if they have governing rules and elected officers for the purposes of Section 501 (c) (3).[48] This section lists exempt organizations as:

> Corporations, and any community chest, fund, or foundation, organized and operated exclusively for religious, charitable, scientific, testing for public safety, literary, or educational purposes, or to foster national or international sports competition (but only if no part of its activities involves the provision of athletic facilities or equipment), or for the prevention of cruelty to children or animals, no part of the net earnings of which inures to the benefit of any private shareholder or individual, no substantial part of the activities of which is carrying on propaganda, or otherwise attempting to influence legislation (except as otherwise provided in subsection (h)), and which does not participate in, or intervene in (including

---

[45]Craig W. Weinlein, "Federal Taxation of Not for Profit Arts Organizations: A Guide for the Arts Manager," *Journal of Arts Management and Law* (Spring 1982): 34.

[46]As will be explained later, a 501 (c) (3) organization is itself a private foundation until it receives a determination letter from the IRS stating that it is NOT a private foundation. The effect of a determination letter is that the heavy excise and other taxes levied on private foundations cannot be levied on 501 (c) (3) organizations of this type.

[47]Weinlein, p. 34.

[48]Council of N.Y. Law Associates, Volunteer Lawyers for the Arts, *New York Not-For-Profit Organization Manual*, p. 73.

the publishing or distributing of statements), any political campaign on behalf of any candidate for public office.

After being organized in one of the above legal forms, an organization must meet certain eligibility requirements. First, it must be operated and organized solely for at least one of the exempt purposes stated above—the two most relevant to arts organizations are "charitable" and "educational" although, of course, "literary" purposes may apply in the case of certain small presses, for example. Definitions of "charitable" and "educational" are considerably broader than one might expect, and most arts organizations seem to qualify for exemption in this area on the basis of one of these purposes. As stated earlier, museums and symphony orchestras are traditionally regarded as institutions involved in educational activities.

After meeting one or more of the exempt purposes, the organization must pass an organizational test that proves it is "organized and operated exclusively" for one or more of those purposes. This test tries to ensure that an organization exists to further a set of specific, exempt purposes which must be stated in its instrument of organization such as the articles of organization, or the corporate charter. Also stated in that instrument must be a provision for the dedication of that organization's assets to an exempt purpose—usually another exempt organization—upon the organization's dissolution.

Exempt organizations are to serve public, not private, interests; therefore no part of their net earnings can be used to benefit any private individual. Only if individuals constitute a bona fide charitable class can they receive such benefits, but there are no real guidelines in this area since "private inurement takes many forms and involves judgments in individual cases which are difficult to quantify."[49] Cooperative galleries have had difficulty obtaining and maintaining tax-exempt status on this basis, especially if work is sold on the premises and the artists receive a percentage of the proceeds. In a 1971 ruling the IRS denied exemption to a cooperative gallery on the grounds that the gallery displayed and sold only its members' works, even though its sale and exhibition activities were "educational."[50] Since that time, some cooperative galleries have expanded their activities to include different kinds of exhibitors and/or memberships in order to gain exemption.

---

[49]Weinlein, P. 37.
[50]Revenue Ruling 71-395, 1971, 2 C.B. 228.

These kinds of rulings are difficult for artists to accept, especially those involved in smaller organizations who watch some of the larger institutions operate profit-making subsidiaries while their exempt purpose remains unchallenged. Equally difficult is what small arts groups may regard as denial for serving what they consider a "bona fide charitable class"—namely, artists.

Unrelated-Business Income

As long as an organization serves public, not private, interests, is operated and organized in the appropriate legal form and exclusively for an exempt purpose, and its primary activities serve to accomplish that purpose, the organization may pursue certain unsubstantial activities devoted to other purposes, such as the earning of unrelated-business income.

The area of unrelated-business income for 501 (c) (3) arts organizations is under new scrutiny as these organizations try to avoid or obliterate constantly mounting deficits by entering into earned-income activities, many of which are described in Chapter III. Unfortunately, reduced deficits have not always been rewarded by those very agencies for whom 501 (c) (3) status was a requirement and funding for arts groups that begin to show a balanced budget has sometimes been reduced in favor of grants to poorer managed, deficit-ridden ones.

If a 501 (c) (3) organization enters into business activities that are not related to its exempt purposes, it must be taxed on its unrelated-business income at the same rate as a business corporation—ranging from 17 percent on the first $25,000 up to 46 percent on income over $100,000. The purpose of this tax is to prevent unfair competition between the 501 (c) (3) organization and any non-exempt business with which it competes. There are three major areas of definition for unrelated-business taxable income: the income must be from a 1) trade or business, that is 2) regularly carried on by the organization and 3) whose conduct is not substantially related to the organization's performance of its exempt functions. "Trade or business" signify activities that produce income from the performance of services or the sale of goods just as with a profit-making corporation. The regularity of the activity—"regularly carried on by the organization"—indicates the conduct of business comparable to profit-making commercial enterprises on a year-round basis. This would probably not apply to the sporadic fund-raising events arts groups frequently organize. The area most difficult to define is the one stating that income is taxable if the conduct of the trade or business is not substantially related (aside from the need for income) to the organization's performance of its exempt purposes or functions. A phrase like "substantially related" makes this area almost impossible to explain, except on a case-by-case basis.[51] Merely using the income generated from an activity for exempt purposes does not make it substantially related to the organization's performance of those purposes. The "character" of the activity is under almost as much scrutiny as the uses to which the income from that activity are put. Generally, "unrelated-business taxable income" is the gross income derived from any unrelated trade or business regularly carried on by it, less allowable deductions directly connected with carrying on that trade or business.[52]

One of the first legal precedents set in this area was in 1973 in Revenue Ruling 73–104 in which a tax-exempt modern art museum offered a series of greeting cards for sale to the public. The cards, which bore printed reproductions from the museum's collection and from other art collections, were imprinted with the museum's name, the artist's name, the name or subject of the work, and the date of creation, if known. The cards were sold in the museum's shop and mail orders were solicited for them through the museum's catalog which was advertised in various publications, and for which there was a small charge. A large volume of the cards was sold at a significant profit, especially since retail stores were given a quantity discount.

The revenue ruling declared that income made from these greeting cards was not unrelated and, therefore, was not taxable.

> The sale of greeting cards displaying printed reproductions of art works contributes importantly to the achievement of the museum's exempt educational purposes by stimulating and enhancing public awareness, interest, and appreciation of art. Moreover, a broader segment of the public may be encouraged to visit the museum itself to share in its educational functions and programs as a result of seeing the cards. The fact that the cards are promoted and sold in a clearly commercial manner at a profit and in competition with commercial greeting card publishers does not alter the fact of the activity's relatedness to the museum's exempt purpose.[53]

---

[51]Arts groups are urged to consult the IRS Letter Rulings Reports published through the Commerce Clearing House, Inc. to review precedent cases.

[52]Internal Revenue Service Code Section 512 (a).

[53]Revenue Ruling 73–104.

The sale of such cards with reproductions from the museum's own collection, and even from other art collections, especially when the museum tries to achieve "superior reproduction" of the object or painting on a postcard, is related enough to the exempt purposes of the institution to avoid taxation. This example seems simple and clear, but when it is extended to reproductions of design it may be harder to draw the line between related and unrelated business income:

> Suppose, for example, a museum sells a cocktail tray bearing a reproduction of a work of art or a historic artifact. Now, is that a cocktail tray or is it a reproduction of a work of art or an artifact?[54]

The Internal Revenue Service is troubled by "adaptations" which change the original's use or size as opposed to "reproductions." The Mona Lisa on a tee-shirt is considered an "adaptation" and may not be related to the museum's programs or purposes. Is a picture of a still life from a museum's collection on a placemat or trivet an adaptation or a reproduction? Is a trivet decorated with the museum monogram instead of an actual reproduction related to the museum's purposes or programs? The IRS says it is not. The IRS seems troubled by the traditional utilitarian aspects of certain items as well. Should the income from a coffee grinder—albeit a designer coffee grinder—sold in the shop at the Museum of Modern Art be taxed as unrelated business income?[55] Further, representations that are interpretational rather than direct reproductions of items are hard to categorize as to their relatedness:

> . . . for example, a stuffed animal sold by a zoo. Let's suppose it is more a Walt Disney characterization of the animal than a scientifically accurate one. Or suppose a maritime museum is selling a painting of a seascape or a sailing ship.[56]

Also, items that bear the logo of the organization can be argued to stimulate the public's awareness of the particular purposes and activities of the organization, although, under a 1980 ruling, items bearing

---

[54]John K. P. Stone, "A Tax Attorney Calls for Clarity," *Museum Stores Association*, Winter 1980, p. 15.

[55]J. Edward Shillingburg, "Museums, Reproduction Sales and Taxes," Workshop of Metropolitan Museum of Art at Asia House, 5 February 1982.

[56]Stone, p. 61.

the logo of an aquarium were considered unrelated to the institution's exempt functions.

One way in which art museums have avoided the unrelated-business income tax on certain items is by licensing various manufacturers to produce reproductions and adaptations of articles in the collection, and then receiving licensing fees in the form of royalties. Royalties are considered passive income by the IRS and thus do not constitute unrelated-business income. [57]

Examples in the museum world are numerous and instructive, partly because of a 1979 national training session on auditing exempt organizations where IRS agents spent a good deal of time on issues relating to museum stores. The operation of restaurants and even parking lots has been found to be related to a museum's exempt purposes in that these facilities help attract visitors, allow these visitors to spend a longer time at the museum attending to exhibits and collections, and allow museum staff to stay on the premises throughout the day. If the parking lot is operated when the museum is closed, however, it is likely that the income from those hours will be taxed as unrelated. And if the restaurant opens onto the street, so that customers can go directly to the restaurant without going through the museum, is the income from that restaurant taxable? Some rulings say if there is no sign on the street the activity is related and therefore untaxable. And, if it is possible to operate a restaurant with direct access from the street, and to offer museum greeting cards through direct mail, what about a satellite museum shop, off the museum premises? The Brooklyn Museum has such a shop in the Citicorp Building. The Metropolitan Museum of Art operates one in the main branch of the New York Public Library and in Macy's Department Store. The Boston Museum of Fine Arts has an exhibit space and shop in the Quincy Market in the Fanueil Hall area. Obviously, a space that has exhibition facilities as well as a sales shop with items that relate to museum materials and are properly labelled[58] has a better chance of justifying its income as related to its exempt purposes.[59] Once the off-premises shop is in existence, what about advertising its wares? To my knowledge, there are no rulings on this particular subject, although there are attorneys who say only shops with direct access to the street should advertise, that an advertisement should indicate that the shop is limited by the mu-

---

[57]See Chapter III for more information on this particular point.

[58]As in the case of the greeting cards.

[59]Shillingburg, Workshop, 5 February 1982.

seum's collection, and that proper labeling as to where the item comes from, who created it and when, and even the address of the arts institution should be affixed.

Although rulings regarding the relatedness of an activity or item are handled on a case-by-case basis, the broader an organization's purposes are, the more chance it has of having items and activities classified as substantially related to them. Additionally, there are items and/or activities that may not be substantially related to the institution's purposes that make a substantial amount of money. If these items/activities are a secondary (as opposed to the principal) activity, the institution's exemption will not be threatened.[60] If they can be deemed cost-effective, it may be worthwhile for the institution to continue them and pay the unrelated-business income tax on them.

There are certain exceptions for the tax on a trade or business that is not substantially related to an organization's exempt purposes where exemption can still be maintained. These include activities in which "substantially all the work" is done by uncompensated volunteers, a trade or business organized for "the convenience of its members, students, patients, officers, or employees,"[61] and one that sells merchandise that the organization has received as contributions or gifts.

Small arts organizations should heed these exceptions since their earned income activities are sometimes run by unpaid volunteers, and since their benefits and short-term fund-raising events often depend on contributions and gifts from others. The category covering trades or businesses that are carried on for "the convenience of its members, students, patients, officers, or employees," however, has engendered very mixed results. Often—and this is true of many areas of ruling under Section 501 (c) (3)—what an organization is doing is without either the sanctions or the approval of the IRS. The organization simply never asked the IRS and assumes that its exempt status will not be jeopardized. Other organizations that do ask are often warned that their exemption will be endangered by activities already engaged in by other exempt groups.

Aside from the legal and financial ramifications of unrelated-

---

[60]Some considerations for determining the secondary nature of such activities have been suggested by J. Edward Shillingburg. They include comparisons of: purchasers to visitors, sales staff to total staff, sales and inventory space to total gallery space and other areas, and net sales receipts to total net investment income, gifts, and other receipts.

[61]Council of N.Y. Law Associates, Volunteer Lawyers for the Arts, p. 93.

business income activities of arts organizations, there are serious ethical questions. These are raised most often within the artistic community itself and concern the "taste" question: is it a reflection of
good taste, for example, to reproduce a Picasso design on sheets and
pillowcases? Is this the function of art, of the art museum? Does this
attract people to the museum and, if so, are they attracted to the museum or the museum shop? Does it help them to appreciate art? And
how does a physical reproduction of a piece of sculpture differ from
sheet designs? Or does it differ? What are the effects of such reproductions on the value of the original?

There are those, like art historian Albert Elsen and attorney John
Henry Merryman, both professors at Stanford University, who believe:

> Exact reproductions of works of art devalue original works by creating
> confusion between originals and reproductions. The more exact the repro-
> duction the greater the potential confusion and the consequent devaluing
> effect.
>
> Authentic works of art are among the most significant expressions of
> the human spirit. They are cultural artifacts, precious evidence of our ori-
> gins and our identity. Exact reproductions, to the extent that they lend
> themselves to confusion with originals, falsify art's history.[62]

Although certain arts organizations may find such practices
unpalatable, can they afford not to engage in them—or in other activities like them—unless they have a permanent endowment or a
wealthy donor waiting in the wings?

Other questions arise. Where does the concept of "marketing"—a
tool that has gained enormous popularity in the arts in the last few
years—end and "taste" begin? Obviously, umbrellas, tee-shirts, and
tote bags are not appropriate for every organization. Are there other
lucrative activities that can help these institutions avoid or erase deficits without compromising their exempt purposes and their *artistic*
purposes?

The great rush for tax exemption under IRS Code 501 (c) (3) was
due, in part, to the enabling legislation of the National Endowment
for the Arts in the mid 1960s. The lead of the Endowment in requiring
an organization to be a not-for-profit corporation with federal tax exemption became a legitimizing procedure in the arts, much the same

---

[62]Albert Elsen and John Henry Merryman, "Art Replicas: A Question of Ethics," *Art News*, 78 (February 1979): 61.

as a grant from the NEA became a stamp of approval. (It should be noted that certain state funding organizations, like the New York State Council on the Arts, require neither incorporation nor tax exemption. To qualify for NYSCA funds, organizations that have received contributions over $10,000 in any one fiscal year and/or have hired a professional fundraiser must file the Registration Statement-Charitable Organization form with the Department of State.

The effect of this legitimizing procedure was so great that many other funding sources adopted the same regulations without assessing whether such procedures were really appropriate for their institutions. Thus, certain private foundations require individual recipients of their gifts to acquire 501 (c) (3) tax-exempt status. As stated earlier, since 501 (c) (3) status exempts certain kinds of organizations, but not individuals, these recipients must ally themselves with an institution that agrees to act as a conduit for the grant money. That institution usually takes an overhead or handling fee. Recently Actors' Equity Association required certain theatres that wished to obtain a certain kind (favored tier) of categorization within its current Showcase Code to have 501 (c) (3) status. There was no discernible reason except that the 501 (c) (3) seemed to lend a kind of credibility to those theatres' operations.[63]

Besides using conduits or umbrellas, another solution for arts organizations needing 501 (c) (3) status but wishing to avoid unnecessary administrative and qualifying burdens is the group exemption. In this case, a group with a number of chapters or arms has the same 501 (c) (3) status, and each arts organization in the group is a chapter. Certain dance managements are currently experimenting with this, offering to do financial record keeping, to establish payroll procedures (so unemployment benefits can be collected), and to receive grants for a number of artist-clients under its 501 (c) (3) exemption. This arrangement allows the individual artist to avoid incorporation as a company or organization and to purchase other services—for touring, for aid with home seasons—on a per-service basis.

Unless they meet the requirements of statutory exclusion, all 501 (c) (3) organizations are private foundations. As private foundations, organizations are subject to excise taxes and heavy regulations. The rationale behind such regulations is the prevention of the use of tax-exempt organizations by private individuals for private, rather than

---

[63]Discussion with Leonard Easter, Volunteer Lawyers for the Arts, 16 June 1981.

public, philanthropic purposes. A 501 (c) (3) organization, therefore, has 15 months after its creation to seek a determination letter from the Internal Revenue Service stating that it is not a private foundation. If the 501 (c) (3) organization fails to seek such a letter within the allotted time, it is considered a private foundation and must remain so for five years before seeking a new status.

While other kinds of organizations can avoid foundation status by virtue of their function and character, an arts organization must pass one of three tests based on its sources of financial support to avoid foundation status. In the first test, sometimes called the "mechanical" test, the organization must prove it is "publicly supported" by proving receipts of at least one-third of its annual support from government grants, gifts, contributions, or membership fees and from gross receipts from admissions, sales of merchandise, performance of services, or furnishing of facilities in an activity that is not an unrelated trade or business.[64] Furthermore, the organization must not receive more than one-third of its annual support from unrelated-business taxable income and investment income.

In the second test, an organization must prove it is publicly supported through the "facts and circumstances" test: it must receive at least 10 percent of its annual support from the general public (including federal, state, and local government grants) and must be organized and operated to attract new and additional public or government support on a continuing basis.[65] In addition to these requirements, other "facts and circumstances" are considered by the IRS in determining whether the organization is publicly supported, including:

a. the extent of public support (How much over 10%?);
b. support from a "representative number of persons," rather than members of a single family;
c. whether its governing body represents the broad interests of the public, not the private interests of a limited number of donors;
d. whether the organization provides facilities or services directly for the benefit of the public (a museum open to the public, a symphony orchestra that gives public performances);[66]

---

[64]Internal Revenue Code 509 (a) (2).

[65]I.R.C. Section 1.170A–9 (e) (3) (ii).

[66]I.R.C Section 1.170A–9 (e) (3) (vi).

e. whether the organization has the participation or sponsorship of community leaders, public officials, or members of the public with special expertise;

f. obtaining a significant part of its funds from a public charity or government agency to which it is held accountable as a condition of the grant;

g. maintenance of a definitive program to accomplish charitable work in the community;

h. other factors that pertain only to membership organizations.[67]

In the third test, an organization is considered publicly supported if it normally receives at least one-third of its total annual support from contributions of local, state, federal governments and the general public, even if the organization is not organized and operated to attract additional support on a continuing basis. As in the previous test, contributions by one individual cannot exceed two percent of the organization's total support.

The last two tests do not allow income from admissions, sales of merchandise, performance of services, or furnishing of facilities to be considered as public support, but neither do they deny an organization tax exemption for having over a third of its income in unrelated-business taxable income and investment income.[68] Their focus is, however, on "pure donations" from public sources.[69]

The organization must now file for a determination letter from the IRS stating that it is not a foundation on the basis of one of the above tests. If the organization is new, it must seek this letter within 15 months of its creation, and will be given a determination letter for two years (one for five years sometimes may be requested) if the IRS expects that it will qualify for one of the above tests at the end of that period. If the organization is not newly created, financial records for the preceding four years will be reviewed, as well as its qualifications for one of the above tests.

If there is no material change in the organization's character, purposes, or methods of operation after it receives tax exemption, its tax-exempt status is maintained, providing each year it files Form 990. Form 990 is a statement that serves as a yearly review of its financial activities and includes the names and addresses of substantial contrib-

---

[67]Council of N.Y. Law Associates, Volunteer Lawyers for the Arts, p. 105.
[68]Weinlein, p. 46.
[69]Ibid.

utors. Form 990-T is required if the organization has received unrelated-business taxable income.

Tax attorneys are quick to warn arts groups of the heavy taxes imposed on them should they retain their private foundation status. These heavy taxes include provisions to prevent self-dealing, failure to distribute income, maintenance of excess business holdings, jeopardizing of investments and lobbying. They are the result of legislation to prevent the use of tax-exempt organizations for private purposes by private individuals. As mentioned earlier, there are arts groups that have called themselves "foundations" in order to sound more organized and more credible for funding sources (this is particularly true in modern dance). But most of these groups are not legal foundations in the sense we are discussing them here.[70]

While it is important to know the basic facts about methods of organization and federal tax exemption, an arts group would be advised not to attempt making a final decision in either area without the opinion of at least one trained professional. Although small and emerging groups are a long way from institutional sophistication by corporate standards, their artists and managers are no longer operating out of a cigar box. While the hand-to-mouth quality of existence of many groups is still painfully present, the knowledge required for them to operate in the marketplace—any marketplace—has expanded greatly. The singular brand of entrepreneurship, through which many of these organizations were created, when combined with a fundamen-

---

[70]Another legal form of organization that has received some attention in the arts is the private operating foundation. Although it will not be discussed in this book, the private operating foundation is often touted as a viable form for an individual wishing to support a favorite arts activity. While the private operating foundation is subject to the two percent tax on net-investment activity and to other requirements that apply to private foundations generally, contributions to private operating foundations are deductible by the donor up to 50 percent of the donor's adjusted gross income. (Contributions to all other private foundations are limited to 20 percent of the donor's adjusted gross income.) Also, a private operating foundation may receive qualifying distributions from any private foundation that does not control it, and it is not subject to the excise tax on failure to distribute income. Essentially, a private operating foundation is any private foundation that spends at least 85 percent of its adjusted net income directly for the active conduct of its exempt activities (the income test) and that meets one of three tests: the assets test, the endowment test, or the support test. (From the *Tax Information for Private Foundations and Foundation Managers*, IRS publication #578, October 1981, pp. 2–3.)

tal understanding of how their organizations can best serve their artistic needs, could ensure them a better chance of survival in the lean and hungry times.

A few years after I wrote this book, arguments surfaced over the unrelated business income of tax-exempt not-for-profit organizations. These arguments were probably rooted in concerns from the 1950s, when requirements for tax exemption of such unrelated income changed from the "destination of income" test to a much less fathomable one that sought to determine the character of the income earned, not only how it was to be expended. It was no longer enough that unrelated business income went back into programs and activities of the organization and was used for public, not private, benefit; the *character* of the money was in question, that is, how the money related to the "exempt purposes" of the organization.

In the 1980s, partly because of the visibility tax-exempt nonprofits gained through their attempts to secure greater control over both their destinies and their cash flows through earned income activities, cries of unfair competition were raised and a major attack was launched by the Small Business Administration. Organizations, particularly those in the arts, felt doubly strapped since these objections came to the fore at the same time that government was cutting back or standing still with its own public arts funds at the federal, state, and local levels, and the 1986 Tax Reform Act was adding restrictions on contributed income. Nevertheless, some objections directed at a broad range of nonprofits seemed to warrant scrutiny. Some groups, like one YMCA with a fitness center, received the ultimate punishment and lost their tax-exempt status. Others, like universities, began to examine charges of unfair competition for products like computer programs. Small firms claimed that tax-exempt universities were creating and selling the same kinds of software on which for-profit businesses paid tax. Even university endowments were being challenged.

As a result of mounting distress, the House of Representatives Ways and Means Committee formed a special committee to look into the matter. Testimony was taken in Washington D.C. from representatives of many nonprofit tax-exempt organizations, including those from the arts and culture. From preliminary discussions in spring 1988, a press release was issued delineating potential changes in the UBIT law. These include tax exemptions restricted to a dollar or "item" cap (such as computer sales to students through university bookstores) as well as a review from current exemption of royalty income used by many arts and cultural groups in licensing arrangements (the licensing of a particular design from a museum's permanent collection to a linen manufacturer for use on sheets, for example).

Although questions of taxability, of "fair" versus "unfair competition," and the financial viability of many of our not-for-profit tax-exempt organizations are of critical importance, another issue must not be overlooked in this discussion. It relates to the recent government push toward privitization, so well explored by the Urban Institute in researching nonprofits in ten sites around the country. As the federal government has encouraged the private sector and for-profit business to take responsibility for the general delivery of many different kinds of human services to the public, "the central premise underlying this approach — namely that government-funded human services are now delivered by government agencies — is not really true."[71] Instead, government traditionally has used nonprofit organizations to deliver government-funded human services, and there is an increasing possibility of a "movement away from a provision of government-financed services by nonprofits toward provision of these services by for-profit businesses."[72]

The heart of the matter concerns whether, with such a change, services will continue to be made available to as broad a segment of the community and whether those services will retain the same level of quality if taken over by the private sector. As the business sector moves into our "charitable" organizations — in areas like unrelated business income, corporate support and sponsorship, services and benefits for corporate employees — issues of mission as well as the law emerge in addition to profitability. As the law becomes clearer, nonprofits will need to do some serious re-evaluation. Arts and cultural groups will need to place themselves in the larger context of their sister organizations to determine their own course of action.

[71]Lester M. Salamon, David M. Altschuler, and Carol J. DeVita, *San Francisco Bay Area Nonprofit Organizations: The Challenge of Retrenchment* (Washington, D.C.: The Urban Institute), 1987, p. 18.

[72]*Ibid.*, p. 19.

CHAPTER TWO

RAISING MONEY

Private, Public, and Corporate Grants and Gifts

WHOSE MONEY IS IT AND WHAT
DO THEY EXPECT?

Peter Drucker describes the "third sector," composed of nonprofit service-oriented institutions and organizations that seek to maintain and even enhance the quality of life as a frontier. Arts organizations bring to mind a kind of uncharted territory, ripe for development. They are places where standard organizational principles are difficult to apply and success is difficult to predict, where groups are frequently run on an ad hoc basis, where institutionalization is not always a desired goal, where "products" change as artistic personnel are changed, and where services themselves are often intangible and hard to measure.

The widespread use of nonprofit incorporation in the arts began in the 1950s when art was associated with a variety of social and political as well as educational and cultural goals. Originally adopted by many groups to allow them to focus on objectives which they felt were not possible in the commercial sector, nonprofit incorporation became, by the 1960s, the routine method of organization for a large number of new organizations. Obtaining federal tax exemption became almost as common, and both procedures allowed an organization to apply for public and many private grant monies. Arts money began to flow to the nonprofit arts sector from the Ford and Rockefeller Foundations in the 1950s and from state art councils (led by New York State) in the 1960s. This culminated in the creation of the National Endowments for the Arts and Humanities in 1965, and the beginning of corporate philanthropy on a national scale through the Business Committee for the Arts, created in 1967 by David Rockefeller. Such monies were a constantly increasing testimony to the growth of arts organizations in this country. Starting with heavy funding for bricks and mortar—there were more museums built after World War II than in the preceding 150 years and arts centers built during this time were referred to as part of the "edifice complex"—support continued over into areas of programming, membership, and management. Maintenance was another story. An area more difficult to justify to a constituency interested in tangible projects, operating costs were hard to meet and many facilities became underutilized or empty with exorbitant maintenance bills and growing deficits.

These early years were not, of course, "golden" years; they only look so in comparison to the current level of funding in direct ratio to the number of institutions, and the promise of a relatively bleak future at least on the federal level. But it was during this time that arts organizations began to realize the necessity for understanding the process that became known as "grantsmanship"—the approach, techniques, and skills for seeking out, asking for, and obtaining arts money. While individual donors still account for more than 80 percent of the money given to the arts, formal public support suddenly provided a new route for survival. Even this public support is a small commitment by European standards where many arts institutions are totally subsidized by their goverments; however, federal, state and local money, coupled with private and corporate gifts, offered arts groups a multiplicity of sources to approach. Libraries, seminars, publications, and university courses in grant-getting became available. At the same time, the nonprofit arts looked to the rest of the third sector for instruction—to the capital fund drives of universities, to hospitals—and to the funding sources themselves for guidance. In their eagerness for funds, many groups failed to recognize the priorities of the agencies funding them; some found themselves, a few years up the road, with programs in areas in which they had no real interest.

With public money came somewhat rigorous requirements of fiscal statistics and accountability, of managerial expertise by board members and artistic and executive directors, of audience development, and of evaluatory procedures. Very quickly arts groups realized they were in a competitive market; the responsibility of raising money for the organization, formerly the sole purview of the board of directors, passed to the development officer. For smaller groups, such a person was usually beyond their means. The already beleaguered artistic director or a committed artist-member fulfilled this function along with too many others. For many groups, the development officer was charged with raising money not only for the organization, but to pay his or her own salary as well.

While the quality of the argument and the worth of the idea are vital in a grant proposal, connecting and presenting that idea to the proper person is as important and the development officer is hired on the basis of his or her actual and potential contacts. It is the development officer's business to know who is giving away money—not just private individuals who might be more successfully wooed by board members or artists, but private and public agencies. In the public sector, this is no mean feat since the personnel change with each political administration and sometimes oftener.

A good development officer understands not only his or her organization's need for support, but the granting agency's need for reassurance. As William Coleman says in *Grants in the Humanities:*

> Like all other human entities, foundations need to be reassured about their choices. Nothing reassures them more than the judgment of others, coupled, of course, with the continued good work of the grant applicant.[1]

While this is generally true of all grant giving institutions, agencies that give money to the arts can anticipate one additional element— exposure. Money given to the arts is money publicized, a fact that corporations have been quick to understand and exploit.

Finding it difficult to separate their own needs from funding agency priorities, some arts groups get sidetracked from their original mission and goals. As grantsmanship talents have improved, groups have realized they are all going to the same "well"—not only the same as the one approached by other arts groups, but often the same as that approached by the rest of the third sector. In anticipation of the well running dry, as a response to cutbacks by major private and public agencies, and in answer to the corporate sector's posture that it cannot be expected to "make up the difference," arts organizations have begun to develop new strategies for survival including those discussed in the following chapters.

Nevertheless, the support structure of public and private money still exists, even though it has dealt some groups a heavy blow. Thus, grantsmanship is perhaps even more important than ever before. Certain groups are rightfully suspect of the permanence of such funds; others are suspect of the funds themselves, but new groups, particularly small, avant-garde, experimental ones that wish to operate as not-for-profit tax-exempt organizations, will have to develop professional fund-raising skills to remain in the funding mainstream.

In view of this, it is important for such groups to learn, and to remember, whose money they are seeking and what are the priorities of

---

[1]William Coleman, *Grants in the Humanities: A Scholar's Guide to Funding Sources* (New York: Neal-Schuman, 1980), p. 3.

the donors. Some will feel contaminated by certain kinds of money—foundation money, specifically from certain families, or corporate money—and will struggle between what Judith Malina calls "the angel of our good conscience and our dirty hands."[2] Some can look now at heavily supported arts organizations and wonder if the purse strings are dictating the program, or if the exposure offered a funding source through its association with an arts group destroys some of that group's professional credibility. Some, with no compunction, will say that money is money and as long as it allows artists to carry on with their work and allows institutions to function, pressure and interference can be withstood. Still others voice the opinion that the restrictions inherent in the whole third sector are too great and they would rather take their chances in the profit-making arena.

Therefore, let arts groups beware. Not only do funding agencies have very real and necessary requirements for giving money, they have similarly necessary requirements for accountability. They have a constituency to report to, and geographic dissemination, wide impact, and per capita funding may be among their highest priorities. Of those agencies that are particularly responsive to the field, they may have very specific notions of what discipline or area of emphasis merits response and what doesn't. Let such groups realize that a grant proposal is, in a sense, a contract. If the project is funded, the proposal becomes a written agreement of mutual needs, plans, and expectations.

ABOUT GRANTS

The following pages include grant proposals from arts organizations in three different disciplines—dance, the visual arts, and theatre. The proposals are to three different kinds of funding sources—a private foundation, a public funding agency, and a corporation. They are for relatively small amounts and are from institutions with annual operating budgets that range from $180,000 to $750,000. The Dance Theater Workshop in New York City applied to the Robert Sterling Clark Foundation for $20,000 for a 15-month project in 1980 and 1981. *and/or*, an artists space in Seattle, Washington, applied to the National Endowment for the Arts for $30,000 for a project from May 1982 to

---

[2]Stuart W. Little, *After the FACT, Conflict and Consensus: A Report on the First Amendment Congress of Theatres* (New York: Arno, 1975), p. 54.

April 1983. The Playwrights' Center in Minneapolis applied for $500 (for summer 1982) to the Continental Bank as part of a larger corporate strategy directed to business in the Minneapolis-St. Paul and Chicago areas. The first two proposals were funded in full, the third request was rejected.

Preceding each proposal is a brief history of the organization to give the reader a fuller understanding of the grant process. Additionally, each proposal is accompanied by comments which have been enhanced through extensive interviews with the directors of each organization. The narrative portions of each grant are reproduced in full. While space does not permit the reproduction of total organizational budgets for each organization, the actual project budget for and/or's proposal is included on the form required by NEA for submission. Although all three organizations have changed and grown even in the short time since these proposals were written, all comments describe activities as they existed at the time the proposals were submitted.

The formats of the three grants are strikingly different, partly due to the sources approached. The Dance Theater Workshop proposal, while written in a dense, packed style, is targeted directly at the Robert Sterling Clark Foundation, and includes certain buzz words throughout the grant to indicate its knowledge of the specific management funding interests of the Foundation. It has more of a "voice" than the other two proposals and seems to be, in part, a response to the personal suggestions of foundation officials who reviewed some of this material in earlier form.

and/or's proposal has the distinct disadvantage of being squeezed into a set of forms required by the National Endowment for the Arts that make it seem unnecessarily repetitive. Additionally, space provided for budget information is so minimal that financial figures do not clearly reflect the needs in the proposal narrative. In this case, a separate, more detailed budget would have helped the reader. The addition of supplementary information and an addendum indicate the way in which and/or dealt with the problem of format.

The Playwrights' Center has put together a proposal with many parts, some of which can be switched around and others added or deleted, as part of a larger strategy aimed at over 30 corporate sources. While it is specific about the Center and its activities, it is extremely general in regard to the funding source which is only mentioned by name on the easily removable cover sheet.

There are certain commonalities in these grant proposals, some of which are typical of proposals by small institutions. Each arts group

includes extensive validation of its activities and, although their methods may be different, their purposes are generally the same: to reassure the funding source of their capability as an arts institution both
programmatically and financially.

Dance Theater Workshop's proposal includes a heavy dose of financial and statistical membership information in the narrative, as
well as a substantial list of other funding sources that have supported
or been approached to support DTW. This information is included,
first, to show that DTW is not a fly-by-night organization, to demonstrate that DTW understands the financial aspects of its operation and
is responsible and accountable for its expenditures, and, second, to
reassure the private foundation to which it is applying that it is not the
"fund of first resort." The inclusion of a small biography of one of its
staff members for whom some of the requested funds will be used is
another kind of validation since the kinds of credentials listed serve to
further enhance the association of such a staff person with the Dance
Theater Workshop.

and/or's application to the NEA validates itself through its successful history and recent past programs, stressing again and again that its
responsiveness to the artist community is an essential component of
its programming and that, in certain areas, such responsiveness often
allows the organization to do little more than short-range planning.
Nevertheless, a documented history of the kinds of programs that
have evolved out of this kind of responsiveness seek to validate the
group's approach.

The Playwrights' Center spends considerable time detailing the
history of its recent merger with a complementary theatre group in the
mid-West. These details serve to reassure a funding source that the
applicant has already avoided one problem endemic to arts institutions—the duplication of services by similar groups with the same
constituencies. Additionally, this theatre proposal includes quota-
tions from director-actor John Houseman and *Los Angeles Times* critic
Dan Sullivan, to validate for corporate sources both the regional nature of the program and some of its advantages for playwrights.

In certain other fields of endeavor, like the humanities, and even
in larger cultural institutions, the tendency to include such validation
is frequently frowned upon. But what appears to be a flaunting of institutional or personal achievements in other areas, becomes a necessity in the arts. For small arts organizations, particularly those with
which a funding source is unfamiliar, the need for documentation,
validation, detailed statistical and financial information, personal biographies, and even critical reviews is paramount.

Another basic difference between grant proposals in the arts and those in the humanities is that arts proposals have spent less time focusing on the art of presentation and the quality of argument, and more time on the worth of the endeavor. Such proposals are clearly a means to an end and make no attempt to join the annals of great literature. Additionally, the expertise reflected in the proposal itself may have little to do with the level of production or performance of the arts institution, especially since the grant writer or development officer may have nothing to do with the actual functioning of the organization. (This is one reason site visits are often paid to the arts institution by potential funders.) Nevertheless, poor style and confusion of presentation, regardless of content, may serve to undermine a proposal's chances for funding. Conversely, a well-written proposal has a better chance of garnering respect and attention. It should be remembered that a first submission to a funding source may be the beginning of a long relationship. Therefore, the initial documents should make as strong an impression as possible.

DANCE THEATER WORKSHOP, New York City
Amount of Grant: $20,000
Funding Source: Private Foundation—Robert Sterling Clark
   Foundation

Founded as an artists' cooperative in 1965 and reorganized in 1975,
the Dance Theater Workshop now acts as both a service organization
and a production facility.[3] Committed to creating performance opportunities and to helping develop new audiences for the individual artist, DTW produces and sponsors activities in dance, music, theatre,
mime, and poetry. As a service organization, its most visible program
is the Membership Services Program which offers companies and individuals a variety of services: press, direct mail and advertising assistance, aid and information regarding postal regulations, graphic
design, video documentation and archival services, a national mailing
list of organizations that sponsor and present dance activities, studio
and theatre rental, a telephone reservation service, an "availabilities
file" of personnel and services frequently used by dance companies
and artists, survival seminars, publications, and a variety of staff services.

   In the true spirit of resisting the duplication of services, DTW has
offered many of its benefits as a courtesy to other service and presenting organizations, including the Brooklyn Academy of Music, the
Alliance of Resident Theatres/New York, Jacob's Pillow, and the
Foundation for the Extension and Development of the American Professional Theatre (FEDAPT). Additionally, it has become a nationally
oriented organization giving advice and aid to companies, regional
groups, arts councils, and individuals throughout the country including the Philadelphia Dance Alliance, the Mid-America Dance Net-

---

[3]The latter, through its production arm, The American Theatre Laboratory,
now called DTW's Bessie Schönberg Theater.

work, the San Francisco/Bay Area Dance Coalition, the Minneapolis Independent Choreographers Alliance, Volunteer Lawyers for the Arts, the North Carolina, Ohio and Massachusetts Arts Councils, the Washington Hall Performance Gallery in Seattle, as well as England's Dance Umbrella and France's Avignon Festival.

Dance Theater Workshop has grown from a small choreographers' cooperative to a solid but responsive institution. Its budget has climbed from $80,000 in 1975 to almost three quarters of a million dollars in 1982. Its Executive Director, David White, has played major roles in the creation of the Dance Umbrella and of the CETA artists' project in New York City. From 1979 through 1981 he was a member of the Dance Advisory Panel of the National Endowment for the Arts. Since then he has served on the NEA's Inter-Arts Advisory Panel.

The following proposal, written by David White, was submitted to the Robert Sterling Clark Foundation—a private foundation funding activities of organizations in New York State. Support of $20,000 was requested for a 15-month period (April 1, 1980 to June 30, 1981) for the development of a complete planning process including a written study that would review the past five years of the organization's development (1976–1981) and project its activity, service, and responsibility for the next five years (1981–1986). In more specific terms, funding was requested for two DTW projects: the Membership Services Program and a series of seminars devoted to economic survival for individual artists and small arts groups. The proposal was funded in full.

Accompanying the proposal, or sent just prior to its submission, were a Membership Kit—a handbook used in conjunction with Membership Services—plus a Press Reference List, a general purpose statement of the organization, a membership services brochure, and a membership list for 1979–80.

The grant grew out of White's perception of the need for a comprehensive planning process for his organization and his knowledge that his already overworked staff could not supply the time to make the necessary commitment to this process. Within this larger planning proposal, in which White wanted to involve and catalyze both the staff and the board, was another impulse to solidify control over the Membership Services Program, an area that had dramatically increased in volume from year to year. There was a desire to achieve both these aims in a non-crisis atmosphere. It is to White's credit that he understood the frequent modus operandi of arts organizations to be crisis management, and that his commitment was to begin planning for the future in advance, rather than as a result, of a crisis. White's thoughts for the future of DTW also included application to

the National Endowment for the Arts for a challenge grant. He knew
that a formalized, written planning study would aid him in substanti-
ating his organization's need for other monies in future.

Unlike the proposal from the Minneapolis Playwrights' Center,
the following proposal was written for one foundation, the Robert
Sterling Clark Foundation, one of the few private funding sources
with an interest in management issues in the arts. Since the Foundation refuses to fund salaries per se, and prefers to fund projects, the
proposal was developed to incorporate the requested salaries into a
larger project and to assure the Foundation that such salary costs
would be assumed by DTW after the grant period (which they have
been). The "strategy" of applying to specific sources for specific projects is one that DTW uses all the time, it was not developed solely for
this proposal. Nevertheless, the kind of planning study developed by
DTW is rare for a relatively small arts organization, a fact the Robert
Sterling Clark Foundation undoubtedly realized.

dance theater workshop, 219 west 19th st., new york, n.y. 10011 (212) 691-6500

dance theater workshop, 219 west 19th st., new york, n.y. 10011 (212) 691-6500

THE ROBERT STERLING CLARK FOUNDATION

The DTW Membership Services Program: A Planning Proposal*

(submitted March 1, 1980)

Dance Theater Workshop, Inc., requests the assistance of the Robert
Sterling Clark Foundation, in the amount of $20,000, in securing and
consolidating the administrative management and delivery of the component
service resources provided by DTW's unique Membership Services program (see
accompanying program description as well as materials submitted to the Clark
Foundation on November 29, 1979). Specifically, the funds requests in
this proposal will enable DTW to accomplish this process of consolidation
in three distinct but complementary stages, during a fifteen-month project
period that begins on April 1, 1980, and ends June 30, 1981.

It should first be noted that Dance Theater Workshop, a non-profit,
tax-exempt organization, is currently in its fifteenth year, its fifth at
its present home on Manhattan's West 19th Street (aka the American Theatre
Laboratory, where DTW is now the single most active dance theater in the
United States, through the production/presentation activities that parallel
the services program) and under the guidance of executive director David R.
White. The carefully constructed concept of cooperative resources embodied
in the Membership Services area and directed towards the massive administrative and financial complexities surrounding dance performance and
production throughout the metropolitan New York region has resulted in an
unabated surge, over the last several years, in DTW's paid artist membership.

In FY 1975-1976, that membership stood at 124; as of FY 1978-1979, it had
climbed sharply to 318; as of the date of this application, in FY 1979-1980,
membership has already reached 335, with more to come in the next four months.
DTW's budgetary growth (with Membership Services accounting for just under
50% of DTW's overall budget) has seen a similar sharp pattern of increase:
at the end of FY 1974-1975, total operating expenses stood at $81,437;
for FY 1979-1980, they are projected at $312,966 – with an accumulated deficit
during the same period that has only gone from ($9,897) to ($14,675).

As can be seen in the accompanying project and organizational budgets, the
volume of these individually inexpensive services, particularly within
what is known as the "DTW Promotional Resource Project" (in-house computerized
direct mail, advertising and press research operations), that has been
brought about by the membership increase has generated a large earned income
potential for DTW. Nonetheless, that same growth in membership and conse-
quent escalation in the artist demand for technical assistance is now testing
DTW's staff capacity in accommodating, virtually overnight, the rising
number of services rendered on a day-to-day basis, as well as in anticipating
additional future service needs of this broadly representative membership
that are not being provided elsewhere. It is in creating a comprehensive
approach to this short- and long-term need, within what DTW considers its
principal responsibility to the community of independent dance artists,
small companies and public audience alike, that DTW now asks the support
of the Robert Sterling Clark Foundation.

*The editor has taken the liberty of dividing the text into shorter
paragraphs for easier reading.

The first paragraph is really an abstract or summary of the entire proposal. It states at the outset the specific dollar request, the general areas those dollars will support, and the time period of the project. It appears in lieu of a cover sheet.

From the start, the grant writer uses a success-oriented tone and a style that invites the Foundation to be a partner in an enterprise instead of the rescuer of a sinking ship.

The word "stages" at the end of this paragraph and at other points in the proposal implies differing and sequential time periods. What the grant writer actually means are activities that occur simultaneously over the grant period, but are dependent upon each other.

This assaultingly alliterative passage ". . . carefully constructed concept of cooperative resources . . ." contains the essence of DTW's mission—cooperation and service, especially in administrative and financial areas, for those who produce and perform dance in the New York City area and who make up DTW's membership.

The inclusion here of membership and budgetary statistics serves as a statement of need. While stressing its growth and impact, the writer also explains the concurrent growth in demand for DTW's services. Additionally, the stature of the organization in terms of its budget and membership indicates a fiscal responsibility and understanding; it also validates the organization for the Foundation

The fourth paragraph uses a number of buzz words that connect directly to the funding interests of this Foundation at this time, including "earned income potential" and "technical assistance." It also specifically defines DTW's market to the Foundation as the community of independent artists, small companies, and public audience.

Dance Theater Workshop, April 1980 (cont'd)

Membership Services - Planning Proposal

The three steps to be taken in planning and implementing the consolidation of the administrative management of the Membership Services program
are as follows:

1) Assurance of current level and quality of DTW service activity -
There is no question of the central and significant role that the Membership
Services program plays in the professional lives of a majority of independent, non-institutionalized choreographers and companies, for whom the
ensemble of services have become at least a partial alternative to conventional arts management, particularly in the pre-production preparation
of concert dance activities. The remarkable membership growth must
count as an important measure of the program's impact: another measure is
the increasing number of theater and music artists and groups as well
as outside service organizations who are beginning to approach DTW for
assistance on different practical issues (see attached interim membership
list for FY 1979-1980). To meet the rapidly rising demand for its
component services, DTW is adding a new staff position to the Membership
Services area, effective April, 1980, to help facilitate the daily flow
of work involved in delivering services to DTW's constituency. In this
regard, and after a six-month search, DTW is hiring Kathy Spahn as
Associate Director for Services and Planning. Ms. Spahn, who is herself
a former dancer, has served as Assistant to the Director of the Cultural
Assistance Center in New York, a service organization established by
Martin Segal. Her background in the research and development of specific
resources available to the broad range of New York City cultural institutions, along with her analytical and evaluative experience in surveying
the spectrum of needs to be met, makes her an ideal candidate for this
position. She will work closely with Robert Applegarth, who now becomes
Associate Director for Programs and who has previously been charged with
the sole responsibility for all aspects of Membership Services. In addition,
DTW has budgeted more funds during the project period for Service
Associates, part-time assistants who work largely in the direct mail
operation preparing the actual audience and sponsor mailings as well as
the critically important periodic updates of the mailing lists on computer;
and for DTW's graphic design staff, who provide advertising design for
both publications and mailing pieces at nominal charge.

2) The creation and publication of a five-year plan for Membership
Services - Central to this proposal, and indeed to the whole of DTW's
obligations as an emerging institution within the New York performing
arts community, is comprehensive planning. At its January 26, 1980,
meeting, DTW's board of directors formally approved the executive director's
suggestion to design a five-year plan for the organization. The overall
plan is targeted for completion and distribution in January, 1981, and
will result at the same time in a major Challenge Grant application to
the National Endowment for the Arts, geared to achieving one or more
priority objectives set forth in the plan. As one of her primary duties,
Kathy Spahn will serve as staff coordinator for the plan, in conjunction
with a newly established Planning Committee made up of both board and
staff members. It is understood that the overriding theme and discussion
within the planning process will be that of service, not only in view of

MORE/...

The three activities in the project are clearly organized in order of their importance to DTW: first, a commitment to maintain the quality of current services which must never be threatened; second, a method for avoiding such threats in the future; and third, the continual development of programs that respond to the needs of its constituency.

This first point is a good example of an activity that is not really a "project," and which therefore lacks the strong appeal of projects that have well-defined, limited lives. Its inclusion as part of a larger whole and the writer's stress on its "alternative" nature strengthen the organization's request for aid.

This section of the narrative which "names names" seeks to do two things at once: it validates the creation of a new staff position through the credentials of a specific person and it illustrates the commitment of the institution to the project and the person.

As mentioned in the history of this grant, the strategy behind DTW's planning process is based partly on an avoidance of the "crisis management" so common to small arts groups. The second point illustrates the institution's support of such a process, through Board validation and approval of the executive director's decision-making and through the institution's plan to reach an even more effective level of planning by using the Robert Sterling Clark money to engender future support, including a Challenge Grant from the National Endowment for the Arts.

Dance Theater Workshop, 3/1/80 (cont'd)

Membership Services - Planning Proposal

of the Membership Services program itself, but equally in relation to
DTW's separate but companion production programs which are also conceived
as a basic service, in the area of sponsorship and accessibility in
performance opportunities, to the artists and audiences of New York.
It is, in fact, this combination within the whole of DTW's work that
makes the organization unique. As noted earlier, a coherent written
version of the finalized plan will be made available during the project
period, detailing the programmatic options and corresponding budgetary
considerations that DTW might be likely to pursue in the years ahead.
One major concern prompting the creation of a long-range plan is that,
in the expansion of DTW's resources, DTW should not forsake or allow to
deteriorate those services already being provided.

    3) Formalization of the "Economic Survival Seminars" series -
Over the past years, DTW has prepared a number of special nuts-and-bolts
seminars and meetings on major administrative issues and procedures that
individual artists and small groups must come to grips with, whether or
not they have an actual management person available. In the last two
seasons, these discussions, grouped under the rubric of "Economic Survival
Seminars" have covered such topics as incorporation and its alternatives;
the relationship between company (incorporated) and individual; creative
payroll and its relation to unemployment insurance and other basic
benefits; dance budgeting and recordkeeping for small companies; and
so forth. In late February, DTW sponsored an open meeting with the
New York State Council on the Arts Dance Program, with key staff members
representing the Performing Arts division, the Dance Program and the
Fiscal office. Again because of the lack of available staff, DTW has not
yet been able to prepare and forecast this seminar series on a truly
regular schedule - ideally of 6-8 seminars annually. The series becomes
especially important at this time because DTW is now beginning to research
and write a survival manual for dance artists, the Poor Dancer's Almanac,
a publication that is projected to be approximately 200 pages in length
and that should be ready for distribution in the fall of 1980. In early
February, the New York Community Trust awarded DTW a $25,000 grant for
the purposes of preparing and printing the Almanac under the auspices of
the Membership Services program. Since the nature of the publication
will be to turn up the gamut of issues and problems, both large and small,
that affect the personal and professional lives of working professional
artists, DTW hopes to adapt some of this material to the seminar format
during the 1980-1981 year, and beyond, for further investigation. The
support of the Robert Sterling Clark Foundation in this application will
allow us the chance to do just that. Responsibility for the "Economic
Survival Seminars" will be shared by Kathy Spahn and Robert Applegarth,
with the participation of the executive director. A final word: the
seminar series also serves to give DTW an excellent perspective on what
particular problems artists are encountering with a given issue; thus,
the series will aid DTW in its planning of what future service role and
functions the organization might best assume.

                                                    MORE/...

The word "service" is stressed here again, and the pairing of programming and budgetary considerations reiterates the institution's understanding of their relatedness.

Point three of the proposal can change as the organization's needs change. It outlines a series of seminars that suggest a responsiveness to the immediate survival needs of the New York dance community.

Dance Theater Workshop, 3/1/80 (cont'd)

Membership Services - Planning Proposal

These, then, are the three main stages of the proposed project to consolidate the management of DTW's Membership Services program. The process, as outlined here, speaks both to DTW's immediate administrative needs, brought about by the large and positive response of the artist community to the program, and to a simultaneous effort of DTW's part to anticipate and plan for such future expansion and/or re-direction of the program as may be called for. The support asked in this application from the Robert Sterling Clark Foundation will be used to help underwrite the appropriate administrative salaries and costs, including the participation of the key DTW staff members - in particular, Kathy Spahn and Robert Applegarth, as well as the service associates and assistants who work on a part-time basis - during the fifteen-month project period.

Finally, what are DTW's plans for assuming personnel and other costs over and above the requested grant assistance, both during and beyond the project period? As indicated earlier, the five-year plan will result in a Challenge Grant application to the NEA, such an application having already been invited by the NEA Dance Program, for a term beginning sometime in 1981. In addition, DTW will also be applying to the Rockefeller Brothers Fund for further assistance with the Membership Services program during the project period (the project budget shows a total foundation need of $30,200) - in this regard, DTW has already held discussions with RBF's Marilyn Goacher. The single most significant cost, the salary of Kathy Spahn as Associate Director for Services and Planning, is also incorporated into DTW's funding applications to the New York State Council on the Arts and the National Endowment for the Arts, which have continued to increase their support to DTW annually. By June 30, 1981, it is safe to assume that all of the proposed costs will be integrated into DTW's normal (and increasing) spread of public and private funding. The latter, through the date of this application, include: the Howard Bayne Fund; Capezio Foundation; Consolidated Edison of New York; Mobil Foundation, Inc; Morgan Guaranty Trust Company Charitable Trust; the Shubert Foundation; and individual contributors.

A brief review section indicates how the requested money will be spent and hits on words that illustrate organizational needs that directly result from client demand.

The last paragraph reassures the funding source that project costs will be assumed by DTW after the project period as well as restating DTW's commitment to the project.

The invitation by NEA for DTW to submit a Challenge Grant proposal reinforces the earlier success-oriented tone of this proposal.

The list of private funding sources at the end of the proposal reassures the Foundation that DTW has built up a strong funding reputation, and that the Robert Sterling Clark Foundation is neither the only nor the first private source approached.

AND/OR, Seattle, Washington
Amount of Grant: $30,000
Funding Source: Federal Government, National Endowment for
   the Arts

and/or is an artists space in Seattle, Washington. There are over 500
such spaces across the country, many of which began in the early-to-
mid 1970s. While it is impossible to generalize about the kinds of activities artists spaces embrace, they are frequently founded and run by
and for artists. They are an alternative to traditional commercial-sector
arts activities (commercial galleries, theatres) and, in many cases, to
traditional non-commercial activities as well (museums, repertory
companies, chamber groups). They support, generate, and present
work that is uncollectible (performance art, video installations), as
well as work that can be bought, sold, marketed and manipulated
(painting and sculpture). They support artists administratively, financially, and psychologically by being concerned with the most contemporary work and with a stretching of traditional definitions in that
work. While many began as exhibition spaces for visual art, they have
since included theatre, music, dance, video, film, performance art,
artists books, literary and interdisciplinary activity.
   Their beginnings in the 1970s were due to the encouragement and
support of public funding. Artists spaces, perhaps more than small
groups in any other discipline, came to regard that funding as a natural and expected part of their yearly operating budgets. Although they
were probably given no promises by funding agencies themselves,
the fact that some spaces were virtually created by public monies led
them to expect its continuation. By 1980, before the current administration took over, the NEA and state councils provided between one-
third and one-half of the budgets for many spaces. Although not a
direct result of the public support, national recognition of some

groups occurred before their place in their local communities was fully understood.

While *and/or* has managed to retain its commitment to the artist community that inspired it, it has grown into an institution whose national recognition overshadows its local reputation. Described as a "conjunction," a "resource," and a "sponsor," it is committed to a position of response, nurturing, and support of ideas, artists, and activities. Its current activities include a contemporary arts library called the Annex, a media center, the Pine Street Warbler and Soundwork Studio devoted to contemporary music activities, the monthly contemporary arts magazine *Spar*, a budding institute for contemporary visual art, COCA, and a group of artists organized around issues of art and social change, Xchange. It is curious that the activities with which the group was predominantly associated at its inception under its Visual/Media Arts Program—the presentation of visual arts and video exhibitions, projects, performances, and showings—have been discontinued, although support and encouragement of visual and media artists and activities have not.

Lack of significant financial support and audience growth within the community contributed to the program's demise and, in part, resulted in an overall evaluation of *and/or*'s position in the Seattle community.

> Although *and/or*'s reputation nationally has always been extremely good and its activities well regarded, from a number of local directions there was an expressed feeling that *and/or* was rather unprofessional (perhaps partly derived from our "unslick" physical space and promotional style), a "scruffy little place" run only by and for artists—an image curiously negative even to many artists. To many who might have been stronger supports, *and/or* was a "$20 place" and therefore in their minds, twenty dollars was a large gift. While staff members thought that this opinion could be changed, it would take an enormous effort where the visual arts program was concerned because that was the nearly exclusive reference point for *and/or*'s image locally.[4]

In response to this evaluation, *and/or* created operating divisions— programs that have reached a certain level are encouraged to become autonomous and independent, with their own staff and their own programming, under *and/or*'s umbrella. One result of the recent

---

[4]*and/or* Reports, "Visual Arts/Media Arts: exhibitions and other presentations," November 1981.

policy of giving each activity a name and, where possible, a space of its own, is that their individual identities are being strengthened so that they are not overwhelmed by the identity of *and/or*.

This is a departure from the original organizational concept of *and/or*. Originally activities were separated into programs with various program directors, but by definition and organization they came under *and/or*. This departure is also a reflection of mature leadership. Unlike artistic director/founders who cannot relinquish responsibility as their organization grows, *and/or* seems to be trying to provide the administrative and fiscal management support (including its not-for-profit, tax-exempt status where appropriate) that allows artists the room to develop.

The guidelines under which this proposal was submitted in the Spring of 1981 to the Visual Arts Program of the National Endowment for the Arts were undergoing certain revisions, many in response to needs from the field. Additionally, it has been the policy of *and/or* to submit proposals for emerging projects in their developmental stages to the Visual Arts Program at the NEA and, as these projects become more specific, to direct them to other divisions (the contemporary music programs to the Music Program at the Endowment, for example) or to help them develop their own funding elsewhere. The difficulty in fitting this proposal to the new guidelines—more severe than ever due to approaching federal cutbacks—was partly overcome through the expertise of *and/or*'s director, Anne Focke. Also Chairperson of the Visual Arts Program Policy panel since January 1981, Focke has tried to balance the challenges she thinks her organization needs with the needs of organizations around the country. Naturally, some might be quick to accuse *and/or* of obtaining funding due to this relationship. The relationship is somewhat complicated, however, since all policy panels and the National Council on the Arts and Humanities (the final review board for all proposals) include artists and managers affiliated with institutions that are applying to the Endowment for money. No panelists attend the actual review of their institutions' proposals. Focke admits the impossibility of remaining totally neutral on certain issues, but it is clear that she was chosen for the Policy Panel for her opinions as well as her perception of the field.

While such a position has its conflicts, there are some very real short cuts in the application procedure that are apparent in this proposal. These short cuts are not limited to *and/or*: they are standard operating procedure for most groups that have established a relationship with a funding source and that are applying for money more than one time. While a listing of key personnel is given both for specific projects and for the staff, board and advisory panels of *and/or*, there is no additional documentation to validate them—no resumes, biographies, critical articles, or reviews of activities. The legal requirements that all organizations must meet in order to apply to the Endowment—for example, a copy of the determination letter from the Internal Revenue Service indicating the tax-exempt status of *and/or* under IRS Code Section 501 (c) (3)—have been bypassed since this is not a first-time applicant and the Endowment has that letter in its files.

It should also be noted that the form of the NEA application, reproduced in toto here exactly as it was submitted, creates a great deal of confusion for the applicant and the reader. It requires a great deal of repetition for some items and not enough explanation for others. While certain items in the narrative seem to be explained endlessly, other parallel items in the budget are left a single line. Although supplementary information has been added, some points remain confusing. For example, an explanation of the activities of the library—in this proposal called Resources in Contemporary Arts, and now called the Annex—is included in a completely separate proposal for library programs alone. In Spring of 1981, NEA changed its deadlines to require all Visual Arts Program proposals at the same time; therefore, Anne Focke felt a reiteration of library activities in this proposal was unnecessary.

In addition to changing its guidelines and deadlines, the Visual Arts Program requested a budgetary system for separating support for artists from support for institutions; therefore, in this proposal the Total Amount requested from the National Endowment for the Arts is $30,000 listed in the following way: $20,000/10,000. $20,000 is for program money for the organization and needs to be matched; $10,000 is nonmatching money for artists' honoraria. Since NEA money is normally divided between organizations and individuals, one application does not usually include a request for both kinds of funds. In the case of artists spaces, the National Council was convinced that one of the main functions of artists spaces is to provide direct services to artists, so it agreed to entrust some of the money earmarked for individual artists to these artists spaces to disburse. There is some question regarding the efficacy of this idea, particularly since no other division of the NEA follows this procedure.

This proposal, for a total of $30,000, was fully funded by the Endowment, but its activities have not yet begun. While a portion of the money has been received (money can be requested in advance on a monthly basis, or the organization can operate on a reimbursement basis), federal law prohibits a recipient organization from investing it,

even in a short-term bank account. Certain funding sources like the
Seattle Arts Commission require total completion of a project and an
invoice for expenses before they offer "payment for services"; other
funding organizations are simply so late with their grant payments
that an organization has no money at all for cash flow or even salaries.
These kinds of restrictions make it necessary for a manager to skill-
fully manage income, to even out the cash flow, to invest only those
funds that can be invested, and to know a dozen little tricks for
maximizing the potential of a little budget.

It should be noted that the grant requested was applied for one
year before activity was to begin and that *and/or*'s firm commitment to
constantly respond to the needs of the artist community is referred to
over and over again as the reason that firm, unretractable programming plans are not set down. This proposal is an excellent example of
a general plan that makes sense in view of the organization's mission
and purpose, but that leaves room for experimentation and renewal.

and/or

OMB–128–R0001

Visual Arts Program

Organization Grant Application Form NEA–3 (Rev.)

Applications must be submitted in triplicate and mailed with other required materials to: Grants Office VA, (Category Name), National Endowment for the Arts, 2401 E Street, N.W., Washington, D.C. 20506

I. Applicant Organization (name, address, zip)	II. Category under which support is requested:	III. Period of support requested:
and/or service 1525 – 10th Avenue Seattle, WA 98122	_X_ Artists Spaces ____ Art in Public Places ____ Crafts Exhibitions ____ Photography Exhibitions ____ Photography Publications ____ Photography Surveys ____ Services to the Field ____ Visual Artists Forums	Starting 5 1 ·82 month day year Ending 4 30 83 month day year

IV. Summary of project description

With this application we request support for the activities of and/or that direct-ly serve the needs of visual artists. and/or is a contemporary artists' organization, initiated by and run primarily by artists in a variety of disciplines. It has a commitment to new ideas and a willingness to take risks on untested or unfamiliar work. An over-riding goal is to remain flexible, both in our programs and in our organizational form in order to respond to new and emerging needs in the artists' community. One result of this commitment is that specific program activities are seldom scheduled more than six months in advance, and generally less.

At this point, and/or can be described as a cluster of groups or programs linked together by shared commitments such as those mentioned above, and supported in a variety of ways by a central operational core. In addition to providing support to its component groups in such areas as management, recordkeeping, fundraising, etc., this core has the ability (and actively seeks) to nurture new ideas that aren't easily supported elsewhere.

The specific programs and projects to be supported through the funds requested here include:

1) The Projects Building — a large (30,000 square foot), two-story (basement and main floor) warehouse building next door to and/or's original location, to become ———————————————— (next page)

V. Estimated number of persons expected to benefit from this project   30,000*

VI. Summary of estimated costs (recapitulation of budget items in Section IX)

		Total costs of project (rounded to nearest ten dollars)
A. Direct costs		
Salaries and wages		$ 27,700
Fringe benefits		3,500
Supplies and materials		2,500
Travel		
Permanent equipment		
Fees and other		36,850
	Total direct costs	$ 70,550
B. Indirect costs		$
	Total project costs	$ 70,550

VII. Total amount requested from the National Endowment for the Arts $ 20,000/10,000

VIII. Organization total fiscal activity	Actual most recent fiscal period	Estimated for next fiscal period
A. Expenses	1. $ 200,662.15	2. $ 211,500
B. Revenues, grants, & contributions	1. $ 200,180.32	2. $ 211,500

Do not write in this space

*doesn't account for artists' projects in public situations

The atmosphere of the 1970s that gave rise to a variety of alternative organizations in the visual arts has been reflected in the Visual Arts Program of the National Endowment for the Arts. Categories, definitions, requirements and deadlines continue to change from year to year. While such changes often seek to respond to important developments in the field, they can also be extremely confusing for the grant applicant. In this proposal and/or has chosen to apply under the Artists Spaces category, in Part II of the form, one in which the Endowment encourages "individual artistic development and achievement by assisting artists' organizations which provide a structure and atmosphere conducive to dialogue and artistic experimentation."

The grant reader must understand the NEA guidelines as they relate to proposal length, since and/or's handling of an unworkable form is testimony to individual ingenuity. After the space provided here for the Summary of project description, the grant writer is allowed only one additional 8½" x 11" page even if the organization is applying for support for more than one activity or project. For the additional NEA Organizational Supplementary Information Form sheets, again only one additional 8½" x 11" page is allowable. Such bureaucratic restrictions have made it impossible to include a grant narrative near the beginning of the grant, where one would expect to find it. Instead, the actual narrative that details points made in the project Summary appears under "Exhibitions—Supplementary Information"—the only section whose page numbers are unrestricted.

The insistence on the new, the untested, and the untried immediately identifies and/or as avant-garde. At the same time, and/or manages to achieve the image of an organization run by and for artists that is also professionally managed.

A listing of projects illustrates the institution's role as an auspice for a variety of activities.

In answer to Part V, the institution once again refuses to be confined by the form and includes information in the margin, reflecting the independence and cleverness of the grant writer.

Items under Salaries and wages, and Fees and other, are discussed in detail later in the proposal.

As explained in the grant history, total amount requested is divided into two separate amounts: $20,000 needs to be matched and goes to a variety of institutional programs; $10,000 is nonmatching money for artists' honoraria.

A close reading of Part VIII reveals not only the lack of a deficit but a slight surplus of several hundred dollars.

Summary Project Description, continued

operational in the fall, 1981, and to include a fairly large (3,500 square foot) exhibition space, a medium (1,500-2,000 square foot) short-term project space, artists' studios, workshops, storage space and a small number of compatible commercial tenants (no more than 25% of the total area). Exhibitions and artists' projects will be the focus and primary public visibility of the building. and/or will provide overall management and direction for the exhibitions and projects as well as for the building as a whole through an advisory committee and project manager.

2) Independent Artists' Project Support. Based on an evaluation of proposals, and/or provides support to independent artists for projects of their own definition which can include the development or presentation of new work, public projects, publications, research, collaborations, planning, etc. The purpose of this program is to support artists' new ideas and directions by providing modest support for current projects which might not otherwise be possible. This will be the third year of the program.

3) Discussion and lecture series sponsored by Resources in Contemporary Arts, and/or's library. A series of six discussions or lectures (approximately every other month) intended to stimulate interaction and dialog among artists and between artists and the community. Among others, potential participants include visiting artists and artists exhibiting in the Projects Building.

4) Special sections of particular interest to visual artists in Spar. Spar is a contemporary arts magazine developed from foundations laid by the and/or Notes (our newsletter of the past three years) and from the critical need in this region for increased quality and quantity of publicly available writing about art. Funds will cover such costs as fees for artists' contributions, a critic-in-residence and guest editors' honoraria.

5) The final activity for which funds are requested is the most difficult to define but is, in our minds, the most important. It consists of partial support for the operation of and/or's core staff, allowing it to respond to new needs and new ideas emerging from the artist community during this grant period. This grant begins approximately one year from the time this application is being written and at this distance it is difficult to identify the specific nature of those needs, though there are several possibilities we can anticipate. One is the need to provide support (resources, fees and honoraria, advice, consultation, etc.) to artists who want to work outside the traditional or formal art exhibition contexts--in public situations, on community projects, on television, etc. Another is the need to assist emerging groups of artists; in the past, and/or has provided assistance to a variety of artists' groups, especially at their beginnings. A recent example is XChange, begun in January, 1981, a group of artists organized around issues of art and social change.

Key personnel at and/or at this time include Laura Brenner*, Irene Eggerman and Anne Focke* (core staff); and a program staff of Claudia Clement*, Rene Fabre*, Carole Fuller, David Mahler*, Heather Oaksan, Norie Sato* and Robert Teeple*. (Artists are starred*.)

Here the grant writer has managed to tread a very thin line. Treating the Projects Building as "working facilities," a category NEA will fund instead of "real estate," a category NEA will not fund, she has managed to use the guidelines to her advantage. Additionally, the plan to earn income from commercial tenants in the building for which and/or will hold the master lease allows for additional support. Beyond this, and/or is exploring the possibility of rental fees from artists as matching funds for the grant.

In point 2 what might seem an institutional risk—support of artists for projects "of their own definition"—is given validation through the last sentence.

Information about and/or's library is not available in this grant, partly because a separate application for library programs was submitted to the NEA at the same time. At the time of submission (Spring 1981) the NEA had just consolidated all their organizational applications in the visual arts which created a certain amount of confusion for applicants.

It is important in point 5 to stress the-time lag between a grant application and its funding results. Applications are frequently required by public agencies a year in advance.

In this section and/or turns a potential weakness into a strength and even gives an example at the end. What might be viewed as a lack of long-range planning skills is changed to a responsiveness and closeness to the artist community that is and/or's main constituency.

IX. Budget breakdown of summary of estimated costs

  A. Direct costs

    1. Salaries and wages

Title and/or type of personnel	Number of personnel	Annual or average salary range	% of time devoted to this project	Amount $
Director	1	14,000	50%	7,000
Ass't Dir.	1	14,000	50%	7,000
Bookkeeper/ Bus. Man. Manager:	1	14,000	25%	3,500
Projects Bldg.	1	14,000	30%	4,200
Work/Study Assistants: 30 hrs/wk @ $5/hr for 40 wks (help with office, discussions, special issues, etc.)				6,000

Total salaries and wages	$ 27,700
Add fringe benefits	$ 3,500
Total salaries and wages including fringe benefits	$ 31,200

    2. Supplies and materials (list each major type separately)

	Amount $
Overall office supplies & postage	1,000
Projects Bldg. supplies (office, maintenance, etc.)	600
Supplies for special Spar issues (layout supplies, etc.)	300
Supplies for Artists' Project Support (PR, postage, etc.)	300
Supplies for discussions (office, PR materials, postage)	300
Total supplies and materials	$ 2,500

    3. Travel

    Transportation of personnel

No. of travelers	from	to	Amount $
Total transportation of personnel			$

    Subsistence

No. of travelers	No. of days	Daily rate	$
Total subsistence			$
Total travel			$

It is unusual that the Director for this project remains unnamed in the grant, particularly when he or she will be receiving a salary of $14,000. While the reality of the situation is that this project is at least a year away from starting and the director has not yet been chosen, it is also likely that the general reputation of the institution will engender trust for future decisions in this area.

The role of the work/study assistants, however, should have been discussed in the narrative. $6,000 is a good deal of money in a $70,000 project and it would be useful for the grant reader to know that such students are drawn from the Cornish Art Institute, the University of Washington, and the University of Puget Sound. Something about the institution's educational relationship with them should also be included.

IX. Budget breakdown of summary of estimated costs (continued)   **3**

    4. Permanent equipment (list each item separately)   Amount

                                                                                         $

	Amount
Total permanent equipment	$

    5. Fees for services and other expenses (list each item separately)   Amount

                                                                                           $

Item	Amount
Rent: general office @ $100/mo	1,200
Rent: Projects Building (exhibition space, projects space, office – ¼ of total) $750/mo x 7 mo, $1,300/mo x 5 mo	9,000
Maintenance, utilities & insurance (office)	500
Publication printing & postage: $800 x 3 issues (includes % of monthly total for Spar)	2,400
Guest editors for special Spar issues: $250 x 3 issues	750
Professional services: carpentry, photography, accounting	2,000
General publicity costs -- for overall programs	1,000
DIRECT PAYMENTS TO ARTISTS: non-matching	10,000
" " " matching	10,000
Total fees for services and other expenses	$ 36,850

  B. Indirect costs

    Rate established by attached rate negotiation agreement with
    National Endowment for the Arts or another Federal agency   Amount

    Rate_____ % Base $_____ $ _____

X. Contributions, grants, and revenues (for this project)

  A. Contributions

    1. Cash (do not include direct donations to the Arts Endowment)   Amount
                                                                                             $

	Amount
Private contributions to Artists Project Support program	7,000
General contributions	5,000

    2. In-kind contributions (list each major item)

Total contributions	$ 12,000

  B. Grants (do not list anticipated grant from the Arts Endowment)   Amount
                                                                                             $

	Amount
Corporate Council for the Arts	5,000
Other foundations (Buckeye Trust, etc.)	7,500
Total grants	$ 12,500

  C. Revenues   Amount
                                                                                             $

	Amount
Rental income from Projects Building (% of total)	15,000
Admissions from discussions	550
Total revenues	$ 15,550
Total contributions, grants, and revenues for this project	$ 40,550

It is unclear both here and in the narrative that the $9,000 figure listed as rent for the Projects Building equals the portion of the total space to be used by the public.

Also unclear are the exact programs for which $2,000 worth of Professional Services are listed.

That there are no indirect costs is not unusual with an arts group that exists under its own auspice.

It should be understood that Section X on contributions, grants, and revenues is entirely projected at this point. Since the grant proposal is written so far in advance, such projections are normal and acceptable procedure.

Future Exhibition Plans

   While and/or's commitment to nurturing artists and to supporting and encouraging the presentation of new ideas in contemporary visual art is as strong, if not stronger than at any time in its history, the method of providing that support is changing, for a variety of reasons.

   In many ways, and/or has, during the seven years since it opened, provided the only, consistent showcase and support system in our area for artists' work that is investigatory, that challenges current definitions and that takes risks in a wide variety of media and disciplines. Until recently, no "alternatives" to and/or emerged here. While perhaps this reflects some degree of our strength, at this point we feel there is a real need for greater diversity in organizations supporting this work. (Among other things this is true because the art/artist community here has grown significantly, not only in size but in depth and understanding.) In fact, there are now a number of young organizations of high quality, each with its own goals, who together have the energy and potential to meet this need. Among others they include: C.O.C.A. (Center on Contemporary Art), created with the purpose of establishing a significant and highly visible center to stimulate the advancement and understanding of contemporary visual art; "BLUEPRINT: for Architecture", which presents and explores new ideas in architecture through exhibitions, presentations and talks; On the Boards, committed to presenting and encouraging performance art and contemporary dance; O.S. (Open Space), a very low budget storefront non-commercial gallery located in the same building and/or occupies; and, a yet untitled group of photographers who plan a series of contemporary photography exhibitions.

   After considerable evaluation and discussion, and/or has decided to re-direct its energy — rather than maintaining an exhibition space for programs specifically under our own direction and selection, we have made a commitment to find ways to support these new groups. The Projects Building, described in this application and included in the budget request, provides one method of support that we feel is critical. With the exception of On the Boards, which has its own space (one oriented to performance), the other groups do not have permanent exhibition space, and, at this point, they don't want it, can't afford it, or aren't ready for a 12-month ongoing exhibition program that becomes unavoidable once a permanent commitment is made to a particular space. And, yet, it is essential that they have access to a good, professional exhibition facility. (Questions of and/or's responsibilities for overall exhibition policies and curatorial selection procedures are addressed on the Artists Spaces Supplementary Sheet).

   The Projects Building is only one program which addresses the presentation/exhibition needs of contemporary visual artists. and/or also has a commitment to supporting the creation and exhibition of artists' work outside traditional exhibition spaces. Since this is a need that can not be met through the maintenance of an exhibition space, this commitment is expressed through two other aspects of our activities (both included in this application). 1) The program of Independent Artists Project Support has assisted a variety of artists in their desire to work in public and non-traditional contexts, and this will continue to be an emphasis. (A list of projects supported in the period Jan-June, 1981 is included in this package.) 2) The continued ability of the core staff to remain responsive and to support projects on short notice will undoubtedly result in support of projects of this sort.

This is the narrative which the NEA format does not allow.

In the second paragraph, the grant writer defines and/or's *role in the arts community over its seven-year history.*

The third paragraph explains the move of and/or *as it grows from a pure artist-run space to an organization difficult to categorize. Providing services and support as well as facilities and sponsorship for activities,* and/or *remains artist-run. The operative point here is that* and/or *is not a simple exhibition space.*

Paragraph four provides some expansion of ideas originally expressed in points 1, 2, and 5 of the project Summary at the very beginning of the proposal.

EXHIBITIONS   Supplementary Information

Highlights: one year of presentations at and/or — September, 1980 - August 1981

Hobie Swan: installation
Shigeko Kubota: videotapes, slides and talk
"R. Dick Trace-it: Image Mass Murder 1976-79": documentation exhibition by
    Vancouver artist Richard Hambleton, with text, photographs & paintings
Chris Burden: "The Big Wrench", videotape showing
Barbara Smith: "Just Passing", videotape showing
Willy Walker and Dana Atchley: an evening of video and humor
Northwest Film/Video Festival: highlights and selections from festival winners
Antonio Muntadas: video installation and talk
Bill Ritchie: "Glimpses", videotapes
Greg Skinner: installation
"The Art of the Handbill": a collection of public art
John Sinclair: "Pyrotechnics Extraordinaries", fireworks performance
AND/OR STORE: exhibition and sale of artists' products
Barbara London: lecture, "Video - through the Looking Glass"
Larry McKim: installation
Gary Reel: wall drawings
Gary Hill: video installation
Alvin Lucier: concert
Video on the Ferries: videotapes presented on the Washington State Ferries
Karen Helmerson: "00:30", exhibition-the art of television public service announcements
Shalom Gorewitz: videotape showing
Karen Helmerson: videotape showing
"Zounds on Tape": audio tape music by local composers
Frederic Rzewski: concert
Howard Fried: talk, videotapes and residency
Stuart Dempster: concert
Adrian Piper: "It's Just Art", performance, discussion and installation
Al Robbins: "Anticastrophy", installation and talk
Jerry Pethick: "The Polarity Strategem/Evolved Distortion", sculpture, wall
    pieces involving glass, metal, diffraction gratings
Michael Winkler: concert
Judith Hoffberg: illustrated informal talk
David Critchley: "London Video Arts" videotapes & talk
Joan Logue: "Video Portraits", exhibition and tape showing with discussion
"The Salvador Deli", food event and benefit
Michael McCafferty: "American Primitive", indoor installation and photographs of
    outdoor work
Paul Dresher: concert
"Oppositions: An Exhibition of Bookworks by Artists"
Warren Shaffer: concert
Martin Puryear: "Where the Heart Is", installation and slide talk
Jay Cloidt:loud sounds and visuals
The Girl Artists: "Split Shift Cafe", a restaurant from a waitress' perspective,
    installation and performances
Co-Lab: "The Two Suitcase Show"
The Art Politik: a national conference of art and politics with Lucy Lippard,
    Judy Baca, Suzanne Lacy, Jerri Allyn, Martha Rosler, Michael Glier, Tim
    Dresher, Carol Deutsch, and others.
Hans Haacke: "The Mobil Series", exhibition, talk and publication
Soho Cable - Selections: interviews with and works by artists
Thomas Peterson: concert
Vito Acconci: installation and talk
Suzanne Lacy: talk and installation
Mierle Laderman Ukeles: exhibition and talk
Mitchell Kreigman: performance/talk

This page validates the group's past and current work and is required by the NEA.

EXHIBITIONS   Supplementary Information

Notes:

Slides of work exhibited/presented at <u>and/or</u> in the recent past did not seem to be requested.
If in addition to the other information submitted, these materials are needed, please let us
know.

Due to our commitment to remaining responsive to the most immediate needs of the artist
community, <u>and/or</u> (and most of the other participating organizations) does not schedule
specific artists/exhibitions/projects/performances far in advance. The fact that this application is written almost one year in advance of the beginning of the grant period (and two
years prior to the end of the period) prevents us from identifying specific artists or projects
to be included in the program. We hope that the list of programs sponsored in the past year
will indicate the quality and breadth of our ongoing and future programming.

In the past, brief biographies and three slides for each artist were also required in some categories, plus an organizational description of future plans. Confusion as to the current regulations is obvious here. Brochures and publicity material accompanied the proposal, but space does not permit their inclusion here.

It is also clear that and/or wants to show itself to advantage but is at the mercy of an inadequate format.

HONORARIA   Supplementary Information

History

With only a few exceptions (during our first few years and for large group exhibitions) and/or has paid fees to all artists who have presented their work here. In our first few years, when the budget was very small, it was difficult to guarantee fees in every case since very often the only source of revenue for a particular show was the income it could generate directly, through admissions or specific contributions. As we grew, programs developed specific restricted income to cover their expenses. At this point, budgets were written to ensure a more reasonable and predictable fee to artists. For at least the past three or four years artists in all programs are paid.

Plan for awarding honoraria 1982-83

Artists' fees included in this application:

Non-matching	10,000
Matching	10,000
Total	20,000

Note: The total spent on fees at and/or as a whole is considerably higher than this figure.

Distribution of Artists' Fees:

Independent Artists' Project Support	12,000
General supplemental artist fee fund	5,000
Discussion/lecture fees for artists	1,500
Fees to artists for contributions to Spar	1,500
Total	20,000

Independent Artists' Project Support

This represents the third year of this program (briefly described in the summary project description). Selections are made by a special curatorial advisory panel which includes a member of the staff. (See staff/board/advisors list included elsewhere in this package.) It is made clear through all information distributed about the program that the definition of the individual projects is entirely in the artist's hands, with as few restrictions from and/or as is legally possible. An upper limit of $1,000 is placed on requests. Although this program perhaps stretches somewhat the definition of "honoraria", we feel this is justified by the program's very direct connection to artists' needs defined as they themselves choose. At the time this application is being made, only one year of the program is completed. Funds available for this period totalled approximately $7,000 ($4,000 non-matching from Artists Spaces grant for 1980-81, and $3,000 from private sources). A summary of the projects is attached.

General supplemental artist fee fund

This fund will be used to supplement funds for artists' fees in any of and/or's programs. This will include the Projects Building, giving us the opportunity to strengthen the exhibitions taking place there by providing support directly to the artists. This fund will also be used by and/or's core staff to pay artists for those unexpected, exciting, last-minute projects beyond the range of our other programs.

A number of the more institutionalized artists spaces in the 1970s began to pay their artists fees as soon as their budgets allowed. The commitment by those spaces eventually resulted in artists' fees being deemed a ''priority item'' in the Artists Spaces category at NEA.

The breakdown of budgetary items clearly indicates which activities are to receive emphasis. The inclusion, however, of the ''general supplemental artist fee fund'' is confusing. It appears to represent point 5 of the original project Summary but the difference in nomenclature makes such an attribution difficult.

HONORARIA   Supplementary Information

Independent Artists' Projects supported during period January–June, 1981

Mary Avery, framing of "Send Slides", a series of xerox works to be exhibited as part of a comprehensive exhibition of her work in Xerography (1973–1980) at the new offices of the American Institute of Architects in Seattle.

Kenneth Grzesik, completion of "The Electric Rain Forest", an open-ended installation of collected objects and sounds to be presented at ARC in Chicago.

Doug Kahn, production and partial distribution on radio of an audiotape, "The Tomorrow Show".

Richard Posner, A production of a publication, "Cope-aesthetic Glass Architecure", a photographic essay on ways people have transformed broken and discarded glass.

Heidi Drucker, a large scale, outdoor environmental performance piece designed specifically for Louise Boren Lookout Park, to take place in May 1981.

Ron Glowen, "The Farm Project", the creation and exhibition of outdoor, site-specific works by a number of Northwest artists on a ten-acre parcel of farmland.

Sheila Klein, production of a pamphlet-brochure about her work.

Donna Kossy, publication of one color postcard in an edition of 3,000.

Barbara Noah, research in holography with the help of an engineering consultant and with the goals of making at least one hologram.

David Sokal, production of a 28-page booklet, "Copyright Violation", with the purpose of "turning the omnipresence of advertising against itself".

The Girl Artists, "Split Shift Care", assistance with an installation and performance series in Seattle by a group of artists from Portland.

Gloria Bornstein, production of a videotape, "Cascade House Tour".

Sherry Markovitz, exploration of the possibilities of painting outdoors – on and in trees and other parts of the landscape.

Larry Reid, support to "Live Like a Human Being".

Paradise Loft (two-person theater group), support for publicity brochure.

Steve Christiansen, research for television documentary on the log export crisis in the Northwest.

Maxine Nelson, black and white slide piece responding to Michael McCafferty's outdoor installations.

Andy Ostheimer, development of a model portfolio/mini-exhibition.

This is actually an "appendix to the supplement". Were it not for the untenable requirements of the government form, most of this kind of information could have been appendixed.

Visual Arts Program
Organizations Supplementary Information Sheet

Please complete this form and return it in triplicate with your application. If more space is needed, please submit no more than one
additional page (8½" x 11") with this sheet.

Name of Applicant: _____and/or service_____

Category under which support is requested. _____Artists Spaces_____

1. Describe the significance of the proposed activity to the field, the objectives sought, the methods by which they will be achieved, and
   the relevance to the community in which the activity is to be conducted.

The overriding goals (and, we hope, the ultimate significance) of the activities proposed
here are an increase in opportunities and support for visual artists whose work challenges
and takes risks, a broadening of the audience (and support base) for contemporary visual
arts activities, and an increase in the level and quality of dialog and understanding of
the ideas and issues of this work. Each of the projects proposed reflects these goals.

Through the Projects building and its exhibition and short-term project space we
hope to support and encourage a broader diversity of visual arts and related activities
than has existed in this area previously (See "Future Exhibition Plans" for more information.) It is an attempt, on the one hand, to recognize and to support the increasing level
of activity and the need for a diversity of voices (avoiding the temptation to respond to
growth by developing an ever-larger "monolithic" organization), and, on the other hand,
to acknowledge the value of a single physical focus in developing a broader audience and
the economic need for groups to consolidate their efforts, sharing expenses and space
with others.

The Independent Artists Project Support is a very direct attempt to encourage artists
to explore new ideas and new directions. Both the library discussion series and the
special magazine issues are responses to the need, increasingly expressed by artists, for
more discussion of the ideas and issues of their work — both in print and in person.   And,
the goal is not simply for more, but for intelligent, articulate and knowledgeable response and criticism.

PLEASE READ SUPPLEMENTARY INFORMATION ABOUT EXHIBITION PLANS AND
HONORARIA. They are important to an understanding of the proposed projects and
their significance.

2. Describe the methods that will be employed to inform the public about the project.

One very important vehicle to be used in informing the public about these projects will
be Spar — a contemporary arts magazine developed through the experience and/or gained
from three and a half years of publishing a monthly newsletter. In addition to the magazine's primary focus (critical writing, articulation and discussion of ideas in a wide
variety of disciplines and special sections each month exploring specific issues) a group
of organizations will be invited to participate by using it for publicity and information
purposes. The groups who currently plan to participate include those operating under
and/or's umbrella, those planning to use the Projects Building and others who share
related goals. Spar, like the Notes, will be widely distributed, particularly throughout
our immediate geographic region — Notes distribution was 2,500 monthly.

In addition, each group and activity will use traditional publicity channels — posters,
handbills, advertising in local daily and monthly papers, radio and TV public service
announcements, press releases, and regular mailings to their own growing mailing
lists.   The publicity and distribution resources developed by and/or over the years
will, of course, be used by programs operating under its umbrella (library, artists'
support project, etc.), but will also be available to any participating group.

An aspect of Spar that we hope will stimulate and nurture an increased audience for
these projects and contemporary art in general is the fact that it will very consciously encourage a dialog between the written word and the spoken word. For example, the publication might sponsor a residency (artist/writer/...) or a seminar which would be intro-
duced the prior month through published articles and information, and, then followed by
reports, evaluations, edited transcripts or other articles generated by the event — the
published materials helping to stimulate the "live" discussion which in turn initiate
new published responses.

The need to manipulate the form makes the writer seem repetitious here; in all probability, she is tired of coping.

The second paragraph plants the seed in the reader's mind that the Projects Building is simply one of many future endeavors for which and/or will seek funding from the NEA.

The last sentence in paragraph 3 is a clear rejection of expansion for expansion's sake and addresses the quality issues of art criticism, dialogue, and communication.

Instructions to read supplementary information remind the reader that, although the format has made it difficult to provide a free flow of information, that information is not "boilerplate."

This section draws together all previously mentioned avenues of connecting the work of and/or with its public. Its particular emphasis on Spar, which will be taking roughly 15 percent of the total project budget, seems to be a major effort in its immediate plans.

Visual Arts Program
Organizations Supplementary Information Sheet (continued)

3. Describe the function and professional qualifications of persons responsible for organizing the proposed activities. (Resumes
   may be attached.)

Laura Brenner, Project Director and Assistant Director of and/or, will provide general
guidance and overview of the program. Laura is a writer, publishes occasionally, has
worked as a proofreader and was an artist-in-residence with the public schools. She has
professionally and successfully held the position of Assistant Director at and/or for the
past year and a half. In the fall, Laura will become full-time editor of Spar.

Anne Focke, Director of and/or, will provide curatorial direction, management support
and planning assistance for the program. Anne is an artist/writer, has been Director of
and/or since it began, prior to which she was Assistant Director of the Seattle Arts Commission. She is a member of the selection group for Artists Project Support.

Claudia Clement is the Director of Resources in Contemporary Arts where she has
worked for approximately two years. She will have responsibility for coordinating and
directing the series of discussions. Claudia is a writer with journalism experience.

4. Briefly describe the history of your organization, including its scope of activities and experience in conducting activities similar to
   those for which funds are being requested.

and/or was established in early 1974, and announced its opening with the following statement: "and/or is a space for the presentation of artwork such as videotape, film, conceptual work, contemporary performance, multi-media situations and other work currently
without opportunities in Seattle for public presentation, as well as more familiar art forms.
and/or will also sponsor workshops and forums, and will direct the production of new works.

Over the years and/or has added programs, clarified programs, occasionally dropped
programs and supported new activities as they emerge. These changes have been the
result of continual evaluation of past activities combined with a responsiveness to new
ideas, and the overall pattern of development has been one of gradual evolution and
change. New and current activities are based on the experience of past activities.
Specifically, the Projects Building is based on our experience with exhibitions of contemporary art as well as our experience collaborating and working with other groups
(In most cases we have spent considerable time with each of the participating groups
during their development, providing advice, resources and support.) The Artists
Project Support program is based not only on one year's experience with the same
program, but on the experience of two earlier related though more limited programs
which invited artists' project proposals. Spar has developed specifically from our three
year experience with a monthly newsletter — and attempts to build on our experience of
its strengths and weaknesses. Since the very beginning, and/or has sponsored discussions
and workshops.

5. Describe your ability to administer the proposed activities. Send a budget of similar previous projects, if available, and a financial
   statement for your organization's most recently completed fiscal year.

A financial statement for Fiscal 1980 is attached.
The best description of our ability to administer the proposed activities is our past
performance administering the activities that provided the foundations for the new ones
(combined, perhaps, with the fact that and/or currently operates without a deficit).
Each of these previous activities is documented in some fashion in this application,
and their relative strengths and weaknesses should be reflected.

Although a listing of staff and board members appears at the end of this proposal, this is the first opportunity the reader has had to become familiar with organizational personnel.

This section fleshes out the statements made in the project Summary about organizational flexibility.

One of the most important points in the whole grant—the operation of and/or without a deficit—appears here. Although it appears in figures on the bottom of page one, it might have been wise to include it near the beginning of the project Summary as a primary example of good management.

Visual Arts Program
Artists Spaces Supplementary Information Sheet

Please complete this form and return it in triplicate with your application. If more space is needed, please submit no more than one
additional page (8½" x 11") with this sheet.

Name of Applicant:_____and/or service_____

1. Describe your organization's structure, including a list of the board of directors, advisory panels, and staff, curatorial selection
   procedures and exhibition policies, and your membership policy, if applicable.

   and/or was initiated by artists and from the beginning has been staffed primarily by
artists. The direction of and/or as a whole comes in large part from the individual
artists who comprise the staff. At this point, and/or consists of a cluster of relatively
autonomous programs or groups linked together by shared commitments and supported
by a central operational core. The "core" is comprised of two full-time people and a half
time business manager who provide assistance in such areas as management, planning,
recordkeeping, fundraising and communication, and who provide, as well, a focal point
for new ideas and support for emerging projects. The program staff consists primarily
of artists who work part-time, responsible for a specific program or service. The individual program staffs set directions and priorities for their own programs, select participants, write grant applications, handle correspondence, and in most other ways implement the program.

   and/or's Board of Directors, provides general guidance for the organization, oversees
overall financial matters, participates in long-range planning and communicates primarily with the core staff. A variety of advisory and policy groups have been established, with specific responsibility to a particular program in most cases. (Staff, Board
and advisors lists are attached.)

   Selection & curatorial policies: Traditionally, responsibility for curatorial selection
at and/or has been assumed by the artist staff in each program, working from inquiries
and proposals and from their own experience and understanding of the field, with the
assistance of the rest of the staff and various advisory groups. The core staff have
selection and curatorial responsibility for projects and activities beyond the range of
other and/or programs.

   Specifically in terms of the proposed projects: 1) a selection panel (which will
change periodically) has been established for the Independent Artists Project Support at
                                        (see next page)

2. Describe the size and composition of the constituency served by your organization.

   Overwhelmingly the constituency served by and/or and the groups and activities
operating under its umbrella or with its support is artists — artists broadly defined,
in many disciplines, from this region and elsewhere. Increasingly, however, our
constituency includes the broader audience interested in contemporary arts and issues
raised by this work.

   At the moment, the specific constituency is relatively difficult to define specifically
as each of our existing programs develops more autonomy and begins to find its own
base, and as and/or begins to serve an increasing number of groups (and their constituencies in an indirect fashion).

   To summarize: and/or's constituency includes:

   1) Artists, in the Northwest and across the country
   2) Other organizations which serve artists needs and which support exploration
      and new ideas
   3) Audiences interested in the work of contemporary artists, both in its actual
      presentation and in information and dialog about it.

This section reassures the funding source that the institution, though run by and for artists, is not a vanity operation. The presence on the board and on various committees of non-artists, including attorneys and businesspeople, and the very number of committees should indicate a built-in system of checks and balances.

Like many artists spaces, and/or *no longer serves only the community of artists. In its move from artists space to service organization,* and/or *finds its audience is changing. It is clear that one of the results of its new direction will be to address that audience's needs.*

ARTISTS SPACES SUPPLEMENTARY INFORMATION SHEET addendum

1. Organizational structure; staff, board, advisors, etc., continued

the invitation of the core staff and including <u>and/or's</u> Director. 2) <u>Spar's</u> editor, with the
participation and approval of the magazine's policy board will select artist contributors.
3) Artist participants in the discussion series will be selected by the library's director
with the participation of the library's assistance group. 4) The Projects Building Advisory Panel, with the active participation of <u>and/or</u> Director will select the participating
organizations to use the exhibition space and <u>will also</u> set guidelines for and select
artists for the short-term project space. Criteria for participating organizations include their commitment to contemporary exploratory work in whatever disciplines they
work, the meaningful involvement of artists in the policy and decision making of their
organizations and the quality of the work presented. The current identification of certain groups (BLUEPRINT, COCA, Open Space, etc.) has been based on these criteria.
Similar criteria are used in evaluating individual artists' work for the project space.
Throughout any of these programs, artists are encouraged to make proposals.

<u>Staff, board and advisory panels</u>   (artists are starred*)

Core Staff
    Laura Brenner*
    Irene Eggerman
    Anne Focke*

Program Staff
    Visual/Media Exhibitions
    (through 9/30/81)
        Carole Fuller
        Norie Sato*
        Robert Teeple*
        Anne Janisse* (work/study)
    SOUNDWORK
        Rene Febre*
        David Mahler*
    Resources in Contemporary Arts
        Claudia Clement*

    Video Editing Facility
        Heather Dew Oaksen*

Board of Directors
    Eric Anderson, architect
    Jack Baker, artist*
    Gloria Bornstein, video/performance*
    Suzanne Tedesko, video producer*
    Kelby Fletcher, attorney
    Robert Kaplan, attorney
    Frank Tenczar, TV producer
    Iris Sutton, gallery owner
    Rex Erickson, computer firm

Board of Advisors (general group,
functions primarily as individuals, participating in a one-to-one manner rather
than as a single body)
    Buster Simpson*
    Andrew Keating*
    Diane Millikan

Board of Advisors, continued
    Ronald J. Ciro
    Julie Anderson
    Stuart Dempster*
    Susan MacLeod*
    Barbara Mooradian
    Ann Ostheimer*
    Cara Wells
    Anne Gerber

Projects Building: Policy & Management Panel
    Richard Andrews*
    Kae Eyre
    Marcia Wagoner
    Jon Gierlich*
    Larry Rouch (rep of BLUEPRINT)

    Eric Anderson
    Artist rep of photo group*
    Artist rep of COCA*

Independent Artists Project Support Panel
    Anne Focke*
    Anne Gerber
    Catherine Hillenbrand
    Norie Sato*

Spar: Policy & Advisory Group
    Laura Brenner*
    David Mahler*
    Bob McGuinley*
    Larry Rouch
    Anne Focke*
    Brian Branagan*

Library: Assistance Group
    Karen Watts*
    Diane Shepardson
    Laura Millin
    and appx. 10 more

Visual Arts Program
Artists Spaces Supplementary Information Sheet (continued)

3. If applicable, describe technical equipment owned and or rented and your policies for making this equipment available to artists.

The Philo T. Farnsworth Memorial Video Editing Facility, which operates under <u>and/or</u>'s umbrella, makes 3/4 inch cassette editing equipment available to artists and other independent producers at a low rate and in accordance with a published set of guidelines (enclosed in this package).

SOUNDWORK, the new music program at <u>and/or</u>, owns and operates an electronic music and tape studio including Buchla synthesizer equipment. Like the Video Editing Facility it is publicly available to artists in any media (composers are, however, the primary users) according to an established set of policies and guidelines. (also enclosed here).

Since these two programs are not included in this request, further information was not included here. Contact <u>and/or</u> if additional information is necessary.

THE PLAYWRIGHTS' CENTER, Minneapolis, Minnesota
Amount of Grant: $500
Funding Source: Corporation—Continental Bank, Minneapolis

In 1980, the Midwest Playwrights' Program and the Playwrights' Center merged. Both organizations shared a commitment to the development of playwriting talent in the midwestern United States and their merger was a stellar example of a natural collaboration that avoids the duplication of services so common to arts groups. This was not a case of two organizations trading tangible assets—a building, for example, or grant monies—since the Playwrights' Center had virtually all the tangible and financial assets. Instead, it was a sharing of services, resources, personnel, and artistic direction.

The background of both the Midwest Playwrights' Program and the Playwrights' Center are stated in the introductory section of the grant proposal, but what is not stated is the funding atmosphere in the Twin Cities when these groups began in the early 1970s. An interest in the individual artist and in keeping that artist in the Midwest had blossomed, with dramatic increases in support to programs supporting individuals. Among such programs were Composers' Forum, the Minnesota Independent Choreographers Association, and a fiction writers' group called the Loft. The Loft's support jumped from approximately $25,000 to $120,000 in two years, while the Playwrights' Center, in grant monies alone, jumped from $11,700 in 1979 to $118,000 in 1980, and to $300,000 by Winter 1982.

The atmosphere was ripe not only for the program described in this proposal, but for the strategy of obtaining small pieces of local cash to support it. Such a plan was completely in harmony with the mission of the program: while Minneapolis houses the Center itself and will continue to do so, the Midwest Playwrights' Program will move each summer to one of 12 different states, committed to creating an opportunity for Midwestern playwrights with the additional hope of keeping them in the Midwest and not losing their talents to the two coasts. Summer 1982, the year for which this particular proposal was written, the Program was hosted by the state of Illinois and housed in Chicago.

When the now-familiar federal cutbacks in the arts became a reality, the Center's original plan for raising contributed income changed. Instead of seeking equal support from the federal government, local sources, and the host state, a strategy was developed that depended more on local and state sources. A strong, aggressive campaign was created that addressed private foundations and corporations in the Minneapolis-St. Paul area, and in the host city. While the Playwrights' Center may run out of local Minneapolis sources, it is establishing a broader funding base by approaching the 12 member states for support.

While the intention was to obtain a handful of leadership grants, that is, grants over $3,000, only one, from Chicago, was received; the Playwrights' Center began the arduous but important task of applying for small grants in amounts ranging from $500 to $3,000. Two-thirds of the support was to come from Chicago and one-third from Minneapolis-St. Paul. The grant included here is an example of this strategy.

Personal contacts were made at each corporation and foundation before a proposal was submitted. Certain issues that do not appear to be resolved in the grant itself—the selection process of playwrights to appear in the summer Program, for example—were resolved in personal meetings with corporate and foundation representatives. The three Minneapolis sources had been approached by the Center before 1982, but the 35 Chicago sources were brand new for the organization and there were several important procedures that helped cement relationships between them and the Playwrights' Center. First, the Center made it quite clear from the start that it was not attempting to raise funds in competition with the established theatre and that, if funding a proposal from the Center meant that grant money would be taken away from an existing theatre, the Center would not submit a proposal. Twenty Chicago sources immediately rejected the Center's request on this basis. The Center stated its aims at the initial contact with a funding source because the success of the Center depends on its relationships with established theatres. Its credibility was thus at stake. While short-term financial gains might be served by competing with these theatres, the long-term development of the playwrights' craft through collaboration with professionals—the essential purpose of the Program—would suffer.

Second, the Center used an existing Chicago arts organization to act as validator and buffer for them. The Chicago League of Theatres both endorsed the Center and acted as a sounding board for all solicitations before they were made. Since the League is a known quantity in Chicago and the Playwrights' Center was not, the League's backing was invaluable as was their expertise with local funding sources.

Third, in an extremely unusual gesture, a private, corporate foundation actively solicited contributions for the Center. The Dayton-Hudson Foundation in Minneapolis wrote letters to all the appropriate Chicago funding sources explaining their own local support, and urging further support by these new sources. Foundation President Richard Contee initiated this because he believed in the program and felt it was extremely important for the organization to secure funds from Chicago sources. The Dayton-Hudson Foundation is one of 45 Minneapolis corporations that contributes five percent of annual profits to cultural and social action programs.[5] This kind of support is perhaps even more important than cash for a growing, emerging organization. It makes it all the more unfortunate that none of the Center's smaller requests was funded.

The funding that was received by the Center included $15,000 from the MacArthur Foundation, $5,000 from the Chicago Community Trust, $3,200 from the Illinois Arts Council, and $4,000 from individual sources. Although at this writing proposals are still pending in several places, the smaller requests seem to have been rejected along with a host of "emergency requests" made by arts organizations suddenly aware of the imminent economic crunch. In a few cases, the Center was led to believe that funding hinged on their obtaining a leadership grant, but even after receiving such funds from the MacArthur Foundation, corporate funds dried up.

Although the following proposal was sent to a Minneapolis corporation that had just opened (the Chicago branch of the same corporation turned down the request), this exact proposal did not go to every corporate and foundation source. Different components were taken out and others added, offering a variety of attractive support features including total support of a playwright—$6,000, travel for one playwright—$250, playwright's stipend—$500, support of one actor for two weeks—$600, support for one director or one dramaturg for the program—$750, and support of props and lights for one read-

---

[5]Alan Kritzler, "The Five Percent Solution," *American Arts*, May 1981, pp. 3, 20.

ing—$100. In this way, the proposal was specifically toned to corporate sources. It was made to appeal to a committee and acknowledged that the committee and the corporate entity needed some publicity and a tangible product for their support. Realizing that arts organizations were competing for money with programs that many funding sources feel are absolute necessities—welfare programs and social services, for example —support for specific items was requested. Nevertheless, the Center had to stress that it could not guarantee the selection of a playwright from the geographic location of the corporation where it sought support; a Minneapolis playwright could not be guaranteed for summer 1982 even if a Minneapolis corporation gave support.

Publicity in the Center's local newsletter and in the Midwest Playwrights' Program's twelve-state newsletter was promised, and relationship building began to ensure the inclusion of supportive corporate and foundation representatives at each event. In addition, due to the nature of the program itself, contacts were begun in Spring of 1982 for the Summer 1983 Program and potential funders were invited to Chicago for the 1982 event.

The proposal itself was the brainchild of managing director Ted Crawford and two staff people, Julie Busard and Christopher Kirkland, Director of the Playwrights' Center. True to the spirit of the organization, the first people consulted at the idea stage were the playwrights. Subsequent to their approval, the Board of Directors was consulted.

The proposal was accompanied by existing and projected Program budgets, a financial report prepared by a Certified Public Accountant, an annual report, and publicity material.

Although one can take umbrage with the proposal in matters of rhetoric and style, one gets the feeling from the sweep of corporate rejections that the proposal itself had little to do with the decision not to fund it. Rather, this situation provides a startlingly clear example of the predictions corporations have been making since 1980—that they would not fill the gap created by federal cutbacks to the arts. And although the procedures followed by the Playwrights' Center are commendable, the result illustrates all too clearly the inequality between effort and reward. It is this very inequality that has made many arts groups contemplate projects in the commercial marketplace to help sustain their operations.

Midwest Playwrights' Program

An Annual Project of The Playwrights' Center

PROPOSAL SUBMITTED TO: Dave Handy
                         Continental Bank Foundation
                         510 Marquette
                         Suite 300
                         Minneapolis, Minnesota 55402

North Dakota
South Dakota
Illinois
Indiana
Iowa
Kansas
Michigan
Minnesota
Missouri
Nebraska
Ohio
Wisconsin

Artistic Director
Dale Wasserman

PROPOSAL SUBMITTED BY: The Playwrights' Center
                        2301 Franklin Ave. East
                        Minneapolis, Minnesota 55406

             CONTACT: Ted Crawford
                       Managing Director

REQUEST: The Playwrights' Center requests a grant
          of $500 from the Continental Bank Foundation
          to support the stipend for a local play-
          wright to participate in the 1982 Midwest
          Playwrights' Program. The Midwest Play-
          wrights' Program is an annual project of
          the Playwrights' Center. It is a unique
          opportunity for ten Midwestern playwrights
          to become involved with the development of
          their craft by intensive collaboration with
          professional dramaturgs, directors, actors
          and technicians. The Program culminates
          in a two-week festival of staged readings
          of the new plays.

INTRODUCTION

     The Midwest Playwrights' Program (formerly the Midwest Profes-
sional Laboratory) was founded in 1975 by Dale Wasserman (best
known as author of MAN OF LA MANCHA and the stage play of ONE FLEW
OVER THE CUCKOO'S NEST) in Rhinelander, Wisconsin. In a span of
five years it grew from a playwriting course taught as part of the
University of Wisconsin Summer Session to a nationally recognized
conference for the development of playwrights in the Midwest. In
1979, the program moved from Rhinelander to the University of Wisconsin at Madison joining forces with the University Theatre and
Drama Departments. Under this auspice, it was able to develop
into a viable and effective program serving playwrights from twelve
midwestern states, as well as increasing its administrative staff.*
As the program grew, however, it became apparent that continued
growth and success necessitated a further move. There was a critical need to expand the work to a broader community throughout the
midwestern states, without any affiliation which might give the
impression of parochialism or in any way limit the promising potential of the program.

     The solution was found in the Playwrights' Center in Minneapo-
lis, Minnesota. The Playwrights' Center evolved out of an organization started in 1971 called the Playwrights' Laboratory. The
Center is dedicated to developing the talents of playwrights in
the regional area by offering such diverse services as: a year
long playwright-in-residence program for six playwrights, script
copying, script distribution, non-performance workshops, cold and
staged readings, job referrals, commission work, a reading and
critiquing resource center committed to promoting, encouraging and
motivating playwrights, with a special emphasis on playwrights
tapping into the resources of their regional heritage.

     The collaboration between the two organizations was a natural
and healthy extension for both. On August 9, 1980, the Midwest
Playwrights' Program became part of the Playwrights' Center's year-
round operation. The integration increased the opportunities for
playwrights to create a more pragmatic and professional alliance
than was possible before. It also made feasible a different location each year for the Program by virtue of becoming independent
of its parochial affiliation. The summer of 1981 saw the first of
the annual allied effort in Northfield, Minnesota. The Midwest
Playwrights' Program, a two-week intensive workshop, combines the
talents and conscientious efforts of the selected playwrights with
professional directors, actors and dramaturgs. The event received
national attention as an unprecedented cultivator of tools and resources necessary for the constructive development of promising
playwrights in the Upper Midwest.

* The twelve states involved are: North Dakota, South Dakota,
Illinois, Indiana, Iowa, Kansas, Michigan, Minnesota, Missouri,
Nebraska, Ohio and Wisconsin.

The first paragraph serves to validate the proposal by referring to the credentials of the founder and to the earlier academic affiliation of the Midwest Playwrights' Program.

This last sentence makes a particularly important point. The writer anticipates any objections that might be made about the program being parochial. Throughout the proposal, regional importance and national appeal are balanced against possible "parochialism."

The validation process continues in the second paragraph which serves to reassure perhaps dubious bankers that the artists know how to solve administrative problems.

One difficulty at this point in the proposal is the reader's confusion with several different organizational names. Although the historical background of each organization and of the merger between organizations is important, it will be less confusing for future funding relationships if the group can solve this problem.

Another example of validation occupies the third paragraph, which points out that a merger of the two organizations served to avoid the common problem of duplication of services. This is generally commendable. Readers familiar with arts groups should see this as a cost-saving and energy-saving strategy. Additionally, the vocabulary indicates collaboration rather than simple merging. The descriptive style of the proposal continually indicates help, aid, nurturing, and development.

From the well-focused foundation already created in Minnesota and Wisconsin, it is the conviction of the Program to extend
itself geographically to the other participating states with projections of building a tight network more completely supportive of
playwrights and arts' supporters in the Upper Midwest region. By
doing so, the Program hopes to develop a real commitment and involvement of each state in the development and support of playwrights, and to develop closer links with the professional
theatres in the Midwest.

Here the reader is again reminded that the Program is not parochial, that the Program's directors have contacts in the field. One could quibble, however, with the last line. The attempt here, to suggest the broad future applications of the Program, might be challenged by a literal-minded reviewer interested in facts and specifics. The inclusion in an appendix of a list of professional theatres which the Program might contact in the future could serve to mitigate such a challenge.

CHICAGO--SITE OF THE 1982 MIDWEST PLAYWRIGHTS' PROGRAM

The goal of the "floating opera" concept is to establish an open and cooperative regional network of playwrights and theatre artists which are integral to the vitalization of American theatre. Chicago, as the second largest city in this country, is obviously a critical and necessary participant in creating this network, particularly in these early stages of growth for the Midwest Playwrights' Program. There is a tremendous wealth of artistic talent in the city of Chicago, in the performing arts as well as in the literary field. It is only natural that Minneapolis/St. Paul, also midwestern cities with national recognition in the arts, form a bond with Chicago in sharing artistic resources and talents. In fact, already there are signs of mutual and eager interest. John Olive, for instance, a playwright-in-residence at the Minneapolis Playwrights' Center, has recently had his play STANDING ON MY KNEES produced at the Wisdom Bridge Theatre in Chicago. John and Bob Falls, Artistic Director of the Wisdom Bridge, worked together on that same play at the 1981 Midwest Playwrights' Program. STANDING ON MY KNEES has received critical acclaim, and is sold out for the duration of its run. By hosting the 1982 Midwest Playwrights' Program in Chicago, the Program hopes to encourage the expansion of those kinds of relationships as well as increasing the opportunities available to theatre-related artists. In so doing, an important, vital connection between Minneapolis/St. Paul and Chicago will develop, providing an important linkage in the cultivation of regional arts and artists.

This page is a variable insert that can be changed according to the specific source from which funds are sought. The "problem" which the page deals with is to reassure the Chicago bankers that the Minneapolis theatre group is not merely interested in Chicago money—that Chicago will profit from the project.

The "floating opera" idea of the first sentence was excised from later versions of the proposal, since many readers found it confusing. The advantage of a proposal of this sort is that it can be constantly revised, if the writer is careful to solicit feedback about it.

NEEDS STATEMENT

There is a growing need to develop and explore skills and visions of new playwrights nationwide. Theatres are hungry for new plays because of the audiences generated as well as the artistic challenge demanded by producing quality original work. By optioning an original play, theatres will profit from future productions of that particular work.

Several projects philosophically compatible with the Midwest Playwrights' Program have responded to this rising need throughout the country. For instance, the Actors' Theatre of Louisville hosts a two-week festival of full productions of new plays as part of their regular season. Most regional theatres have incorporated into their season a program which presents readings of selected unpublished, unproduced plays, usually with the volunteer support of the company actors and assistant directors. The Playwrights' Center in Minneapolis devotes 52 weeks a year to workshops for playwrights' plays-in-progress.

The most visible and intensive of these types of programs is the National Playwrights' Conference at the Eugene O'Neill Theatre in Waterford, Connecticut. It offers two staged readings of each play selected for the four week workshop period. The Midwest Playwrights' Program, affiliated with the O'Neill Conference, works cooperatively with that Conference and, in a variety of capacities, with the other programs.

These examples express national recognition of theatre as a vital arts component of our culture and the need to perpetuate lively new expressions of that culture. It is the unique opportunity of the Midwest Playwrights' Program, by nature of its location and goals, to provide an atmosphere isolated from the commercial pressures which allows for a more comprehensive focus on the playwright. The origi- nality of the Midwest Playwrights' Program is that it has a truly cre- ative, retreat environment in which the playwright is expected and en- couraged to develop the quality of the script. Removed from the buyers' market, the playwright, as well as the supporting artistic staff, be- comes dedicated to the process of play development.

The non-coastal location of the Midwest Playwrights' Program encourages a cooperative and strong regional artistic network. The necessity is to expose the playwright working on a farm in Iowa to these unique resources and opportunities by bringing the focus of the Program to a new state each year in active pursuit of rooting this regional artistic community. Playwrights whose plays were not se- lected are nonetheless invited to participate in the Program, and to share the developmental process.

John Houseman, world famous stage director, said recently, "That's where the action now is--in the regions." It is undeniably true that during these times of economic recession and stress and unstable foreign circumstances, there is a need for the American

The "Needs Statement" is an example of the problem that grants writers often face: that projects must have both artistic and social justification.

The third paragraph offers further validation of the Program by stressing its associations and connections, and by displaying the knowledge of the grant writer of other similar programs around the country.

The proposal then appeals to regional pride. The theatre is recognized as a vital component of our culture. This particular project offers an opportunity to practice theatre in its purest form ("isolated from the commercial pressures"). The writer, however, treads lightly here, perhaps to avoid offense to potential commercial patrons.

The reference to the "non-coastal location" of the Program is a further example of regional appeal. Far removed from the commercialism of Hollywood and New York, the local playwright can profit from the "unique resources and opportunities" of the Midwest.

Houseman's words reinforce the previous point about the region. It is curious that he is one Britisher who is strongly identified with American theatre outside as well as inside New York City. If his associations with the Mercury Theatre and The Acting Company do not spring immediately to the lips of Midwest bankers, it is possible that his television commercials for Smith Barney will.

voice of its cultural heritage, spirit and imagination to be heard. Maintaining special emphasis on regional playwrights enhances two important features: it discourages playwrights from deserting the midwest for either coast and abandoning regional roots, and it encourages playwrights to explore more fully their regional heritage. It allows them to become voices for the conscience of that region.

There is a vigorous and important cultural heritage rooted in this midwestern region, but the access to the essential tools for developing the playwrights' voice will remain limited if the Midwest Playwrights' Program remains stationary. The Playwrights' Center acts as a missionary to the region by asking what they can do for the playwright in Omaha, Nebraska and Chicago, Illinois. The Center anticipates problems specific to the state as well as to the region. The Center also regards its financial responsibility to these playwrights by funding one third of the total Program expense. It is the responsibility of the host state to supply the rest.

The major consideration for the Midwest Playwrights' Program at this point in its growth is the need to extend the roots of the Program to the other twelve states—to develop an extensive community by reaching out to them.

The paragraph develops the previous idea about the strength of the region. Not only does the Midwest have a vigorous cultural heritage, but it can also export that heritage (''as a missionary'') to the rest of the country.

OBJECTIVES

The objectives of the Midwest Playwrights' Program are numerous:

* First, to provide a creative atmosphere conducive to a
  pragmatic application to the problems of playwrights. This
  is dependent on the participation, enthusiasm and support
  generated by all related theatre personnel, organizations
  and playwrights in the region.

* Inherent in a constructive atmosphere is the "right to
  fail," a term used by Dan Sullivan in a LA Times article
  about the Midwest Playwrights' Program to describe the
  willingness of playwrights to explore where and why the
  play fails and to work towards correcting it with the encouragement and support of the thoughtful and concerned
  professionals.

* On a broader level, to lure the involvement and commitment
  of each participating midwestern state in developing and
  supporting its playwrights.

* Another key objective is to build a foundation for a play-
  wright-sustained network of regional artists involving
  alumni of the Program in the total process of outreaching
  and solidifying playwrights.

* To make a commitment to further the growth opportunities
  for promising playwrights and to significantly broaden the
  production opportunities for developed new plays within
  the region.

* To facilitate the growth of a new playwright toward the
  attainment of a professional career with opportunities to
  make a living from their craft, for instance, to expose
  playwrights-in-residence to their local opportunities.

* In terms of wider outreach possibilities the Midwest Playwrights' Program can provide a model for the development
  of future programs nationwide.

* Last, and possibly most important, the Midwest Playwrights'
  Program is striving to become the "Olympics" of playwrighting in the Upper Midwest by organizing extraordinary
  opportunities for talented playwrights to become an actively vital component of regional theatre.

This page and the following one are crucial to this proposal. Up to this point, the proposal has attempted to validate the project, to argue the value of the Playwrights' Program, and to appeal to the regional sympathies of the proposal recipient. The proposal is directed, however, toward businesspeople who will require more specific information about what *the program seeks to accomplish and* how *it will meet these objectives. The list of objectives is as clear as one might find in a stock prospectus or in a company's annual report. The only deviation from this business-like formula is the remark in the last objective, that the Program will become the ''Olympics'' of playwriting in the Upper Midwest. This is a variation on the ''missionary'' theme of the previous page, although the mixing of metaphors is questionable.*

HOW OBJECTIVES OF THE MIDWEST PLAYWRIGHTS' PROGRAM WILL BE MET

The ten fellows selected for the Midwest Playwrights' Program participate in the following activities:

--All of the plays receive 10 to 12 hours of rehearsal with
professional actors and directors. The playwright is actively involved in this process. In fact, the director is a
facilitator instead of a co-creator, so that the playwright
has the rare opportunity to see the play as written. The
director is however, definably a cooperative part of the
process.

--Each playwright works with a dramaturg to deal with specific
problems with the script <u>from the time the script is selected.</u>
(This is a unique feature of the Midwest Playwrights' Program.)

--Each playwright sees the play performed in the form of a
staged reading (limited props, sets, etc.), and always with
script in hand) to an audience. (The audience has the chance
to respond with written critiques.)

--Each playwright individually spends time with Dale Wasserman
(Artistic Director) discussing the play in detail.

--All playwrights attend daily discussions led by Dale Wasserman.
Plays produced the previous day are critiqued by the entire
artistic staff in these sessions (i.e., dramaturgs, directors,
actors etc.) These sessions are taped. The cassette is
given to the playwright for future reference.

--A more general seminar session follows each critique. Herein
the discussion relates to the playwright the trends, styles
and techniques of contemporary playwrights nationally and
internationally.

--Prior to the program playwrights are asked what topics they
would like to have discussed at the conference. (These may
range from copyrighting, to how to get a play produced, to
different writing styles, etc.) The Playwrights' Center
brings in professionals to address these topics and all sessions will be made available to the playwrights.

--All playwrights have access to a library which offers diverse
resource information, newsletters, etc.

--All of the plays will be offered a second reading during the
last three days of the conference, assimilating rewrites or
additions based on the critiques of the first production.

The playwright also receives a stipend and expenses are covered by
the program.

This page "speaks to" each of the objectives listed just previously. For those who are perhaps not aware of the importance of each of these answers, the occasional parenthetical commentary supplements the text.

The bottom line of the list of objectives is quite literally "the bottom line." It is an important reflection of the Program's commitment to the playwright in financial terms.

By moving the site of the annual event to each of the participating states, it is essential for those states to supplement the
funding, identify and establish facilities, help to organize and
channel publicity, and, naturally, provide audiences to become actively involved with the playwrights in their region. In addition,
theatres in the host state will have easier access to the wealth
of presented new works, and become more actively communicative with
the playwrights of their region.

The belief is that the work will continue beyond the two-week
program extending to the broader regional artistic community.
Playwrights are encouraged to maintain relationships with the
various components of the Midwest Playwrights' Program. These
alumni, in a sense, become missionaries for their states' playwrights by virtue of participating in the process of serving the
needs of playwrights. Reaching these playwrights facilitates the
continual search for new playwrights. The communication process
has already begun.

The dual exposure of theatres to playwrights and playwrights
to theatres is an integral part of the process of developing and
motivating playwrights in the region. Not only are theatres and
audiences party to a lively process of depicting mid-America's
cultural roots, but the playwrights are exposed to very professional realities and criticisms. The outcome is a playwright with
a more clear and concise understanding of the craft of making
theatrically workable plays. A better avenue of reaching local
playwrights opens to theatres everywhere. The ultimate winner,
of course, is the arts patron.

The Midwest Playwrights' Program is already being used as a
model for regions in the country which are just now joining efforts
to identify and support their playwrights. The western states and
the southeast region are presently moving in this direction and
are using the Midwest Playwrights' Program as an example and for
counsel. The favorable press is indicative of the richness and
importance of the Program in this capacity. If the philosophical
base of the Program can spread and be effective in the other regions, there is no end to the possibilities and futures of
America's playwrights. This is, however, a long term vision, and
the attainment lies in the success and continuation of the Program
and its ability to excite and intrigue the other regions. An extraordinary patchwork of America's heritage could begin to emerge.

The value of the Program, which has been a constant theme throughout the proposal, continues. Reference to the Program's "alumni" suggests the educational value of the Program and a return to the "missionary" metaphor serves to reinforce its educational component.

The reference to the "arts patron" is perhaps purposely vague: it includes both the corporate sponsor(s) and the viewing audience. Nevertheless, the sudden shift from a vocabulary of service and sharing (collaboration, linkage, development) to one of patronage is a bit jarring.

This paragraph returns to previously voiced themes: national recognition further validates the Program, the Program has strong educational value, the Program will have an impact beyond the region.

The emergence of the "patchwork" in the last sentence is, however, a confusing metaphor.

EVALUATION

    The evaluation of accomplishing the stated objectives will
be determined through a long term follow-up process of qualitative
and quantitative results.   How many plays were rewritten to completion?   How many plays were given productions, or readings at regional theatres?   How many new playwrights were attracted to the
Program?   Were any new projects dedicated to the playwright developed?   How many playwrights were commissioned by regional
theatres?   How many playwrights were convinced that the action
is in the regions? Were any new funding sources attracted? How
many playwrights established new working relationships? Or net-
worked with other professionals in the field? Did the number of
scripts submitted for the selection process increase from the 200
received last year?

    The qualitative evaluation, equally important, addresses the
range, the state and the development of playwriting as art, as
craft, as a powerful and dynamic instrument of social grace, awareness and conscience.   To entertain and to instruct, to satisfy and
to stimulate, to comfort and to provide are traditionally the dual
missions of the playwright.   The Midwest Playwrights' Program holds
itself accountable, with rigorous year by year self-examinations,
to extending the quality and growth of progressive playwrighting.

The Evaluation section is particularly important, especially in its emphasis of the Program's holding itself "accountable" to support "progressive playwriting." Just as the beginning of the proposal emphasized the administrative skills of the Project's directors, the conclusion refers to their moral responsibility (reinforced by the reference to rigorous periodic self-examination). The reference to accountability and the promise of progress are certainly calculated to appeal to the corporate audience of the proposal.

A LAST WORD ABOUT GRANTS

As these three proposals show, there is no set formula for writing a grant. Perhaps the most striking characteristic of these three pieces is their individuality. None of them was written in the how-to fashion of many grants-writing books. None of them has a clear delineation of specific narrative sections in a set order. While all the writers know the general requirements for any proposal, each has gone about the task differently, influenced by the nature and interests of the funding source, its guidelines and requirements, the needs and activities of the organization, its location, its competition, and the needs of the particular artistic discipline at hand.

What these proposals offer the reader is a first-hand experience with actual grant material, with comments on the craft of the grant writer. While they are not meant to be how-to guides, one hopes they will demystify the grant-writing process for some and enhance it for others.

CHAPTER THREE

MAKING MONEY

Financing Techniques and Strategies

EARNING INCOME: PROFIT SUPPORT
OF THE ARTS

"Getting and spending, we lay
waste our powers."

—William Wordsworth,
"The World is Too Much with Us."

Wordsworth's famous phrase is an accurate description of the frustration felt by many arts groups trying to gain control of their destinies by providing their institutions with earned income, rather than relying on grants, gifts, and contributions. With a basic understanding of the tax law and of the Internal Revenue Code section 501(c)(3), some groups have developed ingenious schemes to keep their organizations afloat. These include the creation of separate for-profit corporations, subsidiary corporations, and licensing arrangements where an arts institution receives royalties rather than active income.

While such alternatives may provide increased income for a group, the small arts organization may find that the strain on staff time and morale and its already tight resources is too great a liability, particularly since any new venture requires time to develop and grow. The very real cost to the institution and the difficulty in sustaining enthusiasm for such a project over time may not be outweighed by a source of income that is new, but by no means guaranteed.

It is clear that profit-oriented efforts are frequently market-oriented ones as well and there is a moral and ethical dilemma faced by many artists and managers who fear that artistic products which are essentially dictated by the consumer are aesthetically compromised. Thus, some institutions prefer instead to take advantage of opportunities that rely directly on their presence rather than their product, such as urban redevelopment complexes.

The decision to support an arts institution through these new

127

kinds of ventures is a highly individual one. It depends on the organization's history and management, on its artists and "products," on the support of its board and staff members, on the entrepreneurism of its leaders, and on the perception by the marketplace that the arts institution has something that is worth money, something that can be sold. It also depends on the institution's financial resources, its readiness to enter some relatively uncharted seas, and its knowledge of what is allowable according to the law.

LEGAL RESTRICTIONS

A not-for-profit institution that enters into commercial activities must understand that the money related to those activities is viewed in two ways: how it is earned and how it is spent. As mentioned in Chapter I, activities of a nonprofit tax-exempt institution that are not substantially related to its exempt purposes, that actively compete with activities in the commercial sector, and that are regularly carried on may be taxed according to corporate rates. If such activities seem to be economically worthwhile to the organization they can be continued, and the taxes paid, with no threat to the organization's exempt status. If such activities become the major focus of the organization, however, its tax-exempt status may be revoked.

Common dangers to be avoided when creating the kinds of subsidiary corporations described in this chapter include interlocking directorates (where the board members of the nonprofit corporation and of the profit subsidiary are the same people) and the support of a profit corporation by a nonprofit corporation. For example, if a not-for-profit organization receives a grant which it uses to buy equipment and then leases that equipment to its profit subsidiary at a lower rate than is usually charged for that equipment's use, the not-for-profit agency is using its tax advantage to compete unfairly against the commercial marketplace. Should an arts group decide to form a profit and a not-for-profit corporation at the same time, it would therefore be advantageous for the profit corporation to purchase the equipment and supplies. This would avoid the above conflict and also would allow the advantages of tax credits and depreciation for the profit corporation.

Records as well as actual monies for profit and nonprofit corporations with such a relationship—either as subsidiaries or as separate entities—must be kept separate and distinct. Each group must also employ responsible accounting procedures.

Another potential conflict area in small arts organizations where creation is cooperative and resources are frequently pooled, is the contribution of money by a single individual who is also a staff member of the organization. For example, an individual videomaker who is on salary at a tax-exempt nonprofit media center acts as a cameraman on a network television commercial. The videomaker gets paid a fee for that work, pays personal income tax on that fee, and then donates that fee to the media center claiming the donation as an individual tax-deductible contribution on his or her income tax form. The fact that the videomaker is on salary, or even receives some kind of direct or indirect payment from the media center for services rendered may suggest to the IRS that the videomaker is trying to "launder" that money through a nonprofit organization.

This kind of activity—not at all remote from small arts organizations—often makes artists feel they are engaged in a damned-if-you-do, damned-if-you-don't situation; but it perfectly illustrates the kinds of scrutiny such activities are prone to. Questions of how money is earned and spent, the relationship of the individuals to the source of the money, to the exempt institution, and to the earned income activities all play a part in determining the legal propriety of such activities.[1]

What follows is a series of examples that might serve as models for the support of nonprofit arts institutions through for-profit activities and as a guide to arts-related activities for emerging groups that are considering organizing as profit corporations. While the range of possibilities, as represented here, is quite broad, each example is very much an outgrowth of the particular institution that created it. It is not suggested here that other arts groups seek to duplicate that effort, but rather, that they look to their own strengths and resources in creating individual vehicles and ventures.

Whether their money is earned or unearned, it is possible for arts groups to earn money on their money, to borrow low- or no-interest capital for specific projects, and to garner aid in the form of investment instead of philanthropy. The section on loans and banking seeks to inform arts groups that an uncashed, undeposited, uninvested check on the manager's desk loses money for the organization. Finally, the section on real estate illustrates how many arts groups have

[1]For this example and for a general understanding of this area, I am indebted to the discussions of the Media Alliance of New York State at their conference in June 1981.

achieved progress through adversity by associating themselves with public and urban development schemes.

While some of the following illustrations are about art, all of them are about money or things that equal money in the arts—exposure, facilities, larger audiences. It is hoped that in the getting and the spending of the money, artists and managers are not forced to lay waste their powers of art.

MODELS

Tour Management

Of the smaller, artist-oriented, avant-garde arts groups, The Kitchen Center for Video, Music, Dance and Performance has a reputation for being administratively sound as well as artistically interesting. Nevertheless, its place on the cutting edge allies it with artists more than commerce, and The Kitchen's posture as it enters the commercial marketplace is one of self-protection rather than artist exploitation. The dual commitment—to emerging artists and to newly forming commercial activities—is particularly difficult for the more experimental arts groups that often feel an involvement with "business" deprives them of some of their freedom. The Kitchen's entry into profit-oriented activities is especially interesting when viewed alongside its highly successful track record in the public-funding arena and the kinds of bureaucratic requirements that accompany such funding. Because of its multidisciplinary nature, The Kitchen one year was forced to submit 28 proposals to the National Endowment for the Arts. This duplication of administrative effort can quickly deplete an institution's managerial resources until earning money may be viewed as less complicated than raising it.

In 1980, building on its European reputation as well as its commitment to unknown artists, The Kitchen developed a touring program in which The Kitchen essentially acts as an artist's "personal management" for a period of approximately 18 months. Working with the International Communications Agency in Washington, D.C., with two private foundations, and with foreign posts, it first sent a group of artists to Europe at a cost of $103,280, of which artists received $39,000 in fees and the Kitchen took a commission of $10,000.[2] This

---

[2]Much of the information on The Kitchen comes from press material and discussion with Mary MacArthur, Executive Director, on 8 May 1981.

initial project, developed with the knowledge that many avant-garde artists earn their livings on the road and especially in Europe where fees are good and audiences receptive,[3] gave birth to a series of projects under the rubric "The Kitchen Presents . . ." By June 1981, income from the Touring Program totaled $180,000, of which half went to artists in fees and $20,000–$25,000 to The Kitchen. Work ranged from progressive jazz and new wave rock music to post-modern dance, experimental theatre, and multi-media performance art. Subsequent tours included a summer festival in Cologne, a dance tour of the British Isles, and a series of programs for the American Center in Paris.[4]

The Kitchen's commitment to the career development of new artists has often resulted in a support system through which The Kitchen contributes to an artist's fee level as well as to his or her reputation. In providing support during the early years when an artist is unknown, taking him or her to various festivals and bookings, it allows the artist to become better known and to command greater fees. Why shouldn't The Kitchen then receive some percentage of those fees, especially when it is committed to returning its profits to other emerging artists?

The amount of time that the Kitchen will support an artist in this way is limited to 18 months. This time restriction means that The Kitchen is committing itself to the exposure of the artist, rather than to becoming the artist's full-time manager. The reputation and contacts of The Kitchen, its store of videotapes that allows curators and programmers from around the world to view the work of emerging artists, and this crucial service at a developing stage of their careers make the Touring Program an attractive option for many. This activity, which began in the nonprofit arena as an earned-income activity, may become a separate profit-making subsidiary to help support the ongoing activities of The Kitchen.

Network Television

In any discussion of earned-income activities, it should be understood that some nonprofit arts organizations have skills that are more mar-

---

[3] In some countries outside the U.S., higher fees for avant-garde and foreign artists are a direct result of a country's policies for arts subsidy.

[4] Press material, The Kitchen, July 1981.

ketable than others. Media centers are an obvious source of video and film expertise that can easily be translated into commercial terms.

Downtown Community Television is a small nonprofit community organization in New York State. Founded in 1971, it has a current budget of approximately $250,000. After years of offering free services provided by an overworked and underpaid staff, in 1979 DCTV increased their space, staff, and activities and obtained broadcast quality equipment that included a CMX computer editing system. Certain activities, like the rental of equipment and the distribution of tapes made by independent producers, bring in a small amount of income, but DCTV's entry into the commercial newtork marketplace has provided a way for profit activity to subisidize its nonprofit institution. Networks are traditionally closed to independents, but a documentary and subsequent film footage on Vietnam brought DCTV to the attention of NBC-TV; that success has enabled DCTV to act as producer of certain works for commercial television.

Portable Channel, a media center in Rochester, New York has a similar arrangement with CBS-TV—its earned-income activities include shooting commercials for broadcast television. Interestingly, such activities were a result of a cut in funding from the New York State Council on the Arts some years ago. Although its directors were able to obtain a bank loan at that time to purchase equipment, they are almost at the limit of their current credit structure and are considering the formation of a private for-profit entity to help support nonprofit artist-related activities.

It is important to realize that many of the artists working in such institutions could easily work in the for-profit sector. They could form their own companies or work for other entities and make a more regular and substantial living than they are doing now. Artistic reasons as well as life styles (many media centers began as collectives) have made many choose the nonprofit arts institution as their forum. Both their own growth and certain financial realities have contributed to their search for earned-income activities that allow them to retain their artistic commitments to their institutions while at the same time providing for institutional survival.

Nevertheless, certain groups are beginning to realize that they cannot adequately transform their institutions into surviving enterprises. For those using the commercial marketplace as a measure of future survival, some will decide that the artistic as well as the economic consequences are too great.

Packaging Collections

The Institute for Art and Urban Resources is an umbrella agency for a variety of spaces and projects run under a central administration. Concerned with art and the urban environment, it boasts an impressive Board of Directors including prominent artists, critics, and business people. Its main facility is a public school building in Long Island City called P.S. 1. Acquired for the Institute in 1976, the building acts as an exhibition space, performance space, a place for interdisciplinary programs, and for artists' studios. Its reputation is international and avant-garde and its growth, since its first activity in 1971 in a small space under the Brooklyn Bridge, has been impressive.

Through one of its board members, the Institute has created an interesting mechanism for obtaining money from corporations—not as philanthropy, but as revenue. Christo, the artist famous for environmental pieces like the Running Fence in California, began an Artists' Fund. Artists are asked once and only once to make a donation to the Institute, either in the form of cash (up to $10,000) or in art work (up to a market value of $75,000). After a careful choice of potential art work donations, the Institute packages a collection of works which it then sells to a corporation at a 50 percent discount from the retail price. Corporations range in type and geographic location. They are selected because of their existing collections, their curatorial staff, and their interest in art. A recent year realized $250,000 through this scheme.

It should be noted that while the Institute packages collections in this way, it has no collection of its own. It is an artists' space with programs involving approximately 600 artists a year. Because it lacks a collection in the physical property sense, its packaging scheme is perhaps more acceptable—no one need worry that the Institute is deaccessioning works behind its artists' backs. While the "market value" of the works themselves is probably the area causing the most difficulty in such a transaction, in a sense the Institute acts as a validating mechanism for the corporation, saving it the time of finding and selecting the art work. Additionally, the "one-of-a-kind" nature of the package creates a certain attractiveness for the buyer who is originally "selected" by the Institute.

A parallel suggestion for video artists has been the sale of limited editions of video art in much the same way other visual arts "multiples" are handled. A portfolio of video works might provide a money-making support system for a media center if the right consumers could be identified.

Arts Handling Services

In 1977 *and/or*, the not-for-profit artists space in Seattle, formed a profit-making subsidiary corporation called Artech to provide arts-related services to organizations and individuals.[5] These services had informally filled a need in the surrounding community for some years before the formation of Artech. They included:

- design and installation of art exhibitions for museums, galleries, and corporate offices
- installation of art in homes and offices
- planning, registration, promotion, cataloging and design of temporary exhibitions of all kinds
- custom crating and packing for art works, glassware, ceramics, antiques, scientific instruments, and other fragile materials
- shipping, receiving, insurance and storage services
- pickup and delivery of items in the local area
- appraisals and limited restoration of contemporary works
- fine arts photography service for archival, insurance, curatorial, and publicity purposes
- rental of viewing space[6]

Besides providing arts-related services to the surrounding region, Artech's goals include providing employment for artists who provide these services and the support of the not-for-profit contemporary arts center, *and/or*.[7]

The clearest explanation of the formation of Artech as a subsidiary of *and/or* is provided in the "President's Message" of Artech's Annual Report for 1980:

> Artech, Inc., is a for-profit corporation incorporated in the State of Washington. All the Artech stock that has been sold to date has been purchased by *and/or* (a non-profit corporation) through *and/or*'s endowment fund. As the sole stockholder *and/or*'s primary responsibility is to elect the corporation's Board of Directors, and it is only through this action that *and/or* has an influence on the policy, direction and management of Artech. Being the sole stockholder also means that in the event of a decision by Artech's

---

[5]See Chapter II for a detailed history of *and/or* and an annotated grant proposal.

[6]1981 Annual Report, Artech.

[7]Ibid.

board to increase Artech's capital through the sale of additional stock, the shares must be offered first to *and/or*, and only if *and/or* decides not to buy can those shares be sold to anyone else. Being the sole owner of stock also means that *and/or* receives all dividends paid as a result of the year's profits.

One of the most serious of Artech's problems was its lack of capital. Within the first six months of operation, a bank loan for $20,000 was obtained towards it operation. Frequently, people who are recipients of Artech's services donate money to *and/or* to help in the operation of Artech, but these people remain donors to *and/or*, not shareholders in Artech. Since *and/or* remains the only shareholder, the problem of lack of capital still exists.

There are several possible solutions. First, money from services: Artech has recently adjusted its fees, and money from services may now be enough to turn a reasonable profit for the company. Second, fund-raising: *and/or* could engineer a special fund-raising program to put additional capital into Artech, but that is quite the opposite of what was intended—the whole purpose of Artech was to provide money for *and/or*, not the reverse. Third, more shareholders: *and/or* could seek minority shareholders and issue additional stock, or seek partners. And finally, sale: *and/or* could sell Artech and use the money from the sale to set up another profit-making operation. Anne Focke, President of Artech's Board and Director of *and/or*, is committed to the use of such monies for other self-sustaining mechanisms for *and/or* and opposed to pouring the profit into operating expenses of the space.[8]

Realistically, one must understand that certain problems Artech is having are the problems attributable to any small business. The first year Artech showed a loss. Its second year showed a profit of $1,000. The profit generated by 1980 was $1,500. Most small businesses take at least five years to break even—the recent economic situation has made even this an optimistic average. Artech will have to assess whether its potential profit is worth the continued effort, or whether a sale of the operation might generate better benefits for *and/or*.

The problems of a small business are further complicated in this case by Artech's commitment to hiring artists to perform its services. While there is a salaried full-time director, the core staff of seven work on an hourly basis and many of the artist-employees wish to work

---

[8]Much of this information is the result of information from final reports of Artech and discussions with Anne Focke, 9 June 1981 and 23 May 1982.

part-time. While it would be more efficient for the corporation to use its employees as fully as possible, especially since there is constant additional paperwork and expense each time a part-timer with benefits is added, the artist-employees offer the organization a certain flexibility of schedule and readiness to respond to unusual circumstances in showing, exhibiting, and services.

Museum Marketing

Since 1976, the Children's Museum in Denver, Colorado has been committed to earning income and increasing its audience through a variety of marketing schemes. The Museum has been attempting steadily to "kick the grantsmanship habit" that almost killed it in the three years after its founding in 1973. The Museum's 1981 operating budget of $686,000 thus included only $25,000 of contributed income—from individuals, corporations, government, and foundation sources combined. The remainder of the budget included a great deal of income from corporate clients who use their marketing and advertising budgets (as opposed to the traditional community service or charitable contributions budgets) to buy products made by the museum that are tailored to their corporate needs. Additionally, money from charitable contributions budgets is used as seed money toward the development of new products whose sale aids the museum in its campaign toward self-sufficiency.

More firmly and visibly committed to principles of marketing than almost any other nonprofit arts institution in the country, the Children's Museum follows a basic five-step plan of traditional marketing:

1. analysis of image, including assessment of goals and objectives, users of the organization and its services, and the organization's relationship to the community.
2. strategic planning, including regarding the institution's resources as valuable and saleable to the for-profit sector.
3. market research, to determine the needs of specific clients and to fill them with the institution's products or services.
4. development, through seed grants and through the design of products for multiple uses.

5. sales, including setting prices, preselling, wholesaling and net-working.[9]

Obtaining 95 percent of its operating revenue through the sale of goods and services is testimony not only to the ideas developed by the Children's Museum, but also to the presentation of those ideas. All the literature and promotional material for the museum and its products is visually interesting and exciting, and much of it is fun—it reinforces and reflects the museum's focus on children.

Aside from traditional sources of income from admission fees, membership, grants, and contributions, and from the gift shop, the Museum generates another 86.7 percent in publications, traveling exhibits, a poster service, Halloween costumes, an art auction, community art, and promotions. A description of several activities in each major area should serve to illustrate ways in which the museum has made itself self-supporting through its emphasis on marketing.

Publications alone generate over 35 percent of the total museum budget. Advertising space is sold in a number of them, including a family newspaper, a holiday events guide, and a list of summer activities. Other publications are produced specifically for clients. Among such publications are the *Frontier Flying Funbook*, a free activity book for children to use in flight while on a Frontier Airlines plane, and the *Babysitter's Guide* now being considered by a number of baby product manufacturers as a free premium with a purchase of their products. The Museum has also published activity books related to specific Museum exhibits in science, mathematics, consumer choices, and handicapped learning.

Participatory traveling exhibits on a variety of educational topics are sent to schools, banks, and shopping malls. Educational enrichment, positive community image, increase in traffic and sales, and the promotional aspects of the exhibits are cited as some of the needs they meet for the client.

Future ideas and negotiations include a series of "snoop kits" such as the currently tested "Safety Snoop Inspection Kit" that helps children inspect their homes for safety. Kits on energy and nutrition are now being designed. Also under development is a series of "waiting games" for children to use in supermarkets, doctors' offices, cars, planes and other places where waiting is required.

---

[9]"Kicking the Grantsmanship Habit," *News Monitor of Philanthropy*, 11 (January 1981): 1, 16–18.

The pursuit of large wholesale purchases of 50,000 and up creates an automatic distribution system for the Museum's products through only a single sale. The Museum ran its annual membership appeal in much the same way when it persuaded Safeway stores, a regional supermarket chain, to print six million of its bags with a half-price membership offer to the Museum and an activity for children on the bag. Twenty percent of new memberships are recruited in this fashion.

Exhibits and products are almost always sold as concepts, before they are made. Drawings, presentations, and advance sales, based on a good deal of market research, make the often accepted "wait and see what sells" attitude of the institutional gift shop seem outmoded and expensive by comparison.

With its relatively large product line (for an arts institution), the Denver Children's Museum apparently sees no conflict between its mission as a museum and its profit-making activities. Its spokesmen are extremely vocal, in fact, about the profit motive of these activities. Lisa Farber Miller, the Museum's National Marketing Director, claims that for certain activities, like promotions and benefits, the Museum will not participate unless it makes a profit: "Visibility doesn't meet payroll."[10]

The example of the Denver Children's Museum is a little overwhelming in its totality of approach as well as its successful track record. The "hard sell" of its marketing approach, although partly a result of bitter experience with public sector money, can be off-putting to some arts groups whose hesitation in entering into profit ventures is based on a fear of obscuring their institution's not-for-profit purposes. In addition, the focus of the Denver Children's Museum allows certain services and products to be created that might be inappropriate for other kinds of groups. Nevertheless, the range of activities is instructive and certain ideas might be adaptable even for smaller, emerging groups—for example, the creation of "traveling environments" by videospaces, or membership advertising on shopping bags from a local store.

It should be noted that on all the above mentioned activities the Denver Children's Museum pays no unrelated-business income tax, a tribute to its understanding of the marketplace in which it operates.

---

[10]Lisa Farber Miller, "Creative Self-Sufficiency," speech presented at the annual meeting of the Ohio Arts Council, 17 September 1981, p. 26. (Photocopy.)

While the product development concept of the Denver Children's Museum has been proved possible and even effective, it will not be the road many smaller arts institutions will take, especially if their sales potential is not extraordinarily good. A more likely prospect for them will be the expansion or creation of a shop or store that will sell merchandise related to the institution's purposes, function, or collection.

While Chapter I discusses issues of the relatedness of specific items and their taxability, a word should be added here concerning the selection, acquisition, and/or production of objects to be sold. Although institutions considering the expansion or creation of a shop should undertake a complete market analysis of their public and of their members, certain legal restrictions may prevent the acquisition, sale, production, or reproduction of some items. An ethnic museum showing the works of living artists may wish to sell certain items that are restricted by import-export laws: items made with the feathers of certain endangered birds may be allowable for certain cultures within their own lands, but the reproduction of items using these feathers for sale in the United States may be legally prohibited. Matters of heritage, tradition, and religious practice may be similarly prohibitive, or an object may simply be too fragile to reproduce or not unusual enough to sell.

Equally difficult is the acquisition of merchandise that is of high quality. If the institution does not have the resources to create its own products, it must seek individuals or small entrepreneurial businesses that are frequently out of the trading mainstream. Lisa Koch, General Merchandise Manager of the Metropolitan Museum of Art, gives a brief but challenging rundown of only some of the pitfalls in merchandise selection and acquisition:

> Does anyone want it? Does anyone in our neighborhood want it? Is it priced right? What is the competition selling similar merchandise for? Are we displaying our merchandise properly? What is the real cost of doing business? What are our rent, our salaries, our cost of goods, our promotion and advertising costs, our legal and accounting fees? What is the real overhead? And have we included that terrible killer, the cost of inventory? And that means the cost of money. Would we have been better off to buy a CD than to buy merchandise that isn't selling fast enough? But even worse, what about the merchandise that sells so fast that we can't get reor-

ders to satisfy our customers, not a patient lot? After all, we said we had it and now we don't.

And the sales staff, a revolving door of underpaid people who leave almost as soon as they become knowledgeable about the goods. And let's hope that not too much of the goods leave with them.[11]

Obviously, there are many issues that need to be addressed in the creation of a shop or store, not the least of which is cost-effectiveness. But the fairly recent businesslike entry of arts organizations into this arena has begun to realize a number of revenue producing techniques. One example is the benefit sales shop created by the Cooper-Hewitt Museum in conjunction with the Gardens of Delight Exhibit. Goods with a garden or floral theme were donated by over 50 manufacturers and shops (the donative aspect partly relieves the institution of the taxability of those items), and the shop, in a little over the month it accompanied the exhibition, netted close to $30,000.[12] The Metropolitan Museum of Art has an arrangement with Springs Mills: for the use of certain designs from the Met's collection on sheets and pillowcases, Springs Mills pays royalties to the Met on each sale (royalties are passive, nontaxable income).

The problems for performing arts institutions that lack "a collection" seem more difficult than for museums, since fewer precedents have been set. Besides, the museums have a Museum Stores Association where vendors, suppliers, and museums themselves can annually show their wares. Nevertheless, with a Brooklyn Museum Shop in the Citicorp Building in Manhattan, and a shop from the Metropolitan Museum at Macy's advances are being made.

Low-Power Television Networks

Although the final chapter of this book deals exclusively with the arts in relation to new technology, it is appropriate here to include a description of the recent creation of a low-power network of television stations which might allow a not-for-profit group to have some con-

---

[11]NYC Commission for Cultural Affairs, "Self Help: Earned Income Opportunities for Cultural Organizations,": A conference organized by the New York City Commission for Cultural Affairs at the Dept. of Cultural Affairs, 26 January 1982, p. 46.

[12]Linda Sullivan, "Profile: The Cooper Hewitt Museum," unpublished paper, Columbia University, Spring 1982.

trol of these stations from their inception instead of having to repeat-
edly bargain or pay for air time. The idea behind the low-power network came from Former Federal Communications Commission chairman Charles Ferris. Ferris hoped to provide broadcast capability with
minimal licensing requirements to new, local television stations. This
would be accompanied by lowering the power of a TV transmitter to
1000 watts or less (instead of the hundreds of thousands of watts now
required).

This particular example of profit support of the not-for-profit institution is unusual in terms of its possible breadth. Unlike certain other
schemes that rely on grant money to seed the profit operation, the
low-power network relies on venture capital from the private sector.
Private risk capital is raised and invested in a separate commercial corporation, but the stations themselves are licensed to a noncommercial
entity. The commercial corporation can sell commercial time at commercial rates to commercial entities (cereal companies, detergent manufacturers) for a limited amount of time, say, one-third of the
programming day. The money obtained from these commercial activities can then be used to support the nonprofit organization. The nonprofit organization can both run the station itself and provide work
by independent producers for the remaining two-thirds of the programming day. Additionally, if the arrangement is made so that
the commercial corporation leases programming time from the
noncommercial organization, and then pays that noncommercial
organization a royalty, the income is passive income and, therefore,
not taxable.

Global Village, a media center in New York City and Children's
Television Workshop are both moving in this direction. Of course,
they must be granted licenses by the FCC in order to obtain such stations, but it has been projected that, with less than a dozen stations,
as much as one million dollars might be freed up for independent producers through such a mechanism in approximately two years. Nay-
sayers warn that outfits like Neighborhood TV, backed by the Allstate
Insurance Division of Sears, Roebuck, Graphic Scanning Corporation, ABC and NBC, plus a host of medium-to-large sized newspapers
have obtained a good proportion of the licenses already and their programming will echo much of the routine programming one already
views on television.[13]

---

[13]Bob Brewin, "Spectrum Wars!" *Village Voice*, 22 June 1982, p. 72.

Production Transfers

The most common method of supporting certain small- and medium-sized theatre groups has become the production transfer. Costs of producing on Broadway have become so exorbitant that there is little possibility of seeing a new work there first. It must first be tried out, honed, polished, and seen on its feet elsewhere. Except for some few years after World War II, when the works of playwrights like Arthur Miller and Tennessee Williams were first seen on Broadway, this procedure has been the general rule about most serious dramas on Broadway. Now, however, it is the rule about most plays, and often the rule applies to Off Broadway as well. The reason is cost. Broadway production costs for musicals are up to $2½ to $3 million; plays without music start at close to $1 million.

Visibility, feedback, reward for actors and artists are motivations, surely, for the transfer of a production from a small theatre to Broadway, but a primary motivation is money. The possibility of financially supporting an entire season of plays through the receipts of one production on Broadway is hard to resist even though the odds of reaping such rewards are unfavorable. Nevertheless, the transferring theatre may begin to educate a new audience for the plays at its home base—if there is only one transferring theatre. One of the complications in transferring a production to the Broadway or even the Off Broadway stage has been the number of theatres involved in the gestation, development, and mounting of that production. While the rule is almost always that the theatre that "brings the play in" to Broadway or Off Broadway is the one entitled to benefit, complications with Actors' Equity Association (the union representing actors) and the Dramatists' Guild (the union representing playwrights) have created a certain amount of bad will on both sides of many transfers.

There are some who claim that Broadway producers prefer to deal with plays straight out of regional theatres to avoid union complications endemic to the New York-New York transfer. Regional theatres, however, often need a second company to continue their offerings at home while their "hit play" has a Broadway run. Additionally, along with certain company-oriented Off Off Broadway theatres, regional theatres run the risk of losing whole companies of actors once they have transferred a production to Broadway. Artists are usually more loyal to their careers and professions than to any single institution, no matter how responsible that institution has been in the making of those artists' careers.

In terms of the actual money to be made by the theatre that brings

the play in, there are two different ways the theatre can be remunerated. The most common way is for the originating theatre to option a
work, sell the rights to that work by assignment to a commercial producer, and take a percentage of the gross known as its "fair share."
This fair share is negotiable and the percentage arrived at depends on
how much the Broadway producer wants the property and, as in all
negotiations, how good both parties are at negotiating. Off Off Broadway and regional theatres have become much more sophisticated in
this area in the last few years. Now, when Broadway producers scout
or shop for new properties, the small theatres talk money even if the
production is in workshop form.

The second way for the originating theatre to be remunerated is for
it to move the production itself from its Off Off Broadway arena to Off
Broadway or Broadway. But, most theatres are financially incapable of
mobilizing the capital to effectuate such a move. Also, although it may
provide the perfect example of profit support of the nonprofit institution, many Board members feel that if the nonprofit theatre takes on
the role of commercial producer, its tax-exempt status may be jeopardized.

In the case of such a transfer, it might be possible for the nonprofit
theatre to avoid unrelated-business income taxation on any profits on
the basis that the activity is not regularly carried on and is related to
the institution's exempt purposes. Additionally, royalty payments
from any subsidiary rights resulting from the production (records,
T-shirts) could be viewed as passive income. The person who has obviously been able to use this strategy to perfection is Joseph Papp
who, with the help of certain private benefactors, has managed to
transfer a number of productions from the Public Theatre to Broadway. The most economically successful, *A Chorus Line*, was listed as
an "extraordinary asset" in the New York Shakespeare Festival's annual report. It took seven months to pay off the production costs, then
averaged a profit of $31,000 a week; it received $1,485,000 of the movie
sale and still receives profits from subsidiary rights, and from productions locally, regionally, nationally, and internationally.[14] Currently,
similar strategies are being developed for its production of *The Pirates
of Penzance* in the hopes of providing a large endowment on which the
Festival can depend.

In 1980, the tax-exempt status of a nonprofit theatre was chal-

---

[14]This and other information on the Broadway transfer can be found in Chapter II of this author's *The Emerging Arts: Management, Survival, and Growth*
(New York: Praeger, 1980).

lenged on the basis of a co-production that eventually moved to Broadway. A variation was added to the theme of profit support of the nonprofit organization when, in this case, one of the two nonprofit producers ended up in a limited partnership agreement. In 1977, the Plumstead Theatre Society, Inc., a not-for-profit theatre in Los Angeles formed an agreement with the John F. Kennedy Center for the Performing Arts in Washington, D.C. to produce a play called *First Monday in October* at the Kennedy Center. Each organization was responsible for one-half of the required capitalization; both were to equally share profits or losses from the Kennedy Center production. The Plumstead Theatre had difficulty raising its share of the capitalization and sold a portion of its rights to two private investors and Pantheon Pictures, Inc. through a California limited partnership agreement. For $100,000, the limited partners were to receive 63.5 percent share in any profits or losses from the production. Although the play closed at a loss, accusations were made against the Plumstead Theatre's exempt purposes, including allegations that Plumstead was operated for private rather than public interests (since it had entered into a limited partnership agreement with two private individuals and a corporation), and that the Plumstead Theatre was organized for the furtherance of commercial rather than exempt purposes.

These and other accusations were refuted. A point was made about the one-time nature of such a collaboration and the original specific purposes for which the Plumstead Theatre was organized according to its articles of incorporation, which clearly reflected the exempt purposes of the organization. Judge Wilbur's decision describes important distinctions between commercial and non-commercial arts activity, statements that should have bearing on future arrangements of this kind:

> Admittedly, the line between commercial enterprises which produce and present theatrical performances and nonprofit, tax-exempt organizations that do the same is not always easy to draw. . . . However, there are differences. Commercial theatres are operated to make a profit. Thus, they choose plays having the greatest mass audience appeal. Generally, they run the plays so long as they can attract a crowd. They set ticket prices to pay the total costs of production and to return a profit. Since their focus is perenially on the box office, they do not generally organize other activities to educate the public and they do not encourage and instruct relatively unknown playwrights and actors.
>
> Tax-exempt organizations are not operated to make a profit. They fulfill their artistic and community obligations by focusing on the highest possible standards of performance; by serving the community broadly; by

developing new and original works; and by providing educational programs and opportunities for new talent. Thus, they keep the great classics
of the theatre alive and are willing to experiment with new forms of dramatic writing, acting, and staging. . . . The combination of the shortness
of season, the limited seating capacity, the enormous costs of producing
quality performances of new or experimental works, coupled with the desire to keep ticket prices at a level which is affordable to most of the community, means that except in rare cases, box office receipts will never
cover the cost of producing plays for nonprofit performing arts organizations.[15]

This statement is particularly well-informed about the state of the
theatre and Judge Wilbur consulted a number of excellent works in
the field to help him articulate his decision. The quotation cited here
crystallizes two major issues in the whole area of profit support of the
not-for profit institution. First, the graying of distinctions between
what is profit and what is nonprofit in terms of an arts activity—
although experimental works are frequently produced in the nonprofit sector, there is no such thing as a "nonprofit play." Second, the
general rule about nonprofit organizations mentioned in Chapter I,
that what determines the difference between profit and nonprofit organization is not profit, it is purpose: the purpose of a nonprofit organization is not the making of money, while the purpose of a profit
organization clearly is.

While Broadway producers might argue that nonprofit organizations are not the only ones to educate the public nor to "encourage
and instruct relatively unknown playwrights and actors," these are
clearly not Broadway's primary purposes. Nevertheless, the tax advantages that appeared to be taken by the Plumstead Theatre in this
case are undoubtedly what caused its tax-exempt status to be challenged. It is this area of conflict—the nonprofit tax-exempt institution
that seems to have its cake and eat it, too—that continues to pique the
curiosity of the Internal Revenue Service and certain members of the
commercial community.

Training

One way in which an arts facility can endeavor to earn money is by
offering classes to the public. While certain arts institutions have traditionally run schools, the goals of such schools were not necessarily
monetary. Although we have no real academy system in this country

---

[15]Plumstead Theatre Society v. Commissioner 74 T.C. 1324 (1980).

whereby artists train for a certain time in a learning situation and then move into a company, schools like the School of American Ballet (the official school for entry into the New York City Ballet) do try to duplicate a European model. Many companies are concerned with the training and education of their artists and offer a series of classes for company members; regional and Off Off Broadway theatres and modern dance companies frequently offer classes that range from brush-up or practice sessions to courses in unfamiliar performance styles or techniques. For example, the Circle Repertory Company in New York City has given classes to company members in Shakespearean scene study, and voice, speech, and movement for performing the classics.

This kind of commitment by a company to its members may leave little time, energy, or money for offering training to the outside paying customer. For a small dance company that does not perform year-round, its offering of a weekly brush-up class may serve to further strain an already overworked choeographer who also happens to be the artistic director, business manager, and fund-raiser for the company.

Nevertheless, there are groups that offer training classes to a variety of clients: classes in corporations for employees on their lunch hour, classes and performances on cruise tours, open rehearsals and workships, residencies around the country, classes for gifted and handicapped children, and more, all of which can be used to earn income for the institution.

LOANS AND BANKING

By suggesting different ways to enter the commercial marketplace, the above examples of profit support of the not-for-profit institution may also provide ideas for groups that do not wish to enter the not-for-profit sector. But such schemes, regardless of the organizational format under which they are developed, should not be undertaken without some cognizance of what to do with the money—the profit, or surplus as it is known in nonprofit parlance—once it is made.

As arts institutions become more and more involved in profit-generating ventures, subsidiary corporations, and spin-offs, loans may become part of their routine thinking. It is possible, in fact, that public grants agencies may begin to think in terms of loans in addition to or even instead of grants: loan money presumably can be used more than once, and, in one view, the worst thing that can happen to an unpaid loan is that it becomes a grant. Therefore, while a lending agency will look extremely carefully at an arts group before making any kind of a loan, once the loan is made it will do all in its power to avoid bad publicity.

This is not to encourage an arts group or any other group toward non-repayment of loans, but rather to illustrate what is perhaps the converse of traditional corporate support of the arts. In direct corporate support, the corporation usually gains a great deal of positive publicity through its association with an arts group. Philip Morris takes double page advertisements in *Time* magazine with full-color reproductions from exhibits it sponsors. Its catch phrase, "It takes art to make a company great," appears in each of these advertisements, a successful attempt at deflecting the reader from the fact that Philip Morris' products include cigarettes, soda, and beer.

A bank that makes a loan to an arts group, on the other hand, seeks to keep the kind of low profile associated with banking in general, and have word of mouth serve to attract more clients. The state of banking in most arts groups, particularly in the nonprofit sector, is at such an unsophisticated level and the profit to be made by the bank so minimal that only a handful of banks are truly responsive to the needs of arts groups. Three banks that operate separate nonprofit teams or divisions (originally formed in response to university and hospital accounts, not arts groups) are Chemical Bank and Citibank in the New York area, and the Bank of America on the West Coast.

The most traditional kind of loan commercial banks make to arts organizations is bridge financing to cover the period of time between the announcement of a grant award and the actual delivery of grant monies to an arts group. A letter from the granting agency is usually sufficient evidence to the bank that money will be forthcoming. The late delivery of funds has become quite common in the last few years; it would be interesting if a special fund could be set up by the granting agencies themselves to cover at least part of the interest for those groups requiring bridge financing due to the funding agencies' slow delivery mechanism. As mentioned in Chapter II, certain funding agencies dispense money to arts groups not as grants but as fees for services rendered and only after a project is completed. This frequently necessitates bridge financing for the arts group to meet immediate cash flow needs.

Of course, the interest charged on all bank loans is tied to the prevailing rate for general bank exchanges. While this rate may seem fair in the world of commerce, it is often a tremendous strain on a small arts group, especially since it is an expense the group never planned for. Interest rates are a function of risk: the riskier the loan is for the bank, the higher the interest rates. While such rates are typically based on prime, customers considered fairly "safe bets" might find themselves borrowing at an interest rate of only a quarter of a point over prime, while arts groups, often in the most risky category, might find themselves paying interest on a loan at two points over prime. Risk is not only a function of the institution itself, but also of the total banking relationship of that institution: how long that institution has been a customer of the bank, how many of its accounts the bank handles, and whether any relationship exists between the business manager of the arts institution and the bank's financial officers.

There are, of course, other kinds of loans to arts organizations besides bridge financing. Most often, loans are made to an arts group to help solve its cash flow problems. Sometimes, the organization wants to expand or enter into new activities; more and more frequently groups need money to finance profit-making subsidiaries. But no matter what kind of loans it gives, a bank has certain questions it needs answered, namely, how it is going to get paid back and, if it doesn't get paid back, what its "fallback position" is. In other words, how will the bank get repaid if the source originally identified as the one for repayment cannot fulfill its obligations? A more familiar term for "fallback position" is collateral; some banks use the euphemism "comfort." No matter what terminology is used, what the bank is looking for is a tangible asset it can grab hold of should the loan go into default.

For arts groups, banks will often take assignments on pledges made during fund-raising campaigns. For example, the board members of the group can guarantee a series of formal pledges to the bank for the amount of the loan. An active, effective board of directors is one criterion for such a loan. Further, board members can personally guarantee part of the organization's loan and be personally liable should the organization default. Often, a number of board members guarantee several thousand dollars to make up the total loan guarantee, especially since banks are usually looking for a net worth in excess of 125 percent of the face amount of that loan. If the board members lack this amount of net worth, or simply do not wish to enter into such an agreement, another entity may act as the guarantor, for example, a private foundation. The Ford Foundation does this with its program-related investments.

If the arts group owns a building, the bank can take a lien on it. If the organization has an endowment, the bank can accept the endowment as collateral. (The bank may, however, regard the endowment as signed rather than formal collateral since the loan is made with the hope that the arts group will grow and flourish, not that it will close and require the bank to run after its money.) Any activity that produces a steady income stream and that the bank feels will continue to do so (over at least a three-year period) can be used. The Brooklyn Academy of Music has used receipts from its parking lot as collateral; the New York Shakespeare Festival has used receipts from the box office of *A Chorus Line*. The use of performance contracts as a guarantee for a loan is not generally accepted, because of the old practice of the producer occasionally closing the play and leaving the actors stranded in a town, or—even worse—of the company arriving in a city for an engagement and finding out that it has been cancelled.

There is some question whether a museum can use its collection as collateral for a loan. In one sense, it can: if the museum uses something else as collateral and that asset happens to be worthless, the bank can "go after" its collection for repayment. But, in the sense that museum trustees are actually responsible for holding the collection "in trust" for the public, there may be some difficulty in using that collection as collateral. The question also arises whether art objects that the museum has purchased would be treated any differently from art it has been given. Although a museum might choose to use specific art objects as collateral, it is extremely difficult to perfect a security interest in a piece of art since the bank needs a guarantee that it will be able to obtain the object in good condition and sell it on relatively short notice. Besides, banks have been chastened by several bad experiences, some their own fault, where the art work they took as collateral turned out to be fake.

In recent conversations with some bankers, I suggested a possible variation on this theme in support of loans for cooperative galleries and artists spaces. Suppose ten prominent artists—those with the stature and marketability of Robert Rauschenberg, James Rosenquist, Frank Stella—each donate one work to a coop gallery or artists space, and suppose a prominent dealer or private collector agrees that, if necessary, he would be willing to purchase these works in a distress situation. Would the bank accept the ten works at fair market value as collateral for a loan to the coop or artists space? I received a guarded but affirmative response with the following conditions: the bank would need an up-front guarantee of the purchase of those art works in a distress situation (by the dealer or collector), and the bank would probably want the works physically protected in some way, in a vault or perhaps a warehouse, and not on display. In this way, both accessibility to the objects and potential purchase would be guaranteed for the bank which would then probably lend up to 75 percent of the market value of the objects themselves. I offer this example simply as encouragement for arts groups to begin to think more creatively about borrowing money at a time when new financial strategies are sorely needed.

One of the most detrimental side effects of the grants habit has been the support of arts organizations on a project-by-project, year-by-year basis where money has to be spent within a fixed period of time and spent entirely during that period of time. Even if a project has enormous success, if a nonprofit organization has no other resources at the end of the fiscal year, it must either go out of business or into deficit funding. This situation ignores the capital needs of arts organizations. They, like any organizations, need to maintain facilities, pay staff, and program activities on an ongoing basis. There are some who feel, in fact, that deficit funding in the nonprofit sector is the equivalent of capitalization in the profit sector. Banks, however, have taken note of the situation since it is at this juncture they are frequently called upon for loans.

Another area banks are beginning to enter is the issuance of municipal bonds for use in major capital expenditures. One instance is the development of the Intrepid Museum Foundation. The Intrepid Museum Foundation floated a $14 million bond issue by putting together a tax-free bond that carried an interest rate of between 12 and 13 percent and selling it to the general public. The money from the bond went to the purchase of the aircraft carrier Intrepid which has become a museum whose collection focuses on World War II. This tax-free issue was appealing to certain members of the public who felt they were buying an interest in a tangible structure. While universities have begun to get involved with such schemes, arts groups have not had much opportunity to do so and, technically, although the Intrepid Museum is a museum by title, it is obviously not an art museum. Nevertheless, with arts institutions being integrated into newly developed environments like the South Street Seaport, such bond issues may become more frequent.

It may also be possible for certain groups to issue such bonds through consortial efforts, although they will have to develop excellent credit-worthiness in the public eye and a good deal of visibility first. For example, suppose Lincoln Center for the Performing Arts (which is really a consortium of a number of companies with certain shared costs) might want to construct an additional building and might need $10 million to do it. It might be willing to pledge $10 million of its endowment fund to back a bond issue. If it were able to raise the necessary $10 million immediately without immediately starting construction, it could get the difference between what it was paying out and what it could earn on its $10 million until construction began. If Lincoln Center were paying out at a rate of 10 percent and making 12 percent, it could earn 2 percent of $200,000 on its $10 million, plus the interest it is getting on its endowment (even though the endowment would be pledged as backing for the bond issue). Some of this income would undoubtedly be used to pay interest on the loan itself, but the rest would be income for Lincoln Center.

For a consortium of small arts groups, such a tactic would probably be quite difficult unless the financial conditions of each member of the consortium were good enough so that the bond rating attached to a particular issue was equal to the bank's current bond rating. A bank, not wishing to impugn its credit worthiness with the public, does not like to issue bonds below its bond rating since that tends to drag its bond rating down and make it more difficult to raise debt through floating a bond issue in the future. While it would be difficult for a group of small arts organizations in a specific discipline to make use of such a tactic, it is possible that a group of organizations across disciplines might do so—a number of successful service organizations, perhaps, or a number of different kinds of organizations linked by geographic proximity.

Short-Term Investments

For the small arts group the concept of investments of any kind is usually greeted with some astonishment. In view of its manager, the group has barely enough to run the operation so how could there be enough to invest? Oddly enough, there are certain periods of time when even the small arts group has extra cash—recently delivered corporation money on hand for a few weeks, money from subscription income or a recent fund drive—times that accountant Robert Carr calls "peak periods of excess cash."[16] Many not-for-profit arts groups are under the mistaken assumption that they are not allowed to invest. While some boards of directors and some grant agencies do restrict an organization's funds in this way, groups should consider using whatever legally accessible sources of income they have to earn interest, even if only overnight. Interest is not subject to taxation and

---

[16]Robert Carr, "In Your Best Interest," *American Arts*, September 1981, p. 14.

is not considered unrelated-business income by the Internal Revenue Service.[17]

Some groups feel more comfortable entrusting the investment of their funds, however meager, to an outsider, either a professional accountant or a banker. The bank actually is often willing to assume a great many responsibilities for the arts institution as part of an overall fee it charges and it may be worthwhile for the institution to use its bank in this way.

There are six basic "widely used, short-term, fixed-income instruments" of investment:

> savings deposits, negotiable order of withdrawal(N.O.W.) accounts, treasury bills, certificates of deposit, commercial paper, and money market mutual funds. These vehicles each have common elements. Many permit investments for short periods from one day to one year, and other than the bank deposits, they are all IOU's. All, of course, bear interest. They differ from each other in the amount of interest they pay (their yield); the minimum and maximum amounts that can be invested or deposited; whether they are guaranteed by the United States government or by the Federal Deposit Insurance Corporation or neither (their risk); and how quickly they can be converted to immediate cash (their liquidity).[18]

While savings accounts are guaranteed up to $100,000 by the FDIC and funds can be withdrawn at any time, current interest rates of 5¼ percent a year make this option one of the least attractive. N.O.W. accounts, similar in interest (5¼% currently), $100,000 guarantee, and other features, allow a group to essentially write "a check on a savings account."[19] While treasury notes and bonds can be obtained for a period of one to twelve months, treasury bills have no set maturity period and are sold by the Federal Reserve at public auction, through a commercial bank or security dealer, in original amounts of $10,000 with no limit on subsequent purchases. These bills can be sold before maturity (and are subject to fluctuations in interest rates) and are guaranteed by the United States government. The purchaser pays

---

[17]Ibid.

[18]Ibid. The figures and amounts in the following section are based on rates as of February 1983. Interest rates on savings accounts may vary from bank to bank; interest on N.O.W. accounts are determined on a statewide basis.

[19]Ibid.

"the face amount of the bill reduced by the interest to be earned upon maturity."[20]

Money market mutual funds allow interest to be earned daily, are easily purchased and liquidated through fund managers or brokers, and require a minimum investment of between $1000 and $1500. Although they invest only in "United States government securities, bank obligations, and high-grade corporate commercial paper," their only guarantee is the credit-worthiness instruments themselves and the "credibility of the management."[21] Recently banks have become involved in the issuance of such funds—commercial banks in money market funds and savings banks in mutual funds. Changes in the law have allowed such funds to have a "floating" interest rate which, although competitive with other mutual funds, may change weekly or even daily.

Certificates of deposit, also with up to $100,000 FDIC guarantee, have changing daily interest rates and must be bought from a bank. They are essentially loans by an investor to a bank and can often be obtained for periods as short as seven days. The amount invested, the yield or interest, and the maturity of the certificate (or time deposit) is different from bank to bank. CDs are assignable and, if they are in large denominations, they may be negotiable.[22]

Commercial paper requires a minimum of $25,000, has a slightly higher yield than a CD (interest is paid upon maturity), but the credit of the corporation that issues it is the only guarantee for payment. Essentially, commercial paper consists of IOU's issued by corporations for periods between one and 270 days.

Other short-term investment procedures are available and banks that deal with not-for-profit organizations are quite familiar with short-term "working capital" lending to cover seasonal fluctuations. In addition to formal lending relationships, however, an arts group might be wise to establish a more regular relationship with its bank concerning certain operational procedures. For example, it may be worthwhile for the arts group to "hire the bank" to do its payroll and taxes, and to issue its W2 statements. If an arts group is having a special fund drive, it may be advantageous to have a "lockbox" arrangement with a bank whereby all the checks go directly to the bank.

If an arts group has a more regular relationship with its bank it

---

[20]Ibid.

[21]Ibid.

[22]Ibid.

may be possible for the arts group to obtain what amounts to an informal line of credit with them. While formal lines of credit are possible, any group that has such an arrangement requires a formal commitment from the bank. That commitment, since it costs the bank money, means the passing on of extra costs to the customer. But if an arts group regularly employs its bank in a number of capacities and has an occasional shortfall, it might be possible for that group to have what amounts to an informal line of credit for a specific purpose. Somewhat akin to an informal emergency agreement for a short period of time, such an occurrence could not happen too frequently, and would almost certainly not occur if the group did not have some long-standing continuous relationship with the bank.

Perhaps the other side of the line-of-credit situation is the overdraft on accounts. While a customer who frequently overdraws will be charged interest according to the rate at which the bank normally lends money, banks do realize the very sensitive area they enter when they agree to deal with publicly visible institutions like arts groups. This sensitivity, plus the personal relationships that exist between the arts group's and the bank's personnel, and the general financial rating of the arts institution all serve to prevent a bank from bouncing the check of an arts group, at least on the first go-round. For those arts groups that are not-for-profit institutions, the bank is clearly in the business of making "a profit off nonprofits," and its major access to the nonprofit community is through word of mouth. The bank has its own reputation to protect in the not-for-profit community as well as in the profit sector.

Revolving Funds/Development Banks

While the previous section on commercial banking procedures and loans illustrates possible relationships between arts groups and their money, there are other ways in which arts groups are trying to financially aid each other. Some of these schemes are only in the idea stage, but they should be scrutinized in the company of the artistic goals and objectives of organizations that might implement and benefit from them.

One result of the federal budget cuts has been the suggestion of possible intermediary organizations between the National Endowment for the Arts and arts institutions. Loan organizations, partially supported by NEA funds, that would make monies available to arts organizations much like banks, on an investment rather than a philan-

thropic basis, are one example. Perhaps such an organization could issue forgivable loans that would allow a group to borrow a certain
amount of money and repay only 40 or 50 percent of the original
amount, or loans that could be repaid on a descending percentage
basis. This intermediary organization might even be a profit corporation, one that could make investments of its own, thus stretching the
profit/nonprofit support relationship even further.

An idea discussed specifically for media centers is the creation of a
fund for purchasing equipment. While media centers have long realized the cost-saving they could accrue by purchasing equipment together, they have not made many formal alliances. Problems with
certain state funding agencies over reversionary rights for equipment
purchased through state funds constrained them, and the speed with
which the hardware itself changes has made certain kinds of equipment outdated or obsolete almost at the time of purchase. A purchasing cooperative was suggested, to be originated by the federal
government, with equipment manufacturers and vendors invited to
make their wares available for lease, lease/purchase, or purchase at
the best possible price for media centers. While prices would surely be
lower than individual purchases would allow, federal government initiative and control were seen by many as a dangerous precedent.

A different approach to the same problem was the suggestion to
model a piece of state legislation for media centers on the recent New
York State bill that created a revolving instrument loan fund for all
nonprofit orchestras in New York State. The $1 million bill allows
these orchestras to upgrade their equipment (their instruments),
without affecting their organizational support and at no cost to them.
In some ways, a true parallel cannot be drawn since musical instruments generally appreciate and become more valuable with age, while
media equipment does not.

Revolving loan funds, especially those that make money available
to independent artists who have no permanent institutional affiliation, are another kind of aid now being explored. The Center for New
Television, a nonprofit media group in Chicago, has created a fund
called The Producers' Initiative which began with $100,000 raised
from two private foundations. The intention is to support productions
that can be packaged, marketed, and distributed with other related
works of independent film and videomakers, not only in the arts.
Documentaries on mental health problems and on specific medical
and therapeutic techniques might be sold to mental health institutions
or hospitals around the country; a series of five-minute video art

pieces or ten-minute image-manipulation pieces might be sold as filler to cable or pay-TV.

Such a fund could serve several functions: it could encourage video and filmmakers to jointly package and market their products; it could sensitize certain markets to the work and the financial potential of such work; and it could tap into a broader audience for the work of documentarians, video artists, filmmakers, video journalists and others whose work is difficult for the marketplace to understand or accept. Money from the sale of the packages or products themselves is intended to replenish the loan fund and, while producers own the rights to their productions, any revenue that is generated is split heavily in favor of the Producers' Initiative until the loan is repaid.[23]

The Department of Commerce administers a revolving loan fund where money is loaned directly to a community, city, or economic district for small-business needs like rehabilitation, modification, and refurbishing of buildings. Such a fund offers new possibilities to smaller arts groups, particularly those borrowing in consortial form.[24]

Loans Toward Capitalization: Nonprofit to Profit Sector Transfers

Earlier in this chapter the subject of production transfers was discussed, when a play moves from the nonprofit to the profit sector. While there has been some discussion over the past several years of a revolving fund to help plays make that transfer, one of the few schemes to have materialized is the Loan Toward Capitalization Program of the Theatre Development Fund.[25] TDF's program applies to a play produced either on Broadway or on tour: it puts up a block of money and receives a number of tickets to sell on a non-subscription basis. There is no relationship between the guarantee of the money and the run of the play. If the play closes quickly, the chances of payback may be jeopardized. Occasionally, TDF also makes a special arrangement to underwrite an Actors' Equity association bond for a

---

[23]Many of the ideas and examples in this section are the result of discussions at the Media Alliance of New York State Conference, June 1981.

[24]Louise Wiener, "The Arts and Economic Development," *The Arts and City Planning,* ed. Robert Porter (New York: American Council for the Arts, NYC, 1980), p. 65.

[25]See *The Emerging Arts,* pp. 24–25, for additional examples.

specific performer in a specific touring company by holding one of its certificates of deposit for such a purpose and drawing interest on that CD at the same time.

TDF's other loan program falls under the category "Grants and Loans." This fund, considered a kind of emergency court of last resort, is indicative of the whole posture of the Theatre Development Fund toward the arts community—it tries, within its limited resources, to respond to the needs of that community. Groups applying to TDF for a loan (not limited to New York City-based groups) must demonstrate that they have already approached other sources. While they are not necessarily required to produce "assignments" (a letter from a grant agency promising forthcoming funds, for example), they are required to realistically project sources of income from which they will repay the loan. The loans are short-term (up to 90 days). Default on payment brings a 15 percent interest charge retroactive to the date of issue of the entire loan. Collateral for the loan most often consists of a letter signed by a Board member. The first $5,000 is loaned interest-free.

Formal Loan Programs

Other formal low-interest or interest-free loan programs for arts organizations are run by the New York Foundation for the Arts, the Fund for the City of New York, and the Cultural Council Foundation, to cite just a few examples in New York City which could be replicated in other areas.[26]

The New York Foundation for the Arts offers loans to organizations awaiting grant money from the New York State Council on the Arts and sometimes from the National Endowment for the Arts, and contracts from New York City's Department of Cultural Affairs. Organizations with a contract and a budget form can obtain short-term loans up to $10,000 for a nominal service charge, to be repaid upon arrival of the government check. The loan fund totals approximately $450,000.

The Fund for the City of New York gives loans up to $10,000 to New York City nonprofit groups with contracts or grants from a government agency. If the loan is repaid within two months, half of the 2

---

[26]The following examples are taken from *A Quick Guide to Loans and Emergency Funds* published by the Center for Arts Information, New York, 1982.

percent service charge is refunded; the maximum service charge is
$200. The loan fund totals $437,000.

The Cultural Council Foundation offers interest-free loans of up to
$5,000 to its clients against forthcoming foundation or government
grants or performance contracts. Client loans average between $1,000
and $3,000. Occasionally, even corporations give low-interest or
interest-free loans. The Canadian Brass received an interest-free loan
from Seagrams for a tour called "Seagrams Presents the Canadian
Brass." The corporation received extensive publicity through radio,
television, and print media, and the company repaid the loan through
box-office receipts.

Program-Related Investments

The Program-Related Investment program of the Ford Foundation is
essentially a kind of development bank in terms of the arts groups it
helps. The program invests part of Ford's portfolio in activities it considers "related to" or consonant with the Foundations' programs. For
arts groups, this has meant loans or loan guarantees almost exclusively toward capital costs, particularly the acquisition or renovation
of space and/or buildings. (It should be noted that some public funding agencies specifically prohibit funding for these areas.) Thus, Ford
aided the New York Shakespeare Festival in renovating the Delacorte
Theatre in Central Park. (Papp's fallback guarantee for this particular
project was not only a pledge of funds, but receipts from the box office
for *A Chorus Line*.) Ford also provided a loan guarantee to the Brooklyn Academy of Music, and a loan to the Center Stage in Baltimore
when it lost its theatre to fire.

More appropriate to small arts organizations, however, is Ford's
program-related investment to the Studio Museum of Harlem several
years ago. A New York bank donated a building it had obtained
through foreclosure to the Studio Muesum on Manhattan's West
125th Street. A Ford Foundation consultant helped the Museum obtain an Urban Development Action Grant (UDAG). While the UDAG
money helped the Museum pay all but $250,000 of the necessary reno-
vation costs, UDAGs are almost always paid out in piecemeal fashion
by the government at each stage of construction and the money is pro-
cessed by the city before it gets to the grantee. Contractors are often
leery of accepting UDAG jobs since they know it will take them a long
time to get paid. Ford made a program-related investment which was

90 percent secured by the UDAG so the Museum could pay its contractors on time and begin construction immediately.

Although Ford does not deal with numerous arts groups in this way, the above examples should indicate that such aid is sometimes possible. Generally, however, arts groups should recognize that program-related investments focus on loans and loan guarantees, and on investments not on grants.

There are other examples of such aid that, while they are not officially called program-related investments, have all the trappings of being so. Theater Row on Manhattan's West 42nd Street began as a block of buildings occupied by a number of off-off-Broadway theatres.[27] In order to obtain a loan to renovate the spaces, the 42nd Street Development Corporation had to demonstrate to the banks that these spaces were actually needed. The Theatre Development Fund agreed to take the leases for a number of theatres before there were tenants in them, essentially guaranteeing to pay the rentals should tenants not be found. It was never necessary for TDF to be responsible for those spaces, but its key position as both a validating agency and a guarantor enabled the project to move ahead.

The Artists Foundation in Boston, Massachusetts is an organization whose main focus is to aid artists. Through its Art Space Project, the Foundation secured a loan from the First National Bank of Boston for construction costs in an artist-owned condominium with eight studio/loft spaces.[28] By assuming certain leadership, development, and liaison roles for a group of artists, the Foundation was able to convince the bank that artists could meet their financial commitments as condominium owners. While it finally made no difference to the bank whether the owners were artists or not, the Artists Foundation provided an auspice through the early stages of the project, when the fact that potential owners were artists could have worked against their ownership.

Although not a program-related investment in the actual cash terms of the Ford Foundation, the Artists Foundation's investment was one of commitment as well as staff time and money, a commit

[27]More detailed information on Theater Row and its development appears later in this chapter.

[28]Through the excellent study, *Artists' Space,* the Foundation learned about many artist-needs in the Commonwealth of Massachusetts, not the least of which was the need of many visual artists to have a space that serves both as their living and their working quarters.

ment to help "provide living and working space for visual artists in the Commonwealth; to revitalize urban areas of the Commonwealth through the introduction of 'new populations' into existing vacant and underused buildings; and to provide private investors with the opportunity to participate in the revitalization of Massachusetts cities while receiving a fair return on investment."[29]

Like the Theatre Development Fund, the Artists Foundation assumed the role of broker between two formerly unallied sectors, and of validator when credibility for the artists' community was sorely needed. This role may be even more important than an actual cash investment, since it allows certain groups to foray into support areas formerly closed to them by providing them with a stamp of approval acceptable to the world of commerce, investment, and trade.

REAL ESTATE

In the world of buying and selling perhaps no area has received more news coverage or greater scrutiny than real estate. Arts groups, like others, have realized not only that space is at a premium, especially in urban centers, but that space is no longer as narrowly defined as once it was. Living and working space today represents everything from converted fire houses to the air rights above one's head. While the trend in the last several decades was toward the design and construction of lavish, large arts complexes, the trend in the 1980s is toward renovation, revitalization, and the use of existing spaces to earn income and to revitalize communities, as well as to house artistic programs. What follows then, is a series of examples of real estate projects in which arts groups play a prominent part. Some examples are drawn from large arts institutions and, while they may not be replicable, they may serve as models for smaller groups. Others are concerned more with individuals than groups, since the world of small arts institutions finds many groups with their base in the studio, loft, or living space of one person.

That many of these projects do not have as their original impetus any artistic impulses or purpose has caused a certain amount of ambivalence by some artists. The words of director Alan Schneider are

---

[29]The Artists Foundation, *Artists' Space: A Study of the Development of Artists' Living and Working Space in Boston* (Boston: The Artists Foundation, 1981), p. 38.

particularly apt: "I'm not sure how the Parthenon got built, or the Acropolis, but certainly it had nothing to do with revitalizing the neighborhood."[30] Nevertheless, such strategies are being approached and the arts institutions involved are not always of the mammoth proportions of those that constitute Lincoln Center.

Towers in the Sky: Air Rights for Arts Organizations

In 1976 the Museum of Modern Art announced a plan to erect a 42-story apartment tower above its present site on West 53rd Street in Manhattan. The apartment tower was construed as a way to finance not only the Museum's planned future expansion, but its ongoing operating expenses and its annual deficit of $1 million plus. While the plan was made possible through an amendment to municipal legislation, creating something called the Trust for Cultural Resources, the implications for similar legislation and similar financial solutions for other arts organizations are obvious. Although a brief description of the plan will be included here, it should be understood that, "The project is so complicated, involving so many questions of finance, urban design, and even ethics, that only the few movers-and-shakers directly involved with this scheme on a daily basis really know what's going on."[31] As Lee Rosenbaum stated in 1977, "there is little middle ground in this controversy: there are those who see the scheme as the museum's ultimate salvation, and those who are certain that this project will destroy MoMA."[32]

The legislation creating the Trust for Cultural Resources attempts to provide support for "museums and other cultural institutions in the state" by allowing private developers to develop the air rights of those institutions through the creation of a public benefit corporation that exempts the property developed from real estate taxes and allows payments to be diverted to the cultural institution in place of real estate taxes.[33]

---

[30]Arthur Ballet and Lindy Zesch, eds., *The 1978 TCG Conference Report* (New York: Theatre Communications Group, 1978), p. 50.

[31]Lee Rosenbaum, "MoMA's Construction Project: Reflections on a Glass Tower," *Arts News*, November 1977, p. 12.

[32]Ibid.

[33]1976 Session Laws, Chapter 902, Trusts. Cultural Resources Trusts. Article 13-E NYS Cultural Resources Act, 27 July 1976, section 303.

While over $7 million in museum money has already been spent on the project, the developers of the "Museum Tower" will pay the museum $17 million for air rights. These monies, as well as those provided through the Trust arrangement, will be aided as well by a $38 million fund drive.[34] A 50 percent increase in earned income is projected—from merchandising activities, memberships, admissions, restaurants, and related activities.[35] The condominium apartments, to begin at the seventh floor are expected to range from $200,000 to $1 million with a maintenance cost of $3,000 to $7,000.[36] All this income should help finance the museum's expansion and its increased operating costs.

Progress on the tower has been complicated by disputes over the land, buildings, and air rights that surround the Museum. There have been discussions and, in some cases, legal action concerning rights and/or space of the Hotel Dorset, the Museum of Contemporary Crafts, and nearby real estate owned by CBS. Further complications have arisen over financial and hierarchical positions of certain patron families like the Rockefellers. Involved in the founding of the Museum of Modern Art and still active on its board, they also hold positions on the board of the American Crafts Council, overseer of the Museum of Contemporary Crafts. Additional criticism has resulted from the change in the "character" of West 53rd Street between Fifth and Sixth Avenues that the tower will create, and the shadow that it will throw over the Museum's sculpture garden.[37] Finally, in early 1982 the Museum announced it would close its doors for approximately five months for construction purposes. Fears surfaced of the adverse effect of such a strategy on current and potential members, especially if construction took longer than expected.[38]

But the most vocal criticisms center around ethical issues. The MoMA tower project seems to crystallize the most obvious fears of profit support of the nonprofit institution:

---

[34]Lee Rosenbaum, "A New Foundation for MoMA's Tower," *Art News*, February 1980, p. 64.

[35]Ibid.

[36]Ibid.

[37]Rosenbaum, "MoMA's Construction Project," p. 16.

[38]At least one foreign exhibit has already been refused by the Museum as a result of the renovations.

The dilemma . . . is that its [the Museum's] performance is measured not just by box-office returns and by the prosperity of its commercial operations. It is a repository of values as well as of objects, and there is a point at which the museum, like any other nonprofit institution, will decisively compromise its character by succumbing to the siren appeal of commercialism.[39]

Pitting the "repository of values" against the "siren appeal of commercialism" aptly describes the uneasiness of the arts community in general, but the MoMA tower project raises specific questions about the appropriateness of real estate activity for the art museum:

On the most profound level, the question is: Is involvement in a money-making real estate deal consistent with a museum's mission as a disinterested scholarly observer of culture? On a more basic level, the question is: To what extent will MoMA be associated in people's minds with the management of the tower, and will Richard Oldenberg [the museum's director] get called by irate tenants when the pipes leak . . . already the museum's staff and trustees have found themselves fielding telephone inquiries about the availability of apartments.[40]

Even amid all the controversy, the attempt by the Museum of Modern Art to become self-sustaining should be applauded, at least in its willingness to look for new solutions in the support of arts institutions. Its very unconventional approach to financial support may prove that MoMA is indeed ahead of its time and provide a model for other institutions across the country, or it may force the museum to return to more conventional forms of money making—raising the endowment to cover the annual deficit and provide for expansion. In fact, other arts institutions are already involved in similar schemes—City Center on West 55th Street and Carnegie Hall on West 57th Street are two examples. While most small arts organizations do not own enough property to make such an opportunity available, a similar plan might be appropriate for groups involved in the early stages of downtown redevelopment and revitalization projects.

---

[39]Karl E. Meyer, *The Art Museum: Power, Money, Ethics* (New York: William Morrow, 1979), p. 110. This quote actually refers to the Metropolitan Museum of Art, but the universality of the idea is applicable here.

[40]Rosenbaum, "A New Foundation for MoMA's Tower," p. 75.

Local Development Corporations

In 1976, a local development corporation, the 42nd Street Development Corporation, was created under the auspices of the Municipal
Arts Society of New York to "save" West 42nd Street in Manhattan.
An area filled with pornography shops, derelict tenement houses,
and peep shows—yet in the heart of Manhattan, immediately accessible to Broadway theatres, the Port Authority Bus Terminal, and the
Garment Center—the street had suffered from 40 years of neglect and
abuse. In 1978, efforts were expanded to include the entire Times
Square area from Sixth to Eighth Avenues and 41st to 50th Streets.
Phase I included eight theatres on West 42nd Street between Ninth
and Tenth Avenues collectively called Theater Row: Black Theatre Alliance, the Harlem Children's Theatre, The Harold Clurman Theatre,
INTAR—International Arts Relations, the Lion Theatre, The Nat
Horne Musical Theatre, Playwrights Horizons and the South Street
Theatre, plus a residential building whose ground floor is now
occupied by a French restaurant.

New York State law mandates that a local development corporation have "broad economic development purposes, i.e., the creation
of jobs. The statute specifies that an LDC is to act 'in the public interest' and to 'lessen . . . the burdens of government.' "[41] The 42nd
Street Development Corporation is a public, not-for-profit corporation with federal-tax exemption. As the "project-implementing arm of
the local government" in its local development role it receives support
in the form of tax equivalency rentals (instead of full real estate taxes)
on Theater Row from the City of New York. These payments are equal
to 50 percent of profits.[42]

The tax relief that Theater Row received under the Mayor's Business Investment Incentive Program with Urban Development Corporation ownership has reflected the City's position that theatres are
important to the city's economic vitality in a very specific way. This is
the first time New York City has provided up-to-code theatre space for
Off Off Broadway theatres and, while it was not necessarily the city's
intent, these spaces have served to legitimize a number of groups
whose names and work were less well-known before their common
association on West 42nd Street.

---

[41] "Profile: The Theater Row Story," Press Kit, 42nd Street Development Corporation, January 1982.

[42] Ibid.

Essentially, the New York State Urban Development Corporation (a public benefit corporation similar, in certain ways, to MoMA's Trust for Cultural Resources) was allowed by the State Legislature to have all UDC-owned properties declared tax exempt. The 42nd Street Development Corporation obtained the properties, donated them to the UDC which then removed them from tax rolls through its tax exemption, and leased the properties back to the 42nd Street Development Corporation for 30 years for a tax equivalency rental equalling 50 percent of the profits.

The 42nd Street Corporation sublet the properties to the theatre companies, who had to, first, undergo an application process in order to be allowed to rent the space; second, pay a rental on an initial five-year lease (with renewal options of three years, six years, and six years) of $1,000 per month for the theatre space itself and $500 a month for each additional rehearsal/office floor (maximum increase of 15 percent allowable on initial lease, and 10 percent on six-year renewals); and, third; separately finance any and all improvements including the stage, lighting, seating, partitions, and anything else needed to change the raw space into a theatre complex. Additional proportionate charges for heat, insurance, and water are paid to the landlord.

The Black Theatre Alliance, with five floors including a theatre, is paying somewhere in the neighborhood of $42,000 a year in rental fees, as is the Actors and Directors Lab.[43] Many companies have spent as much as $50,000 improving their space and one theatre had a July 1981 electricity bill of $2,100.[44]

As attractive as it was for many theatres to have their own spaces, there was tremendous misunderstanding on the part of funding sources regarding the tenants' financial arrangements with their landlord; many funders simply assumed that the spaces, and related costs, were subsidized. Other problems—impending and continuing cuts in government arts money, the fact that some companies were undercapitalized from the beginning, and increasing costs—found many theatres facing eviction by the Spring of 1981, while others remained dark, a real threat to the level of traffic and activity that the

---

[43]Several theaters, including the Actors and Directors Lab, have been added to the original eight.

[44]Marilyn Stasio, "The Reprieve—for now—of Theater Row," *Newsday*, 30 August 1981, sec. III, p. 1.

theatres provided to the area. At that point a five-year plan was initiated, along with the development of a centralized service organization
for the theatres, and the hiring of a central booking manager to rent
out the spaces to outside groups for part of each year in order to keep
them open and lit, maximize their usage, and help them meet their
costs.[45]

Rental has become a very lucrative form of earned income for several companies around the country including The Wooster Group in
New York City and N.A.M.E. Gallery in Chicago. The American Ballet Theatre earns money renting out its rehearsal and studio space on
Broadway. Some arts organizations rent their parking lots to farmers'
markets and civic groups. But the questions that arise in the case of
Theatre Row are very much involved in the advantages and disadvan-
tages of such arrangements on an artistic level:

> How can a developmental theater do its work properly when it can't use
> its own facilities for half a year? Won't a theater lose its artistic integrity
> when transient shows start sharing its space? Don't the companies on
> Theater Row deserve some kind of cold-cash support for helping to de-
> velop the current high real estate value of their once-blighted neighbor-
> hood?[46]

In fact, when Frederick Papert, president of the 42nd Street Development Corporation, began to emphasize the corporation's business as
one of economic development as opposed to theatre, rumors began to
circulate that he might foreclose on some of the theatres that could not
come up with the necessary cash within a certain amount of time.

Phase II of Theater Row has already begun. It covers West 42nd
Street between Dyer and Tenth Avenues as well as the completion of
the Ninth to Tenth Avenue block. It includes a four-story building
housing the Douglas Fairbanks Theatre, the Raft Theatre, the Image
Theatre and Studio, plus office and workshop spaces. Another four-
story building housing a 260-seat theatre for the Clark Dance Center is
planned as is a Theater Row Market Place including a restaurant, a
public sculpture garden, retail space and rehearsal facilities. Other
plans include a mini-Shubert Alley, improved sidewalks, trees and
signs, a large wall painting by artist Richard Haas, and a stable for police horses, upgrading of the 350-room Holland Hotel on 42nd Street

[45]Alan W. Petrucelli, ''42nd Street Theater Row,'' *Showbill*, April 1982.
[46]Stasio, p. 2.

between Eighth and Ninth Avenues, construction of a 450-unit apartment building at 42nd Street and Eleventh Avenue (Manhattan Plaza, a subsidized housing complex for performing artists, already exists across the street from Theater Row's Phase I theatres), the restoration of a number of legendary theatres in the area, and the possibility of a 42nd Street Trolley running from the United Nations to Eleventh Avenue.[47]

Part of the success of Theater Row's Phase I is due to the relative ease with which it acquired the 42nd Street Ninth-to-Tenth Avenue block. At the time, a nonprofit organization could enter the private market with very little cash and obtain quite a bit of property: less than $10,000 in cash and about $300,000 in obligations purchased the Phase I block. Additionally, almost 50 percent of the Phase I project came from grants from the government, from foundation and donor funds, from the Port Authority, and from New York City. Phase II required greater private market credibility, other kinds of financing, and the existence of an anchor tenant (National Recording Studios) to pay substantial rent, lend credibility, and support bank financing.[48] It was organized through a complicated plan including a cash-flow mortgage, continued city-tax abatement, an Urban Development Action Grant, government assistance, private investors seeking tax shelter benefits, plus an in-depth understanding of the 1981 Economic Recovery Tax Act.[49]

One view of this kind of local development concerns the city as landlord. What if the tenant groups will not or cannot meet the obligations of maintenance and upkeep on the property (as has been rumored several times about certain groups on Theater Row)? When the city is the recipient of funds from nonprofit organizations, do these organizations have an overly sympathetic landlord? If tax advantages are given to such groups that in turn help to revitalize a neighborhood, do emotional issues and the potential of "bad press" for the City prevent it from treating nonprofit groups, particularly arts groups, as any other tenant?

The echoes resound of the misfortune of certain regional arts complexes of the 1960s (and even urban ones like Lincoln Center and its

---

[47] "Profile: The Theater Row Story."

[48] NYC Commission for Cultural Affairs, "Self Help: Earned Income Opportunities for Cultural Organizations," Conference Proceedings, 26 January 1982, p. 35.

[49] Ibid., pp. 35–41.

Vivian Beaumont Theatre) where mammoth plants built in the heyday of private and public funding lived to incur huge maintenance costs on unused or under-used spaces. But in Theater Row, where small, experimental theatres have tried merely to equip their spaces modestly, with the basic necessities for office, rehearsal, and stage, the costs seem crippling. And perhaps because these groups are still small, still emerging, still reliant on a core of artistic people, still intensely personal companies, their position as part of a real estate complex is even more ironic:

> By helping to develop a prime piece of real estate, the theaters have indavertently gotten into the real-estate business themselves. As artists, they have realized their dreams, and yet can't survive on them. As entrepreneurs, they will undoubtedly do better, once they start renting out their real estate. Which, of course, will take them even further away from the job of making theater themselves.[50]

Public Buildings/City Space

While the subject of actual works of art in public places is discussed elsewhere in this chapter, there are certain arts groups that house their activities, either temporarily or semi-permanently, depending on lease arrangements, in publicly owned buildings. Certain organizations like the Organization of Independent Artists exhibit and perform only in public places, avoiding rental charges, and sometimes making use of legislation like the Public Buildings Cooperative Use Act which makes certain space in federal buildings available for "public" use. The artists space Creative Time uses sites awaiting development for "interim use" projects, like its current Art on the Beach exhibits and events on ten acres of the north part of the Battery Park City landfill in lower Manhattan.[51]

In the cities, arts groups have learned either to adapt their needs to existing structures or to use those structures to give form and even inspiration to their work. City Walls is a nonprofit organization responsible for many of the large murals found on the outside of buildings in urban areas; these murals often express community and ethnic themes. Some years ago a group called Graffiti Alternatives was

---

[50]Stasio, p. 2.

[51]Cultural Assistance Center, *Partners: A Practical Guide to Corporate Support of the Arts* (New York: Cultural Assistance Center, 1982), p. 53.

formed to persuade certain "graffiti artists" to turn their talents elsewhere; contracts were obtained for interior painting and design on several public buildings.

Perhaps the greatest Cinderella story of the arts and city-owned space is the one about the Institute for Art and Urban Resources in New York City. The very first activity this artists space undertook was in 1971 when it obtained permission from the city to organize an exhibit under the Brooklyn Bridge in exchange for cleaning up the area where the exhibit was to take place. The Brooklyn Bridge Event was followed by a series of activities in burned-out warehouses, empty factories, police precincts, the clocktower of a city office building, storage depots, and abandoned buildings. Finally, in 1976, the Institute obtained an abandoned school building in Long Island City, Queens with more square footage than the Whitney Museum of American Art. P.S. 1 became the primary residence of the Institute, although other urban sites and a clocktower on Leonard Street were still used.

A good deal of political jockeying resulted in a twenty-year lease to the Institute from the Board of Estimate (not the Real Estate Board), and a $150,000 three-year balloon mortgage guaranteed by private foundations and private personal co-signatures. This kind of private commitment has been especially important to the Institute, particularly since public monies were erratic at the time and since it is always negotiating with the city for more space.

One recent idea is the placement of artists in a hundred tiny surplus office spaces throughout the five boroughs. If these offices are in buildings that are already maintained and the Institute could charge the artists a nominal fee, perhaps $50 per space, several aims would be served over a twelve-month period: the artists would get sorely needed studio space at a more than reasonable fee; the Institute could produce revenue; and the artists might act as a holding effect in otherwise unutilized or underutilized space in a variety of neighborhoods. The Institute would be adopting a slumlord mentality for a good end. Nevertheless, it is difficult to convince City administrators to donate space which they would often rather rent at commercial rates or not at all.[52]

---

[52]Some of the ideas in this section are the result of discussion with Stephen Reichard, the Institute's former business manager, on 1 June 1981.

Amenity Strategies

For those involved in urban revitalization it has become clear in the last several years that jobs follow people and not the reverse, as was previously thought.[53] The post-World War II loss of a major part of city populations to the suburbs has begun to be reversed by the urban adoption of a strategy that attracts both businesses and residents to an area for economic and "quality-of-life" reasons. The creation of a critical mass of cultural, residential, and commercial activities has provided a particular niche for arts groups to survive into the 1980s. While such strategies are usually not generated for any artistic reasons, they may provide the normally deficit-ridden arts group with a support "package" of shops, restaurants, stores, urban parks, and other amenities which makes it an attractive investment proposition.

Cultural planning is the relatively new phenomenon of integrating the arts into the "everyday experience of urban residents."[54]There are a variety of ways cultural planners have begun to use the arts, among them, historical preservation, conservation of the natural environment and public spaces, public art for those and other spaces, restoration and adaption of facilities for arts uses, and artists districts.[55]

HISTORICAL PRESERVATION   Perhaps the most familiar kind of historical preservation is that in which town squares, old towns, and even specific buildings are preserved for their cultural value—either due to their architectural singularity, the historic image they project, and/or their specific design. The city of Cleveland is restoring three run-down theatres in the heart of downtown to be called Playhouse Square. Throughout the country old movie palaces are being restored to their former glory and turned into centers of cultural activity—the Palace Theatre in Danbury, Connecticut, the Paramount in Denver, the Fox-Oakland Theatre in Oakland, California. Joseph Papp's Public Theatre is housed in the renovated landmark Astor Mansion on Lafayette Street in lower Manhattan.

---

[53]Both a 1977 Rand Corporation study about the urban impact on federal policies and a 1979 study by the Joint Economic Committee of Congress made this basic point.

[54]Michael J. Pittas, "Planning for the Arts," in *The Arts and City Planning*, ed. Robert Porter (New York: American Council for the Arts, 1980), p. 19.

[55]These categories are taken from a study by James L. Shanahan in his study, "Using the Arts in Economic Development Strategies," Cultural and Leisure Studies Unit, Center for Urban Studies, University of Akron.

Less familiar is the preservation of industrial facilities that, instead of being renewed to their former uses, increasingly are being converted to other uses. Particularly true in the cities of the northeast that lack the recognizable glamour and charm of certain southern counterparts, these "gritty cities" very often provide abandoned mills, silos, breweries, warehouses, and lofts that can be adapted to arts uses.[56] In Patterson, New Jersey, the city is renovating "two 19th century mills, the Essex and the Phoenix, into space for 146 artists to live and work. Patterson has no central artists space, and planners hope that by encouraging artists to locate in the mill district, the city will develop a lively arts community that will draw visitors from around the area to observe and shop."[57] Alexandria, Virginia, not exactly a Northeastern city, boasts a space used and run by artists, named for its former industrial use, the Torpedo Factory.

CONSERVATION OF THE NATURAL ENVIRONMENT, PUBLIC SPACES, AND PUBLIC ART The natural environment of our cities is a precious commodity, moreso since so much of it has disappeared to make way for social services, transportation, industry, and technology. The protection, use, and enhancement of that environment are in evidence in many major cities as they seek to redevelop certain areas: Boston and Baltimore have centered new developments around riverfronts, Pittsburgh plans re-use of industrial land for recreation, Seattle plans urban greenbelt preservation, and urban cultural parks that combine history, culture, and natural elements are starting in Lowell, Massachusetts and in six communities in the Hudson-Mohawk area of New York State. The man-made environment is of equal concern: street furniture and sign improvements in Pittsburgh, public thoroughfare improvements in Rockville, Maryland, streetscape planning in Milwaukee, and open space planning and enhancement in Easton, Pennsylvania. The systems that service this environment are becoming equally cognizant of the "amenity value" they can provide, often via the arts, in many communities. Art works have appeared in the Atlanta subways, while New York boasts "Poetry on the Buses," and Boston is

---

[56]Carol Rifkind, "Cultural Tourism: A New Opportunity for the Industrial City?" *Environmental Comment*, January 1981, p. 4.

[57]"The Economics of Amenity," *Economics of Amenity News*, 1 December 1980, p. 12.

planning a new extension to its subway system with art as an integral
part of the process in its "Arts-on-the-Line Project."[58]

Public spaces, walks, plazas, malls, and gardens are being designed, changed, and enhanced and public art is often being placed in
them. The issue of public art in public spaces has engendered more
publicity than almost any other environmental issue in the arts. Serving to increase, re-route, deflect, and control traffic, to provide a visible monument of community spirit, even to humanize an area, public
art has been criticized for its "public" value and for its value as "art."
It ranges from Christo's "Running Fence" that wound through miles
of the California countryside, to the highly controversial "Tilted Arc"
of Richard Serra in New York's Federal Plaza and Claes Oldenberg's
"Batcolumn" in Chicago. Public art has been financed by public monies through the National Endowment for the Arts, the General Services Administration, state Per-Cent-for-Art programs, as well as
private sources: Christo financed "Running Fence" by selling
sketches of the piece to the 59 landowners on whose land the piece
was to stand.[59]

The public art experience has been referred to as a community
event and an aesthetic travesty; it has created fierce loyalties both pro
and con, and some communities have found that by involving the artist in the urban planning process at an early stage, a more positive experience ensues for the community. Nevertheless, the art that is
commissioned and therefore is the original work of a living artist
will ultimately have to be a representation of the personal vision of
that artist, and perhaps its greatest value as an amenity is its singularity.

RESTORATION AND ADAPTATION OF CULTURAL AND OTHER FACILITIES
"Adaptive-use" restoration is one of the most popular amenity tools
for arts groups. Aside from the many performance spaces, halls, and
theatres that have been repaired and restored for arts activities across
the country (50 of the 130 buildings on the National Register of Historic Places have been restored for these purposes[60]), other spaces like

---

[58]Martin Convisser, "The Arts and Transportation," in *The Arts and City
Planning*, ed. Robert Porter (New York: American Council for the Arts,
1980), pp. 80–87.

[59]Gene R. Brooks, "Arts Amenities in Comprehensive Plans," in *The Arts and
City Planning*, ed. Robert Porter (New York: American Council for the Arts,
1980), pp. 46–47.

school buildings, fire houses, town halls, breweries, and banks have been renovated for arts uses.

The Puerto Rican Traveling Theatre is now located in a former firehouse on Manhattan's West Side. In Boston, Atlanta, and Seattle, artists have redeveloped former public school buildings into combined living/working space for visual artists. In Charlotte, North Carolina, an abandoned church was turned into a cultural center. In St. Paul, Minnesota, a combination post office, custom house, and court house now houses five nonprofit arts and humanities agencies, recital, rehearsal, and exhibition spaces, private meeting rooms, and shops.

Adaptive-use facilities are frequently mixed-use ones as well. In purely economic terms, mixed-use facilities have proved to aid "economic multiplier effects" for an area: the facility attracts employees and consumers who spend substantial amounts for basic needs and services such as food and transportation. Increased revenues and neighborhood security result from merely keeping the streets active and the neighborhood open for longer hours per day.[61] Traditionally, mixed-use facilities combine residential and commercial activities, but some arts groups like and/or in Seattle and the Municipal Arts Society in New York have found that one way to subsidize real estate and even program costs is for a nonprofit organization to own a building in which commercial tenants pay rent. Proper "packaging" of such projects can often free up the public and private money needed to get them off the ground.

Economist Dick Netzer feels that the multiplier effects of the arts are relatively conventional except in rare circumstances and "therefore, contribute nothing distinctive in an economic context. He proposed that concentrations of cultural activity can be helpful to old downtowns, but rejected the notion that a declining area could be saved by an infusion of the arts. He suggested that major central cities may be helped considerably by the arts in the urban/suburban context, but only marginally in improving an area's competitiveness with alternate urban areas."[62]

---

[60]Shanahan, p. 4.

[61]Artists Foundation, *Artists' Space*, p. 3.

[62]*Cultural Resources/Economic Development, Strengths and Limitations: A Roundtable, December 8, 1980:* Final Report for the U.S. Department of Commerce (Washington, D.C.: The Brookings Institution, 1980).

ARTIST DISTRICTS   It is noteworthy that cities like Patterson, New Jersey include artist districts in the redevelopment of their downtown area. While this kind of city planning is fairly recent, artist districts—not always within the legalities of zoning law—are not.

In America, the advent of zoning in the late 19th and early 20th centuries divided cities into residential, commercial, and industrial zones, with building regulations and restrictions in each zone. Developed for the essentially private interests of politicians, realtors, and those in the urban power structure, the zones made it difficult for any alternative use to be made of a space zoned for a particular kind of use. The joint living and working space arrangement required or preferred by so many artists including painters, sculptors, craftspeople, and choreographers, has created its own history of urban redevelopment. The rezoning of the Soho (and now Noho and TriBeCa)[63] district of Manhattan to permit artists to live and work in industrial zones backfired on the artists themselves. After moving into former manufacturing buildings, and renovating and restoring them with their own money, artists succeeded in making the area a desirable place to live. Landlords then raised the rents and artists were forced to move out. While the economic redevelopment of the area has certainly occurred, the artists' needs were met for only a limited period of time. After "fighting the zoning battle, making the area safe, and filling the streets with energy, and the buildings with boutiques . . . [artists] have been left to the forces of the market."[64]

Rezoning for "live/workers," as they are sometimes called, has taken place right alongside economic development in Minneapolis, Boston, Berkeley, Los Angeles, Seattle, and San Francisco.[65] Strategies for artist ownership of their spaces are also being developed, particularly in response to experiences like Soho's gentrification—"the displacement of existing residents by newer, more affluent residents"[66].

Several studies have been undertaken that characterize artists as

---

[63]Soho, Noho, and TriBeCa are acronyms for three areas of New York City—the area South of Houston Street, the area North of Houston Street, and the Triangle below Canal Street.

[64]Artists Foundation, *Artists' Space*, p. 10.

[65]Artists Equity Association of Northern California, Inc., *Artists Live/work Space: Changing Public Policy* (San Francisco: Artists Equity Association, 1981), p.

[66]Artists Foundation, Artists' Space, p. 23.

risk-takers, willing to pioneer in neighborhood revitalization, with needs that differ greatly from other tenants—cheap rent, contact with fellow artists, the need for an atmosphere where they can freely express themselves.[67] At the Piano Craft Guild in Boston's South End, artists were actively solicited to lease apartments and the area has been partly marketed as "anchored" by artists' housing. Property values have risen and condominium conversions have begun. Nevertheless, artists are limited in terms of any renovations or alterations they can make on the space, since the owners are concerned with future rentals.[68] One anchor for the whole Theater Row plan in New York was the Manhattan Plaza, a subsidized apartment building for artists on the north side of West 42nd Street between Ninth and Tenth Avenues, directly across from the Phase I theatres of Theater Row.

The Arts at the Center

In fairly recent urban history, arts facilities, art works, and even artists themselves have been used as aids for urban revitalization. New York's Lincoln Center, the Columbus, Indiana Commons, and the Pompidou Center in Paris are visible demonstrations of the symbiotic relationship between arts facilities and commercial activity. Rarely, however, have cities sought to elevate arts and cultural activities and institutions to a priority position in the planning stages. In Winston-Salem, North Carolina, the arts are literally the cornerstone on which downtown revitalization is being built.

Winston-Salem, home of the first city arts council (1949), has the highest per capita donation of arts money in the country and a strong history of private patronage. The creation of a critical mass of downtown activities, with the help of that patronage, will revolve around two projects: 1) the conversion of a 1920s movie theatre, the Carolina, into a 1400 seat theatre, the Roger L. Stevens Performing Arts Center, which will house traveling and local shows and concerts, various productions of the North Carolina School of the Arts, and other performing activities, and 2) the creation of Winston Square. Located on two blocks adjacent to the Stevens Center, the square will be a complex of galleries, exhibition space, a theatre, a restaurant, an outdoor park, and artists' studios.

---

[67]Ibid., p. 21.

[68]Ibid.

A description of downtown Winston-Salem just prior to construction of the arts complex and of the method attempted to reverse the exodus to the suburbs provides a startling picture of one of our oldest cities:

> After the 5 p.m. whistles blew, the streets emptied. There were no theaters, concert halls or restaurants to attract people. Only winos and derelicts haunted the streets at night.
>
> The city fathers tried many things to reverse matters. Winston-Salem prettied itself up by taking down unsightly signs, refacing the stores, burying overhead wires, building the 32-story Wachovia Building to entice more buildings to remain in the heart of town.
>
> Nothing worked . . . a downtown mall was built, but it failed. Continued urban flight seemed almost certain.[69]

This description is of a town that currently houses three symphony orchestras, ten art galleries and museums, three chamber music groups, a repertory theatre, a dance company, two craft shops, four colleges and universities, a reconstructed 18th century village, "Old Salem," and one of the largest collections of manuscripts of 18th century music in the world.[70] A textile and tobacco town of approximately 145,000 people, Winston-Salem also houses some excellent private art collections through the Hanes and Reynolds families.

Since downtown revitalization began, downtown owner occupancy has increased by 50 percent, and the arts have helped attract $20 million for the Radison Hotel, $17.5 million for the Integon Insurance Corporation Building, and $5 million for a former cotton mill converted into shops and restaurants.[71]

In San Francisco, the improvement of 87 acres in the South-of-Market area known as Yerba Buena Center includes a 22 acre mixed-use development where cultural facilities are not an amenity but a requirement. Although YBC is still in the planning stages, discussions have begun among the San Francisco Redevelopment Agency, the Canadian firm of Olympia and York, and San Francisco's art community concerning high quality programs that will appeal to a wide range of groups for 12 to 18 hour days seven days a week. Everything from

---

[69]Helen C. Smith, "A Culture Boom Is City's Boon," *The Atlanta Constitution*, 14 December 1981, 1-C.

[70]"Culture: A 'Miracle' in Carolina," *U.S. News and World Report*, 26 December 1977-1 January 1978, p. 64.

[71]Smith, p. 5-C.

street activities to traditional production in proscenium theatres is en-
visioned, plus the possibility of a theatre built specifically for dance
companies that can also be used for other activities. (San Francisco
and the Bay Area boast 110 dance companies and not a single
medium-sized performance house.)

As interesting as the artistic possibilities are, attempts to seek financing that would enable facilities to be self-supporting are equally
interesting:

> . . . tax increment financing, developer contribution in the form of capital
> and operating costs, and the possible use of a portion of the hotel tax from
> the YBC hotels to fund YBC arts activities instead of going into citywide
> arts support.[72]

Several other cities have looked to the hotel tax mechanism, long a
part of San Francisco's arts funding tradition, as a subsidy for downtown revitalization and arts activities. Tax assignments from hotel,
motel, and beverage taxes in Duluth, Minnesota, account for 42 percent of the operating costs of arts activities in the central business district.[73]

Other cities are creating mixed-funding packages that complement
the mixed-use facilities and activities they are developing. A typical
funding scheme is the one in which the city sells a property to a private developer. The developer then syndicates it to investors. The
1981 Economic Recovery Tax Act allows investors substantial investment tax credit for investment in cultural buildings; in the case of the
rehabilitation of National Landmark Buildings, it allows a 25 percent
investment tax credit against other income. The city "leases the property back from the developer and sets up a nonprofit corporation to
run the arts organization. After a certain number of years, ownership
of the building returns to the city."[74]

In St. Louis, Missouri, the multi-block development of the National Historic District is being implemented by the City Center Redevelopment Corporation, a limited for-profit corporation representing
the interests of five nonprofit organizations—St. Louis University, the

---

[72]Harold Snedcof, "San Francisco: Cultural Overkill?" *Federal Design Matters*,
Fall 1981, p. 14.

[73]"Cultural Resources/Economic Development, Strengths and Limitations,"
p. 7.

[74]George Clark, "Footlights Districts," *The Cultural Post*, January/February
1982, pp. 5–6.

Symphony Society, the Urban League, the Third Baptist Church, and the Scottish Rite Cathedral—and two local banks. Plans include redevelopment of the Fox Theatre, a 4500 seat movie palace, and the concentration of existing arts activities in the midtown area including major television and cable franchise office and production facilities.

St. Louis projects are funded in a variety of ways, including Community Development Block Grant money for public capital improvements and major projects like the Fox Theatre, tax-exempt revenue bond financing through city agencies, and acquisition funds through a consortium of civic corporations. It is intended that "these projects will be packaged by City Center Redevelopment Corporation and 'spun off' to qualified redevelopers."[75] In addition, private financing through syndication will be sought for individual commercial, retail, and residential projects, and more traditional fundraising will be used to support other projects. Funds from such national sources as the Department of Commerce, the National Endowments for the Arts and Humanities, and the Educational Facilities Laboratory will be sought.[76]

It is projected that downtown redevelopment of the eight-block National Historic District will "increase economic activity by over $50 million in five years."[77] While financing approaches are suitably varied, coordination of key project elements, responsiveness to community needs, and sustaining enthusiasm over a period of time will be paramount in the District's success.

Saving the Cities

In the Spring of 1980, the Partners for Livable Places, a nonprofit coalition of institutions and individuals concerned with the conservation and development of the physical environment and with the quality of life in that environment, began a five-year research and technical assistance program called The Economics of Amenity. Its purposes are the demonstration of the "marketplace value" of amenities—parks, urban design, cultural attractions, clean air—and the encouragement of local solutions to problems of tourism, conservation, quality de-

---

[75]Geoffrey S. Simril, "The Arts Edge," *American Arts*, January 1982, p. 191.
[76]Ibid.
[77]Ibid.

sign, managing public spaces, natural resources, and cultural planning.

Over 30 pilot cities have received advice, aid, and resources from Partners. In its concern for the quality of the amenities that it so strongly feels are a complement to the "future economic health of our nation's cities," it has encouraged the development of arts and cultural activities to stimulate employment and economic growth.[78] Partners offers advice on investment strategies, zoning, tax incentives, design, and planning, and materials on adaptive reuse projects, arts impact studies and cultural facility planning. Many of the cities described in this chapter have received help from Partners. Each city is treated in terms of its specific history and needs, but is encouraged to use the experiences of other Partners cities as models for instruction. A strong local commitment is required for any participating city, including the appointment of a local coordinator, an advisory committee, and a participation fee of at least $10,000. Capitalizing on the negativism inspired by "big-government solutions" and current federal antipathy toward both the environment and the arts and culture, Partners seeks to emphasize local solutions to local problems.

PROFIT VS. PURITY

It is difficult to say whether the trend toward making money, as opposed to raising money, is a direct response to recent economic trends and cutbacks in arts funding or whether arts groups have begun to realize over the last several years that subsidy in this country is both finite and diminishing. Once past this chicken-and-the-egg kind of theorizing, however, it becomes important to understand that in spite of the very real cries for help that arts organizations express, and even the probability that numerous groups will be forced to close up shop should their federal grant monies be withdrawn,[79] arts groups have been remarkably resilient and inventive when it comes to matters of survival. Nevertheless, it is not without great soul-searching that both artists and managers have tried to adapt to a changing economic environment by creating alternatives for their institutions, alternatives

---

[78]"Partners for Livable Places," *Economics of Amenity News*, 1 December 1980, p. 4.

[79]A front page *New York Times* headline of 19 February 1982 reads, "Cuts in Federal Arts Budgets to Hit Small Groups Hardest."

that require new skills including selling, marketing, and distributing their services and products in more tangible and aggressive ways.

This chapter has addressed those skills in the context of a financial climate that is moving from philanthropy to investment. As this climate changes and arts groups begin to adapt or go under, to change, or to scrap what exists and begin again somewhere else, there is a tremendous ambivalence, not only about adopting "more businesslike procedures," but about "business" in general and, more precisely, about the advice and suggestions from the business-oriented sector.

The failure rate for new businesses in this country is generally agreed upon to be between 50 percent and 80 percent during the first five years with as much as 50 percent during the first year alone. In the current economic environment, it would not be surprising to learn that the failure rate is even higher for arts organizations. What is more surprising, perhaps, is the truly creative ways in which arts groups try to cope, to find new solutions, to grow. Many are trying to translate their innovation, creativity, and commitment from the artistic process into business survival terms. Nevertheless, it is a difficult exasperating procedure, one in which the "getting and spending" take as much energy and perseverance as the art itself.

CHAPTER FOUR

SAVING MONEY

Survival Sharing

While some companies may be ambivalent about earning money through commercial activities, many smaller groups do not have the staff or the capital to enter into sustained earned-income projects in any long-range capacity. Some find that the effort required to implement even the best profit-oriented scheme is simply not worth the outlay of time and resources. One answer for these groups may be found in a variety of tactics employed to "save money" by avoiding certain costs before they are incurred. One of the most effective ways to avoid extra costs while maintaining and sometimes even expanding operations is through sharing.

The variety of networks, brokerages, shared resources, and joint projects that has sprung up over the last decade is testimony to the inventiveness of small arts groups and committed artists and managers. Everything from equipment to computer time has been pooled, rented, or discounted. Cooperative efforts in production, information-sharing, publication, and fund-raising have been initiated. Health plans, marketing services, and artists materials have been offered for less than usual rates and to groups and individuals that might otherwise not have been able to obtain them.

The advantages for small groups entering into joint arrangements do not always produce immediate, tangible results, but they seem to center on a few major areas. The psychological support gained by group members sharing their problems and jointly seeking solutions seems to be a major benefit. The sharing of one's burdens as well as one's ideas, the knowledge to be gained from one's colleagues, and the realization that groups exist as part of a larger field often seeking the same audiences, the same funding, the same services, and the same recognition often help such groups avoid duplication. Additionally, it is easier for some small groups to seek assistance, publicity, financial support, and administrative aid if they band together. Certainly, funding sources find it bureaucratically easier to deal with a consortium of groups as opposed to a number of single companies.

(Some funding sources also feel, however, that a commitment to one consortium takes care of their commitment to a particular field, making it harder for subsequent groups to obtain support.)

Many of those who put all their eggs into the basket labeled "artistic excellence" are realizing that the basket itself may be of greater initial importance in making an impact than the eggs. "Marketing," "packaging," and "selling" have crept into the vocabularies of even the more esoteric groups that realize that sheer excellence of product alone cannot garner support.

One of the major motivations behind joint efforts for certain small groups is the possibility of saving time by learning from others. While the managers of many small companies have an instinctive idea of what needs to be done for their groups, they sometimes have no notion of how to go about doing it. Joining together often forces them to articulate, to plan, to formulate strategy, to budget their time and money, and to call on the strengths of several people at one time in order to reach another level of operation. For managers who are also artists, the time consumed "learning the ropes" is time away from their art and time unrecaptured.

While there are definite advantages to cooperation and collaboration, certain problem areas mitigate against such sharing for some groups. Perhaps the greatest worry of artistic directors when contemplating a shared project is the loss of their company's artistic identity. The individuality that makes many companies special is something they have worked long and hard to obtain in the eyes of their public and their peers. It is something they have nurtured and for which they may have received financial assistance. In small companies, the artistic identity may have originated in a collective experience where artistic goals were colored by a variety of non-artistic factors. In companies where the founder is still the organization's artistic director, there may be a highly personal as well as individual atmosphere in which the founder-director feels he or she is personally responsible for activities of the company. This kind of personal leadership—quite common among emerging groups—may, in fact, dictate the kinds of shared activities in which a company engages. For example, sharing box office services with another performing group is not as threatening to a group's artistic identity as jointly producing a play. Buying reduced-rate computer time does not require the commitment of a long-term joint fund-raising strategy.

Additionally, small groups may be prevented from sharing with each other due to the nature of their relationship as competitors in the marketplace. A small opera company that tours the southern United

States might benefit from shared marketing services with regional operas in the area, but the regional operas may feel that the touring company is competing for the same audience. In a field like opera, with what is often perceived as a very limited audience, this kind of resistance might be very sound. On the other hand, it might be possible for both groups to expand their audiences through some creative collaboration.

Financially, certain groups may not have even a small amount of money to contribute toward the implementation of shared efforts. In some locations this problem is addressed by service organizations that provide a mechanism through which such cooperation can take place. While service organizations frequently serve a local or state constituency, some exist on a national scale (Opera America, Theatre Communications Group), while others are attempting to create cooperation nationally through networks and alliances (The Mid-America Dance Alliance, Southern Opera Conference).

In terms of actual physical space, many arts groups are sharing audiences by virtue of their location, either as part of a local development project like Theater Row in New York City, an amenity scheme, or a mini-cultural center like the W.P.A. in Washington, D.C. As marketing studies have shown, a person who comes to such a space to witness one event often stays to sample another. But for some groups, those that are attended by a small, specialized but faithful group of audience members, gaining a new audience may mean losing part of the old one and an arts group may be reluctant to exchange old fans for new converts. Additionally, in the new "urban spaces," the arts do not stand alone—they are part of a larger physical environment, one that includes commercial businesses, shopping malls, clubs, and eateries which sometimes compete in "entertainment value" for the arts audience and which, quite subtly, may change the nature of audience commitment. Arts as accessible as fast food may need to be as quickly consumed—and as easily forgotten.

For companies that are organized on a cooperative basis, the idea of shared projects with other companies may threaten to stretch their democratic mode of organization to the breaking point. If too much diffusion of responsibility results, the groups could find themselves (as they sometimes do within their organizations) spending more time on the one-person-one vote process and less time on issues needing immediate attention.

Finally, and this is true in any venture, arts groups may shy away from shared projects if they have had a negative experience with one in the past. If they feel that the nature of their work has never been properly understood and that association with other organizations diminishes their importance and understanding, if they feel, as one consortium member said, "There's an artistic turkey in the group," or if they feel that the lack of proper administrative coordination of such a project will guarantee its failure, they will be reticent to attempt joint efforts. Nevertheless, the reality of their financial situations may make it necessary for them to cooperate on some level.

"Survival sharing" need not mean the diminution of a company's worth or image, but it is not for every group in the same way that a subscription audience is not the proper seasonal plan for every theatre. But, like subscriptions, formulas are tempting, especially when they work and, often, the long-term results cannot be calculated in the immediate future. What is offered here, then, is not a formula, but a series of options drawn from examples of groups around the country that have found ways to save money, cut costs, and avoid expenditures, usually after serious and thorough consideration of their artistic missions.

Examples are given, too, of joint efforts that failed, in order to underline the kinds of risks involved for small groups. While the examples covered here are representative, they are by no means inclusive. Many other efforts exist around the country and any small group interested in learning more should contact the groups themselves, and local and national resource groups like the Center for Arts Information in New York City, to better understand the ramifications of such ventures.

MEMBERSHIP/SERVICE ORGANIZATIONS

A number of organizations have grown up in the last two decades that are essentially service organizations for small companies and individuals who become "members" in order to obtain services. Sometimes involved in advocacy and production, these organizations can represent many activities in an urban center while simultaneously serving a variety of groups in outlying regions and, in some cases, whole states. Of the groups described below, it is interesting to note not only the kinds of service offered, but the kinds of constituencies served—from individual artists to nonprofit galleries, art and science museums, exhibition and art centers, libraries, community arts organizations, historical societies, and performing arts organizations.

The Metropolitan Cultural Alliance serves cultural organizations in Massachusetts; the Greater Philadelphia Cultural Alliance serves the greater metropolitan area of Philadelphia; the Cultural Alliance of Greater Washington serves cultural organizations in Washington, D.C., Maryland, and Virginia; the California Confederation of the Arts serves institutions and individuals throughout the state of California; and the Gallery Association of New York State serves institutions and individuals throughout New York State. All stress goals of cooperation, collaboration, and communication.

Frequently, such organizations, at least at their inception, are a direct response to the needs of the cultural community and are begun by people fully active in that community. Thus, the Metropolitan Cultural Alliance was begun in 1969 by people from a half dozen cultural organizations concerned with such problems as the isolation of metropolitan arts groups from each other and their duplication of services. Serving a membership of approximately 130 cultural organizations throughout the Commonwealth as a resource and an advocate, the Alliance offers a fairly traditional fare of standard services: management training workshops and seminars, a monthly newsletter, a library, group purchasing, employment listings, and health insurance plans. Some of its more unusual offerings include a central answering service for groups that lack telephone box-office capabilities and the Boston Arts Computer Hook-up (BACH) that provides monthly computerized financial statements and other reports including forward balances for the next fiscal year, a year-end cumulative general ledger, and "thirteen month runs"—the auditor's year-end adjustments. Special programs to encourage corporate contributions to member organizations, to locate prospective arts board members and match them up with appropriate institutions, and the publication of an annual *Cultural Directory* listing over 150 arts organizations in the metropolitan area are other activities undertaken by the Alliance.[1]

The Greater Philadelphia Cultural Alliance has institutional and cooperating memberships that offer health and dental plans, a group purchasing plan, a book purchasing discount from B. Dalton, and discounts on computer/word processing supplies and rental cars. Its Culture Pass allows numerous arts event discounts and it has developed a pilot program to encourage matching gifts with the Western Savings Bank. In addition to seminars, workshops, technical assistance, employment information, a resource library, and a series of publications specifically attuned to the Philadelphia arts community in everything from raising money to garnering publicity, the Alliance also offers a li-

---

[1]Metropolitan Cultural Alliance, Publicity Packet, Spring 1982.

ability insurance plan for directors and officers of its member institutions—a benefit more and more arts board members are beginning to seek as they understand the legal responsibilities that come with the prestigious but voluntary position of board member.[2]

The Cultural Alliance of Greater Washington offers cooperative mailing, purchase plans, health, life, and dental insurance, directors' liability insurance, technical assistance, employment information and a cultural directory to over 600 arts organizations and over 600 individual artists in the greater Washington area. Since 1981, the Alliance has been responsible for TICKETplace, a half-price, day-of-performance ticket booth for performing arts events, similar to the TKTS ticket booth in Manhattan's Duffy Square and the BOSTIX booth in Boston's Quincy Market area.[3]

The California Confederation of the Arts is a membership organization incorporated in 1975 with the broad and exciting goal of encouraging and enabling "the artists and citizens of California to continue to amaze, delight and educate one another.[4] It has a clear mission of advocacy for arts groups and artists, but it also provides a number of important services on a statewide basis. It encourages resource sharing and information dissemination, has created several "chapters" under joint dues structures such as the California Association of Museums and Dance California, and is working on a Literary and Small Press Chapter.

Since 1981, the Confederation has offered tax-deferred annuity plans for employees of member arts organizations, comprehensive health and dental insurance plans, and a special range of business services through its Business Volunteers for the Arts (BVA/LA). BVA/LA, modelled on New York's Skills/Services/Resource Bank program of the Arts and Business Council, matches skilled corporate volunteers with member arts organizations where they offer their expertise in fund-raising, marketing, management, planning, and public relations. Originally tried with Los Angeles-based corporations, BVA/LA plans to go statewide.

The Gallery Association of New York State (GANYS) was formed in 1973 with the encouragement and backing of the New York State Council on the Arts. Like the artists space movement, this consortium

---

[2]Great Philadelphia Cultural Alliance, Publicity Packet, Spring 1982.

[3]Cultural Alliance of Greater Washington, Publicity Packet, Spring 1982.

[4]California Confederation of the Arts, Proposal Package, 23 February 1981, p. 1.

serving visual arts and educational institutions was the recipient of the beneficence and influence of public funding from its inception. It has served as the model for similar consortia to aid exhibiting institutions in Ohio (the Ohio Foundation of the Arts) and Connecticut (Arts Resources) which had also been supported from the start by state council monies. It is important to note that the above three programs, all begun in the 1970s, were nurtured and financed in part by public agencies interested in encouraging state groups to share resources. By the end of the decade, certain arts groups were providing, on a fee basis, the same kinds of services as these consortia. They were translating their "service expertise" into attempts to financially sustain their organizations. Seattle's Artech, the profit subsidiary of the artists' space *and/or,* is an example.

In 1980, the Gallery Association had 270 institutional members sharing collections, curatorial, and technical skills. Historical houses, university museums and galleries, and even the Pierpont Morgan Library are members. From an organization that began by providing low-cost transportation and insurance for visual art objects around New York State, GANYS has grown to an institution providing a wide range of services—production and design services for the presentation and protection of artworks for exhibition and handling, distribution of museum catalogues for reference and lending library use, and an exhibitions program of over 30 shows. Shows range from small pre-mounted installations to comprehensive presentations and include everything from labels and installation instructions to interpretive material; they are "delivered, retrieved and insured by the Association."[5] A detailed instruction booklet and an accompanying questionnaire go to each institution to ensure proper preparation of artwork for travel, environmental, security and fire controls, storage and shipping availability, and conditions of temporary and permanent exhibition facilities. A sample of recent exhibits includes Iroquois Silverwork, Walker Evans: Photographs of New York State, American Hooked Rugs, Figurative Art, Europe in the 1950s, and The Hudson River 1850–1918: A Photographic Portrait.

A closer look at the exhibition offerings indicates certain limitations faced by GANYS—no large sculptures, many exhibits in easy-to-handle, easy-to-travel media, a stress on crafts and on exhibits lending themselves to small objects, and a focus on many New York

---

[5]Gallery Association of New York State, *About the Gallery Association* (Harrison, N.Y.: Gallery Association of New York State, 1980).

State themes. But the use of such services by member institutions that lack the collections, the money, and the staff to originate and/or transport a constant variety of offerings allows institutions to show more themselves and to share with other institutions. More sophisticated institutions like the Pierpont Morgan Library can also share the wealth of their collections with smaller spaces around the state with the assurance that their objects will be carefully cared for, insured, and transported.

Other consortia of exhibiting institutions are springing up around the country on a state and a regional basis. The Western Association of Art Mueseums (WAAM) is a consortium headquartering in California but serving organizations throughout the United States. Membership is open to trade unions, individual artists, arts councils, artists cooperatives, universities and schools, libraries and almost any facility with a desire and a space to exhibit. The kinds of resources to be shared are expanding as new needs surface: currently both WAAM and GANYS are involved in aiding museum administrators to sharpen certain managerial skills through conferences and workshops.

MATERIALS, SUPPLIES, JOINT PURCHASING

In the last decade, groups have emerged that allow arts and cultural organizations to jointly purchase items and supplies in bulk for substantially less than they would pay as single buyers. In addition to joint purchasing groups, organizations have been created that offer industrial byproducts and manufacturers' rejects at token cost, and organizations that offer a variety of materials—from used typewriters to museum exhibition cases—for free.

The area of joint purchasing has been addressed by a number of service organizations in the arts. The Cultural Alliance of Greater Washington offers its members between 20 and 60 percent discount on office and art supplies sold through specific companies, and a 25 percent discount on car rental. The Greater Philadelphia Cultural Alliance offers members a 15 to 30 percent discount off the listed retail price for office supplies, paper goods, and furniture, and 25 percent discounts off standard computer and word processor supplies, a 15 percent book discount at B. Dalton, and a 15 to 20 percent car rental discount. Boston's Metropolitan Cultural Alliance offers up to 75 percent discounts on office supplies, some printing costs, and word processor equipment.

In New York, through the Cultural Assistance Center or directly through the purchasing agent, the Joint Purchasing Corporation, arts and cultural organizations are given a wide variety of purchase options. Begun over 50 years ago as part of the Federation of Jewish Philanthropies, the Joint Purchasing Corporation was originally designed to serve the needs of social service agencies and hospitals. Over 80 suppliers remit a small percentage on contracts to support the organization, while participating agencies are not charged a fee. Due both to its history and to the size of the constituency it serves (over 445 agencies) the Joint Purchasing Corporation is able to offer up to 50 percent savings on general institutional items like fuel oil, housekeeping supplies, paper, furniture, car rentals, and office supplies. New contracts negotiated to meet the purchasing needs of arts organizations include the supply of discounted arts and crafts supplies, audio and video supplies and equipment, photography equipment and film, plexiglass, picture frames, specialty lamps, and air fare.[6]

A similar organization has recently begun in Chicago through a United Way affiliate called Comprehensive Community Services. Like the Joint Purchasing Corporation in New York, the Chicago program serves a variety of not-for-profit organizations including arts groups.

Some organizations, while not targeted directly at the arts, have made materials available to arts groups at token cost. Recycle, a resource center of the Boston Children's Museum, offers shoppers the option of filling a grocery bag for $3.50, or the group purchase of a $35 discount voucher for 20 $3.50 bags filled with industrial surplus, byproducts, and manufacturers' rejects, including foam rubber and rubber, plastic, wood, metal, styrofoam, paper, cardboard, lenses, and fabric. Additionally, workshops teach the use of such materials for educational and recreational programs, and a publication, *Recyclopedia*, develops science, game, and craft uses for the material. Open to the public, available to individuals as well as groups, and offered to members at a 10 percent discount, Recycle is also a mechanism to earn income for the museum. The material, donated by industry and with museum requirements of cleanliness, safety, and volume, needs to be picked up, stored, and sold. But even with these expenses, Recycle estimates a gross of about $70,000 with a net of $20,000 for 1982.[7]

The Bay Area Creative Reuse Project has major depots in San Francisco, Oakland, Santa Rosa, and Redwood City, California and

[6]Joint Purchasing Corporation, *Index of Purchasing Agreements* (New York: April 1981).

[7]Len Gottlieb, Boston Children's Museum, personal letter, 8 February 1982.

mini-depots throughout the Bay area. These depots distribute over $3 million worth of surplus solid waste materials and usable discards from manufacturers and businesses to nonprofit arts groups, community organizations, parks and recreation departments, and schools. Committed to the recycling of material, and to the provision of new jobs, job training, and increased tax revenues as a result of such recycling, BACR bills itself as "a community partnership working to conserve and re-use California's resources."[8] Although BACR makes no elaborate pitch to the arts community, everything from paper to computers is a possible donation, a gift which may also "free up enough money for an additional staff person, provide a salary increase, or even serve as an in-kind contribution when required for grants or contracts."[9]

At least 12 states have recycle programs, most affiliated with educational institutions and open to institutions and individual artists; information is available through a national clearinghouse, the Teachers' Centers Exchange.[10]

Materials for the Arts, a New York City-based "clearinghouse," goes further than these programs by being directed solely at the arts community. Materials accepts "practically everything" from "manufacturers, distributors, corporations, partnerships, individuals, institutions, cooperatives, as well as city, state, federal, and international agencies,"[11] and offers the donor a tax deduction. Profiled as an organization that matches the donor with the recipient, Materials for the Arts arranges gifts for both individuals and institutions. Begun by an artist for the Department of Cultural Affairs, Materials has accepted and passed on such items as carpeting, canvas, musical instruments, exhibition cases, tape recorders, slide and movie projectors and film, beads, buttons, sod, and limestone. Warehouse space is provided by the Institute of Art and Urban Resources through its Long Island artists space, P.S. 1.

Materials for the Arts has provided one way to make inroads into medium-sized companies that normally donate little or nothing to the arts. Using campaign slogans like "How to contribute to the arts without spending one cent," "This is not a request for money. This is a re-

---

[8]Bay Area Creative Reuse Publicity material, Winter 1982.

[9]Ibid.

[10]Cultural Assistance Center, *Partners: A Practical Guide to Corporate Support of the Arts* (New York: American Council for the Arts, 1982), p. 56.

[11]Materials for the Arts Brochure (New York: n.p., 1981).

quest for something you don't need," and "If you can spare it, we know who needs it,"[12] Materials stresses the painlessness of supporting the arts in this fashion. Pulling together a number of disparate sources—not the least of which is the New York City government under whose auspice it exists—Materials for the Arts provides an interesting example of arts aid that, while it is not directly financial, has provided over a quarter of a million dollars worth of materials.[13]

SHARING PRODUCTIONS AND STAFF

Co-producing and the sharing of both artistic and administrative personnel require a commitment that many groups are unwilling to make, but there are instances where such cooperation can be fruitful. The tremendous expense incurred in producing opera has given birth to the production that is sponsored and developed by more than one company and that tours to a number of locations in a given season. A number of the larger opera companies have been coproducing since the mid-1960s and some smaller ones have followed suit. Although there can be tremendous artistic differences, the money saved may be reason enough to continue the practice for some time. Competition, local pride, problems of making financial commitments more than a year ahead and of production ownership and maintenance are frequently weighed against constantly rising production costs and the desire to create a more even repertory and to present rarely performed works.[14] Additional problems occur with limited storage space, either backstage or in warehouses, and with any productions shown in rotating repertory that necessitate a daily set-up and take-down of sets and scenery.

Among the smaller institutions over the last few years, companies in Cincinnati, Pittsburgh, and Connecticut shared a *Carmen;* the Kentucky, Augusta, and Mobile Operas shared a *Don Giovanni;* the Kentucky, Augusta, and Piedmont Operas a *Tales of Hoffman.*[15] The Piedmont Opera in Winston-Salem and the Mobile Opera in Alabama have been involved in several co-productions, always adding a differ-

---

[12]Materials for the Arts Publicity Material (New York: n.p., 1981).

[13]Ibid.

[14]Ulrike Gottliche, "Shared Opera Productions," unpublished paper, Columbia University, NYC, 1981, p. 15.

[15]Ibid., p. 21.

ent third company to their roster each year. In 1982–83 the Charlotte
Opera joined them to produce *Madama Butterfly* using the same cast,
the same set, and the same stage director but a local orchestra, chorus,
and conductor in each city. Since the theatres themselves are not necessarily similar, productions must be designed and staged to fit the
smallest operation or to be adaptable, just as with a touring operation.
Piedmont, Mobile, and Charlotte are seeking joint funding for this
project and hope to promote cooperation among the companies as
well as to reduce their expenses.

Although there are certain artistic factors that work against shared
productions—the difficulty in a company developing a personal style,
using sets and concepts originally designed to accommodate a number of different theaters—financial considerations often leave a group
with the choice to share a production of a specific work or not to perform that work at all.

While the sharing of artistic staff in the co-productions of performing groups can be difficult, it is at least seasonal. Sharing of administrative staff seems to be a longer-term proposition, but in some areas
duplication of services and expenses can be avoided. In the early
1970s, a common need for docents by three Fort Worth Museums—
the Amon Carter Museum of Western Art, the Forth Worth Art Center
Museum, and the Kimball Art Museum—gave rise to the Fort Worth
Docent Council. Needing docents who were trained in art history and
in museum methods, the museums developed a cooperative training
program and a position for tour coordinator to schedule all guided
tours for all three musuems.[16] Staff training, particularly of volunteers, can create unexpected expenses for an organization and although each institution has an individual character and individual
needs, the pooling of such resources can provide important cost-
saving benefits.

JOINT SUPPORT FACILITIES

The idea of joint facilities to support the activities of an arts organization is just beginning to take hold among small companies. While the
use of performance and exhibition space by more than one group has
long been in practice, the creation of joint scene shops, joint property

---

[16]Barbara Y. Newsom and Adele Z. Silver (eds.), *The Art Museum as Educator*
(Los Angeles: University of California Press, 1978), p. 253.

collections, joint costume collections, common box office space and services, and the combining of activities that have often been duplicated from one company to another are beginning to gain attention.

The Southern Opera Conference (SOC) is a membership organization begun in 1978 for companies that produce at least one opera a year and pay most of their people some fee or salary. In its information-gathering and sharing activities, SOC makes its 18 members aware of the possibilities for sharing productions, rental and/or sale of sets and costumes for specific productions, and joint auditions for future singers. Richard Marshall, Manager of the Charlotte Opera, estimates that his company has saved approximately $20,000 of a $750,000 budget by participating in the Southern Opera Conference.[17]

Marshall has an idea (that is just in the talking stage at present) for the creation of a central scene shop that might save money for member companies. Most small opera companies are not equipped to build their own sets; they either have to rent sets or go out and bid for contracts. If they rent sets, they may be limited in choice of production since the set has to be both affordable and one that fits dimensions of their stage. Marshall's idea is for a central scene shop owned and financed by members of the Southern Opera Conference, and managed by a professional manager charged with running it as a profit-making business. SOC members would make requests for sets to the shop within a certain period of time. The shop would then evaluate the request and give the member company an estimate of the actual cost of building the set. After comparing this price with other shops (obviously the Central Scene Shop would attempt to provide inexpensive, quality service), should a member company decide to use the Central Scene Shop, its set would be put on the annual schedule. While member companies would get preference in terms of early reservation, the shop would also go on the open market and make itself available to any group anywhere on a straight profit basis. The scene shop might also involve a separate warehouse space for storage of unused sets, a rental business, and even a transport system.[18]

The Alliance of Resident Theatres/New York is considering a similar joint scheme—the creation of a joint scene shop for Off Off Broadway member theatres usable by others as available. Many Off Off Broadway companies rent spaces that do not afford places to build and/or store sets. Therefore, the end of each season finds large set

[17]Telephone interview with Richard Marshall, 14 January 1982.
[18]Ibid.

pieces being given away or destroyed. Should a joint scene shop allow companies to store, rent, and even build sets, the amount of money saved in lumber alone should make it financially worthwhile. Already in existence for its hundred-odd member companies is a props collective, overseen by the Theatre Development Fund.

The Costume Collection, created in 1969 and assumed by the Theatre Development Fund in 1973 "provides costumes and related services to not-for-profit arts and educational organizations at low cost."[19] Offering 50,000 costumes and accessories, the collection also provides a fully equipped workroom for organizations that want to have costumes made but have no facilities of their own. As well as earning income for the Theatre Development Fund, the Costume Collection provides another centralized service to high schools, universities, Off Off Broadway and community theatres, regional operas, and civic and community groups.[20]

42nd Street Theater Row is a service organization for companies located on Manhattan's Theater Row. The services it provides are intended to reduce costs and personnel demands or to increase income for the individual companies through a variety of joint activities.

Ticket Central is a Theater Row information center and centralized box office service staffed seven days a week. Audience development procedures include group sales, discount programs, and a bimonthly calendar of attractions. Funds are raised jointly to be equally disbursed among the member companies and for specific projects serving collective needs. Maintenance, security systems, property and public liability insurance, facade, and beautification programs are offered. A special discount plan is offered to employees of corporations contributing $5,000 or more to Theater Row, including discounted theatre tickets, meals, drinks, parking, and classes.[21]

While joint marketing and promotional efforts strive to tout the area in general, as well as the individual companies performing there, the financial difficulties of many resident companies have resulted in the rental of theatre spaces to outside companies when resident companies are not in production.[22]

Film and videomakers have had access for some time to the Media

---

[19]Theatre Development Fund, *Annual Report, 1979–80* (New York: n.p., 1980), p. 22.

[20]Ibid.

[21]42nd Street Theater Row, Publicity Project, Spring 1982.

[22]See Chapter III for a discussion of this point.

Equipment Resource Center (MERC) of the Young Filmmakers Foundation. MERC lends sound, video, and film equipment to New York state individuals and organizations and offers "in-house studio, editing, dubbing, and equipment-maintenance services."[23]

All of the above solutions share a lack of intervention in the artistic process, while at the same time they provide arts groups with certain options for survival. There is, of course, much informal sharing of equipment and facilities among groups, especially of an emergency nature among groups with similar goals and philosophies, or in close geographic proximity to each other.

A somewhat more daring commitment has been made by four visual arts spaces in downtown Manhattan: two cooperatives, one service organization, and one other small gallery are renting roughly 5,000 square feet of space, renovating it and leaving it open, divided only by partial partitions. For 14 Sculptors, Pleaides Gallery, the Association of Artist Run Galleries, and one other gallery, the commitment to share space is much more than financial as evidenced by the proposed layout. One of the galleries, 14 Sculptors, has managed to stay together as a cooperative for over a year despite its lack of exhibition space. While each organization has separate rental arrangements with the landlord, the "package" was put together by the spaces and it was their decision to leave the space relatively unencumbered.

JOINT PRINTING AND PUBLISHING

Cooperation among institutions may be particularly important when production costs and volumes of merchandise create inordinate expenses. Costs for typesetting and printing, for example, can frequently be reduced if an arts organization uses, instead of a commercial outfit, another nonprofit arts organization whose equipment is not tied up full time. The Museum of Modern Art often allows other nonprofit arts organizations to use the services of its phototypesetting machinery at a rate lower than commercial facilities charge.

The Publishing Center for Cultural Resources in New York City offers groups a cooperative production plan. Groups can jointly purchase printing services for small images—for post cards, note cards, small color reproductions, and small promotional materials, at a

---

[23]Dick Netzer, *The Subsidized Muse* (New York: Cambridge University Press, 1978), p. 142.

greatly reduced cost from comparable commercial services. An institution can get post cards, for example, that are run 36 at a time, for about a quarter of the cost of buying the same quality product on a single-card basis.

Although it has successfully tackled cooperative production in one area at least, it has yet to see many developments of cooperative publication among arts institutions that publish a variety of materials from catalogs to scholarly works. One model is the Center's forthcoming publication of a book covering all 20 national parks that are concerned with the Civil War. The publication is being produced for the Eastern National Park and Monument Association, a consortium of 90 national parks.

In the arts, a fairly recent arrival is *Museum Magazine,* a publication of general museum interest that specific museums and visual arts institutions are buying as a membership benefit. In each bimonthly issue, *Museum Magazine* inserts a section on the specific museum using it. Additionally, the mailing jacket is printed with the specific museum's name and logo.

Cooperative publication efforts are few and, unless someone approaches institutions with specific funding for such a project, many rarely enter into them. Possibilities for sharing seem endless: 12 institutions joining together to produce one calendar with one color reproduction from each institution, a number of institutions with a joint package of post cards, a group of museums with complementary collections producing a joint catalog, even a cooperative distribution point for materials produced by a number of institutions. Aside from feelings of rivalry and competitiveness, institutions may not have entered into such agreements because their already overburdened staff simply cannot afford the time to coordinate what might ultimately be a cost-saving, time-saving venture.

JOINT FUND RAISING

There are several models for joint fund-raising efforts, which are instructive for their failures as well as their successes. Small arts groups however, often neglect models created by larger, more established institutions and also those that exist in disciplines other than their own.

The National Corporate Fund for Dance (NCFD), while it represents the interests of companies with budgets over $1 million, is a highly successful model for obtaining corporate support. In existence since 1972, NCFD is a consortium of seven major American dance

companies—American Ballet Theatre, Joffrey Ballet, Alvin Ailey
Dance Theatre, Paul Taylor Dance Company, Merce Cunningham
and Dance Company, Twyla Tharp and Dancers, and San Francisco
Ballet. Money is raised for general operating support—a category
many companies have difficulty funding (there is little glamour in a
donation that pays the light bill)—and is distributed to each company
on a proportional basis of their annual operating budgets.

A model of the NCFD for small dance companies has been discussed for some time. It is possible that the Dance Alliance, a new
dance service organization expected to replace the now defunct Association of American Dance Companies, may be of some help in moving this idea to fruition.

More recent than these attempts has been a consortium of early
music groups representing two performance groups, one dance company, and one presenter (sponsor) of early music group performances. The New York Cornet and Sacbut Ensemble, the New York
Consort of Viols, The Court Dance Company of New York, and Music
Before 1800 formed an alliance called the Advancement of Early Music
and Dance in New York City in order to obtain funding for a three-
year pilot project. Expressing the joint needs of member companies
for artistic development, audience development, and financial development, the consortium hopes to implement managerial efficiency by
sharing a full-time administrator. (Partial funding for this position has
been obtained.)

Recognizing the identity afforded them by banding together, the
four companies felt they would not have been able to garner sufficient
funding as individual groups. Each group was also facing a problem
common to small arts groups—the depletion of energy due to the
sharing of administrative duties by artist members. It is difficult for
many small groups to justify paying an administrator more than an individual artist makes from his or her work with the group (without
artists there would be no group in the first place, runs one argument).
However, consortial efforts like this one demonstrate that full-time
management is necessary for these groups to reach a higher level of
operation, in terms of number of performances, greater audience attraction, new bookings, and more substantial, ongoing funding.

Joint managerial efforts in the early music field might be seen as an
extension of an artistic reality: music before 1800 is composed of
mixed groups as well as specialized ones, and larger scale Renaissance
and Baroque masterpieces tend to use a mix of brass, string and
woodwind players, a chorus, solo singers, and often a dance company. Groups that join together to present a representative evening of

early music or a specific piece like a masque, pull together a diversity of elements that are artistically as well as financially valid.

The growth of chamber music groups in the last two decades is partly evidenced by the growth of at least one major service organization formed to help them—Chamber Music America—and partly the result of the great number of fine, highly trained musicians who derive personal satisfaction from playing with small groups. Even within this corner of the music field, there is further specialization among companies in the type of music they play, the kinds of instruments they use, their artistic philosophies, and the nature and length of their performance seasons. Many groups perform sporadically throughout the year since their members must depend for their livelihoods on other jobs like teaching and orchestral work. This diversity makes it even more difficult than usual for funding sources to differentiate one group from another, and makes strategies like consortial fund raising even more important.[24]

The Corporate Fund for the New American Theatre enabled three Off Off Broadway theatres—Circle Repertory Company, Manhattan Theatre Club, and Playwrights Horizons—to obtain $250,000 each in cash reserve grants[25] over a three-year period from the Ford Founda-

---

[24]Pilot Project for Advancement of Early Music and Dance in New York City, proposal package, Spring 1982.

[25]The cash reserve grant created by the Ford Foundation began with support for regional theaters and dance companies and is now almost completely phased out. Its greatest attraction was that it allowed money for general operating expenses—a category many other sources refuse to fund. The basic procedure under which an arts group operated was as the recipient of a portion of the total funding each year over a several-year period with requirements to maintain a balanced budget and erase its accumulated deficit. If the grant period ended successfully for the organization, the arts group was given the total amount as capital for future survival. The benefits the cash reserve program were set up to provide included aid in changing what has been called a "deficit mentality" in nonprofit arts organizations where deficits were not only increased each year but were expected as part of the overall financial picture, education in sound accounting procedures and financial reporting, and more responsible management. The program's more famous failures include the Stratford Shakespeare Festival in Connecticut which forfeited its cash reserve grant when its major patron died suddenly, leaving the theater without its expected annual donation, and the Joffrey Ballet which actually cancelled an entire season in order to retain its cash reserve status—both institutions have been in severe financial difficulty ever since.

tion.[26] The theatres were similar in philosophy at the time—all produced plays by new, emerging, and/or unknown playwrights and all could make a case for strong artistic leadership and individual identity. Their operating budgets, however, were not similar. While the Circle Rep and Manhattan Theatre Club were in the same budget range, Playwrights Horizons went from a $45,000 budget in 1975 to a budget of $450,000 in 1978, largely as a result of the Ford money which left it with an unusual challenge: developing programmatic and performance goals to meet its budgetary good fortune.

The consortium format in this case represented a marketable concept that enabled three theatres to obtain substantial money. Since the artistic directors of these theatres were in frequent communication with each other anyway, the idea was merely an extension of their working relationship. Nevertheless, the time and energy required to see such a scheme through required a major group commitment.

The Bunch (formally called A Bunch of Experimental Theatres of New York, Inc.), founded in 1973 and disbanded in 1977, was important even in its failure to secure funds for the eight collectives and various guest troupes it represented, since it developed from the real cutting edge of American theatre. The eight founding members were far from the mainstream in 1973 and even those that remain today are considered by many to be experimental, innovative, and difficult to fund individually. The Performance Group, Mabou Mines, Meredith Monk/The House, the Ontological-Hysteric Theatre, the Ridiculous Theatrical Company, the Manhattan Project, the Cutting Edge, and Section Ten represented nontraditional, collaborative theatre. Run by directors or director/writers, their intention as Bunch members was to collaborate in seeking funds and sharing resources.

Trying to expand audiences and attract community involvement, the Bunch ran a series of biweekly forums for the public, and planned for a subscription series for its eight member companies—an idea only now being discussed again for Off Off Broadway theatres by the Manhattan Punchline, the WPA, and the Second Stage in downtown Manhattan. While most of its energies went into booking activities for its member theatres, the Bunch did produce a three-week festival of Bunch Theatre works in the winter of 1977. Although the festival began to address the real needs of collective producing, greater visibil-

---

[26]For further discussion on this point, see Joan Jeffri, *The Emerging Arts* (New York: Praeger, 1980), p. 33.

ity, and audience development for member groups, the Bunch disbanded soon after.

Causes for the Bunch's demise have been attributed to financial instability, an ineffective fund-raising effort, and conflicts of interest and functions among member companies, the Bunch management, and outside agencies. Additionally, there are those who feel the avant-garde direction of all the member companies made funders shy away from supporting them, even in a consortium. Nevertheless, in its attempt to attack specific problem areas of small experimental companies—problems of audience, financing, marketing—the Bunch was a pioneer in its choice of the consortial format.

Interestingly, some of the same problems and the same results occurred in the formation of a more recent consortium of artists spaces. In the visual arts, some artists spaces are so large and so diverse they consider themselves consortia. Places like the Institute for Art and Urban Resources in New York, the Los Angeles Institute for Contemporary Art (LAICA), and *and/or* in Seattle might be viewed this way since they all act as presenters as well as developers of artwork. Nevertheless, even spaces of this size and diversity occasionally attempt consortial activities.

In 1980–81, six New York City artists spaces joined together to develop a "public profile," to let the public know who they were and what they were about. While each space agreed to maintain its own fund-raising efforts, the development of a profile was directed at long-range funding needs with a particular eye on corporations and foundations. The spaces involved in the New York Consortium of Contemporary Artists Centers, also called the Downtown Consortium, were the Institute for Art and Urban Resources, The Kitchen Center for Video, Music, Dance and Performance, Franklin Furnace, Artists Space, Creative Time, and Just Above Midtown.

Since their beginnings a little over a decade ago, some artists spaces have become the research and development laboratories of contemporary art by allowing a kind of experimentation and innovation prohibited in the commercial gallery and the museum. With $10,000 from the National Endowment for the Arts (in the tradition of their individual beginnings in the early 1970s when artists spaces were founded and sanctioned with public money), the consortium held a huge weekend event where each of the spaces advertised, presented programs and lectures, and tried to interest and attract the public at large. The event appeared to be a dead end, partly because the intentions and missions of each space are so different, and partly due to the consortium's exclusivity—the "big six" left little room for even other local artists spaces to be represented.

An additional reason may have its roots in the general awareness by many artists spaces that nothing is done without its price. This consortium successfully avoided a "united way" funding appeal, which is dangerous if it allows a funding source to fulfill its total commitment to a field by making one donation ("I gave at the office"). But it failed to generate the kind of time, energy, and commitment required for its sustenance. Additionally, the competitive nature of some spaces may have pushed them to maintain their independence far removed from any joint arrangements.

Although these examples are of New York City-based organizations, the problem of joint fund-raising outside New York should be addressed, especially in relation to the relationship between small arts groups and their communities.

While joint fund-raising appeals on a mass scale (United Arts funds, United Way campaigns) have been popular with community groups for a long time, arts groups that consider themselves beyond the community arts level in staff, budget, and operations often do not want to compete for local money with smaller, younger groups. Neither do they want to be placed in direct competition with the community's "cultural vaults" (the museum, the symphony orchestra). In arts groups that deal with expensive equipment like media or film centers, there is often no understanding by local groups of the budget required to maintain facilities and equipment. Therefore, if a media center receives a $25,000 grant from its state arts council, even if that figure represents a decrease in relation to its percentage of the annual budget, local arts groups may view that organization as the highest state-funded cultural organization in the region. Those local groups may not want such an organization joining their united campaign for local monies. The arts organization may find itself in a kind of no man's land in relation to funding sources—too small to be a major institution and too big to be a local one. Such an organization might consider a joint fund-raising effort with other similar-sized institutions in other areas of the state.

Another example of a participatory scheme for artists spaces may add resonance to their reservations toward joint efforts. Several years ago, some of the larger New York City spaces were approached with the idea of developing a voucher program for the public. This would resemble the performance voucher program developed by the Theatre Development Fund, where a customer buys a low-priced booklet of passes that enables him or her to attend any of hundreds of New York area events for the price of a voucher (currently $2.50). The performance sponsor is subsequently reimbursed by the Theatre Development Fund, thereby creating a subsidy for both the customer and the performance sponsor. When several artists spaces were approached with this idea they rejected it. They cited their policy of not charging admission for entry (a policy that may have to change with growing economic stress) and argued that such a voucher program would demand additional expenses such as extra lighting, security, and insurance.

It is also possible that the apparent mass-audience nature of this scheme may have contributed to the negative response. (I say apparent because an organization like TDF could do a great deal to identify an organization's audience.) Still, anything that seems to threaten the individuality of these groups will have to be studied seriously even if its financial possibilities appear positive.

An exciting extension of joint fund-raising is joint commissioning. While some larger institutions have commissioned works by living artists, most notably the Brooklyn Academy of Music and the American Dance Festival in Durham, North Carolina, and while certain public funds have been available for such purposes, small arts groups have been understandably shy of such arrangements. Richard Marshall, Director of the Charlotte Opera, suggests the commissioning of a new opera by three to five companies in different geographic areas. The opera would premiere for each company in its own region over a one-to-two year period after being jointly funded, and would be videotaped for future exposure and possible financial gain.

The idea of joint commissioning may seem somewhat advanced for small companies, but it is one that predicts the basic artistic health of our organizations since it illustrates true institutional support of the individual artist and a real nurturing of new work.

NETWORKS

A strategy for sharing information as well as resources that has begun to take hold, particularly on a regional level, is the network. In an attempt to link communities, counties, states, and even regions to each other, groups have been created that have attempted to overcome geographical and other boundaries in order to learn, to share, and to find new mechanisms for support.

As they are now developing, networks may be a direct descendant of regional mechanisms set up by the National Endowment for the Arts, often in cooperation with state agencies, to create communication between the government and the institutions it funds. The Mid-America Dance Network seems at least a partial response to a specific program of Endowment, the Dance Touring Program. Although it was scheduled for demise in 1982–83, the Dance Touring Program raised the level of dance exposure across the United States. The Mid-America Dance Network embraces the dance communities of Arkansas, Kansas, Missouri, Nebraska, and Oklahoma. Formed in 1980, its stated purposes include:

> encouraging cooperative efforts and strengthening the artistic and managerial quality of dance companies in five states; providing a forum for communication, visibility and advocacy for dance in the five-state region as well as encouraging newspaper coverage of dance events; fostering block-booking of nationally recognized dance companies by presenting organizations as a complement to regional dance activity.[27]

To these ends, the Network publishes material listing all dance residencies and performances with the appropriate contact names, holds issue-oriented conferences, and has published a resource book with information about companies, choreographers, sponsors, and dance teachers in the five-state area.

In Oshkosh, Wisconsin, a challenge by Chancellor of the University of Wisconsin-Oshkosh, Edward Penson, in October 1980, for renewed commitment and support of the arts in that region resulted in the formation of the Lakelands Consortium in Support of the Arts. One of the most interesting things about this consortium is its founding—the presidents of Ripon College and Lawrence University, the directors of the Paine Art Center and Arboretum, the Oshkosh Public Museum, and the Bergstrom-Mahler Museum, the presidents of the Kimberly-Clark Foundation and the Miles Kimball Foundation, and a vice president of the Post Corporation met with Chancellor Penson or his assistant, Dr. Clifford Wood, for nine months to explore ways of meeting the chancellor's challenge.

The combination of a state university, two private colleges, one public and two private museums as consortium members with start-up funding from the two corporate foundation members and the University of Wisconsin-Oshkosh Foundation provided the basis for a highly credible organization. With the former president of Lawrence University, Thomas S. Smith, as its first executive director, the con-

---

[27]Mid-America Dance Network, Publicity Material, 1980.

sortium has begun to address itself to information and resource sharing, event planning, and a conference on arts volunteers. Information
for the public (through a telephone hotline), for teachers through a
"Teacher's Guide," and for member institutions and individuals describes artists' performances, residencies, events, and availability.
Not at all a fund-raising consortium, the Lakeland group might be
able to pool resources for block bookings, scheduling, computer use,
humanities as well as arts events, and to be a cultural clearinghouse
for an eleven-county region.[28]

While national networks are rare and can be difficult to manage
while maintaining relevancy for the groups involved, the Dance Theater Workshop (DTW) has been developing a plan for a support mechanism for performing groups around the country. Taking up, in a
sense, where the Dance Touring Program of NEA will have left off,
the National Performance Network may provide a similar validating
auspice for funders and sponsors, as well as a central voice in targeting new monies to small companies.

To better understand why Dance Theater Workshop is the potential auspice for such a project, one should refer again to the brief history of its development in Chapter II. The only other nationally
oriented dance organization, the Association of American Dance
Companies, recently met its demise and a new national organization,
Dance Alliance, is still in the discussion stage. The reputation that
DTW holds for a commitment to new artists, new work, and new audiences makes it a logical place to house the National Performance
Network.

The purposes of this network are to stimulate more performance
opportunities and to stabilize existing ones. More specifically, the network's intentions are:

1. to stimulate and stabilize the producing activities for artists and
   performing spaces,
2. to address the sponsorship of non-local artists and companies
   by encouraging cooperative booking, combined fundraising,
   and centralized technical assistance,
3. to increase and regularize the traffic of these artists throughout
   the country,
4. to develop new sources of earned income,

---

[28]Lakelands Consortium in Support of the Arts, Publicity Material (Oshkosh,
Wisconsin: Spring 1982); Thomas S. Smith, personal letter, 31 March 1982.

5. to develop new audiences and new awareness for the work on a
    sustained basis.[29]

Addressing itself to the small performance spaces around the
country (those seating 75–300 people), such as those found in small
theatres and artists spaces, the NPN can act to legitimize their roles as
presenters of artists and performing companies to the private sector.
It can serve as a mechanism to get money to individual artists—the
very constituency that funding sources find the most difficult and the
least cost-effective to deal with.

Acting as a central voice as well as a central fund-raiser, the NPN,
under the auspice of the Dance Theater Workshop, would raise the
necessary funds and then parcel those monies out on a matching basis
of at least one-to-one for each of the participating spaces. This is an attempt to avoid the random decision-making process that currently
exists in most corporations funding small spaces, with DTW acting as
the qualitative judge of theatres and performing spaces. At the same
time, it is an attempt by DTW to bring certain artists and companies to
spaces outside New York that normally have to wait until those artists
are in the vicinity for some other purpose (a teaching stint, for example). Because these spaces have to wait for attractions, they cannot
properly promote an event nor can they develop an audience on any
sustained basis.

Implementation of the National Performance Network will be
through DTW's selection of ten performing spaces of "primary sponsors," each of which sponsors at least four artist/company performance residencies in one year, with each residency at least two
weeks long.[30] In certain cities, a number of groups might band together to form the "primary sponsor" with each space sponsoring
different artists to make a total of four or more residencies. For example, the Margaret Jenkins Dance Studio and the Oberlin Dance Collective Performance Gallery might agree to co-sponsor a total of six
residencies, three at each space.

Selection of artists and companies will be up to the presenters with
two stipulations—no artist/company may participate in more than two
residencies a year and in each four-residency series at least one out-of-
town artist must originate from somewhere other than New York. Additionally, the host space must offer multiple performances of an

---

[29]*Dance Theater Workshop: Ten Year Report*, 1 April 1981, Appendix A.
[30]Ibid.

event and must work to engender feature publicity for the groups/artists.

In each major location—centralized by one of the ten original spaces picked by DTW—all residencies will be publicized together as a single series of events under NPN's auspices, to begin to develop an audience on a sustained basis. DTW will continue its own commitment to this kind of activity through its "Out-of-Towners" production series in New York City and will be one of the ten participating performance spaces.

While the National Performance Network is not a reality at the time of this writing, a feasibility study is underway for a two-year pilot project. The Network hopes to address the needs of artists and companies in music, dance, theatre, and performance art that are normally housed in small theatre and performing spaces, but the pilot project will address only the needs of the dance community.

While the idea is exciting, the responsibilities for DTW are tremendous. Aside from its normal activities, DTW's NPN will be forced to deal with "central coordination, contracting, logistical arrangements, trouble-shooting, and technical assistance with both local fundraising and audience development."[31] It will end up involving regional organizations like the Mid-America Dance Alliance and the San Francisco/Bay Area Dance Coalition; it will attempt to facilitate a flow of traffic of companies from all over the country (not just the topheavy dance communities of New York and San Francisco); and it will be an attempt to reinforce existing spaces, companies and artists rather than creating monuments, mausoleums, or more spaces.

JOINT MARKETING AND DISTRIBUTION

If management was the watchword for many emerging arts groups of the 1970s, marketing shows signs of becoming the panacea for a variety of ills in the '80s. Such subjects as client-centered product creation, targeting the audience, positioning, and pricing are but a few of the topics of special workshops, seminars, university courses, and gatherings stressing survival for the arts. While there are obvious lessons to be learned from marketing techniques as they are applied to products and services in the commercial marketplace, many arts groups are skeptical about the relevance of such techniques to the mis-

---

[31]Ibid., Appendix, c.

sions of their cultural institutions, especially those in the nonprofit arena. A study conducted by Steven Permut of Yale University revealed a common perception of many performing arts administrators: not only did they view marketing as "normally identified with profit-motivated business" (note the phrase profit-motivated, not profit-making) but the "*role* of marketing within the organization was also viewed as potentially conflicting with artistic considerations."[32]

Despite such skepticism, there are institutions, like the Denver Children's Museum, that have sought to make marketing not only a tool, but the whole planning strategy around which the institution is focused. Still, most arts groups have not gone to the extreme that the Denver Children's Museum does; whatever marketing techniques they have absorbed have been assimilated on a much quieter basis. Some of these techniques are joint efforts, across a number of institutions, that serve financial needs and address issues of visibility and audience development as well.

In the late 1970s, five major modern dance companies banded together in a joint subscription series called the Masters of American Dance. Four of the companies were "permanent" members—Merce Cunningham and Company, the Jose Limon Dance Company, Murray Louis Dance Company, and Nikolais Dance Theatre. The fifth member was a "guest" each year—in 1979–80 it was Alvin Ailey Dance Theatre; in 1980–81, the Joffrey Ballet. The series offered discounted tickets to subscribers for one performance of each company at New York's City Center, although each company continued to sell individual tickets to performances (which usually generated more money than subscriptions).

The subscription allowed the companies to begin to research their audiences and to try to turn one-time ticket buyers into repeat attenders; it also provided greater visibility for each company through a joint promotional campaign. Nevertheless, there was originally tremendous resistance to collaboration among the companies. Their participation in the subscription plan came only with a promise of democratic treatment. Thus, the promotional brochure included five "equal" and separate flaps.

This democratic treatment may possibly have been at the expense of cost-effectiveness and there was a drop in income from the first to the second season of MAD, but without such concessions to the artis-

---

tic directors of each company, the subscription plan would never have happened. It should be understood that Masters of American Dance was not an organization—although there was some talk of incorporating as a nonprofit corporation. It was a marketing strategy partly inspired by continuing problems of rising inflation, increased labor, production and touring costs, and the heavy losses incurred by a company's performing in New York for at least part of the season—an artistic and critical imperative for most companies.

Although consideration was given to the growth of MAD into a management arm of the core companies that might centrally control financing, fund-raising, and audience development in television and cable as well as the live theatre, 1980–1981 marked its final season. Some companies moved to the new Joyce Theatre on 19th Street and Eighth Avenue, a former movie theatre renovated specifically for dance companies. City Center—where the MAD companies performed—subsequently picked up where MAD left off and is currently running a subscription series of its own.

Although there are those that deem Masters of American Dance a failed experiment, in reality it must be viewed not as an isolated scheme but as part of a continuum that began in the early 1970s with the formation of the Dance Umbrella. The Dance Umbrella was a production organization that showcased modern dance companies, providing them not only with stage and rehearsal facilities, but with managerial services. It used a strong marketing strategy to develop a series of discount dance passes, a variation on the subscription theme. Although the Dance Umbrella officially opened in 1975, it was in the planning stages for several years before that. The decade between its beginnings and the City Center subscription plan was a period during which a slow and gradual seduction of dance companies took place, a seduction that convinced at least some of them that it was possible, even desirable, to collaborate. Without MAD, the collaborations of the present and perhaps of the future might not have been possible.

The joint marketing via subscription idea is not only being applied to companies the size of Merce Cunningham's. Three Off Off Broadway theatres—Manhattan Punchline, the WPA, and Second Stage— are currently considering a subscription season, to be tested as a pilot project with the possible backing of the Alliance of Resident Theatres/New York.

Joint marketing techniques have also been used in visual arts institutions: in 1979 the Cooper Hewitt Museum organized Museum Mile in conjunction with the Project for Public Spaces, Inc. and nine other museums. Museum Mile is a group of ten museums along upper Fifth

Avenue in New York City, between 86th and 105th Streets, involved in a joint marketing campaign to promote greater visibility. Brochures resembling subway maps include a picture and description of each museum, plus information about its collection, hours, and admission charges. Although most of the museums are quite different from each other in character, it is their geographic proximity and their desire for visibility that made Museum Mile possible. The museums are the Cooper Hewitt Museum, El Museo del Barrio, Museum of the City of New York, International Center of Photography, The Jewish Museum, National Academy of Design, The Solomon R. Guggenheim Museum, YIVO Institute for Jewish Research, Goethe House New York, and the Metropolitan Museum of Art.[33]

One of the Museum Mile institutions, the Solomon R. Guggenheim Museum, is currently involved in a program that centers on the distribution as well as the marketing of their goods. The program is particularly interesting because it provides a mechanism through which a large established institution can aid smaller, less affluent museums. The Collection Decentralization Program addresses two very specific problems: the wealth of artwork owned and stored by large art museums, much of which is rarely shown or seen, and the meager budgets, small staff, and incomplete collections of many small museums around the country. The Program is an attempt to bridge the gap between these two worlds by lending the smaller museums works from the Guggenheim's permanent collection. Parts of this collection have been organized into categories representing its strong areas such as European Sources of American Abstraction (Albers, Arp, Feininger, Gleizes, Kandinsky, Klee, Leger, Metzinger, Moholy-Nagy, Lissitsky, Ozenfant, Pevsner, Valmier, Vantongerloo, Villon, and Vordemberge-Gildewart) and Modern Sculpture (Rodin, Maillol, Duchamp-Villon, Archipenko, Pevsner, Giacometti, Palozzi, Etienne-Martin, Hadju, Dubuffet, Chamberlain, Trova, Kelly, Lichtenstein, Samaras, Ipoustéguy, Chryssa, Nauman, Bell, Duff, and Benglis). Applicant institutions can choose a category that meets their specific need—the San Antonio Museum, for example, is borrowing a group of Latin American paintings t o"present its audiences a subject of local interest not represented in its own collection at this time.[34]

---

[33]C. Ray Smith, "A Tour of Museum Mile," *Cooper Historical Newsletter*, 3 (Winter 1980).

[34]Collection Decentralization Program, Solomon R. Guggenheim Museum, Brochure (New York, Spring 1982; Solomon R. Guggenheim Museum, Press Release, 23 October 1981.

Loans will last from six months to two years and will be accompanied by educational programs, lectures, and performance events where desirable. Scholarly publications and didactic aids will be produced, some local courses will be developed, and curators from borrowing institutions will work with Guggenheim curators on study and selection of works. Joint fund-raising efforts will also be developed for individual presentation needs.

The 1982–1987 roster of participating museums includes: the Allentown Art Museum, Pennsylvania; The University of Michigan Art Museum, Ann Arbor; The High Museum of Art, Atlanta; University Art Museum, University of California, Berkeley; Birmingham Museum of Art, Alabama; The Ackland Art Museum, University of North Carolina, Chapel Hill; The Helen Foresman Spencer Museum of Art, The University of Kansas, Lawrence; Elvehjem Museum of Art, University of Wisconsin, Madison; San Antonio Museum of Art, Texas; and Worcester Art Museum, Massachusetts.

Some institutions across the country are involved in large-scale marketing efforts known as "cultural networking." Membership organizations like the Station Independence Program, the marketing arm of the Public Broadcasting Service, acts as a marketing umbrella for over 170 independently licensed public television stations providing them with help in marketing, fund-raising, on-air promotion, and advertising copy.[35]

Cultural networks for direct mail have been created through city-wide consortia and through commercial and nonprofit direct marketing or mail outfits like the Arts and Science Development Service on Long Island, N.Y. and Philadelphia's Cultural Communication Corporation.[36]

Another example of an institution where marketing and distribution are simultaneous organizational functions is the Independent Cinema and Producers organization (ICAP). Founded in 1975 to act as a clearing house for Home Box Office (HBO), it now has over 800 films and tapes to market to the entire industry including cable, pay cable, and public and prime TV. Although there are a number of commercial services that distribute films to cable systems, ICAP is a nonprofit organization set up specifically to handle films and tapes by independent producers, and which returns 75 percent of the profit to those

---

[35]Stephen Belth, "Cultural Networking," *American Arts*, November 1981, p. 10.

[36]Ibid., p. 11.

producers. Using a catalog format to market much of the work, ICAP lists films in different series categories, plus information about content and running time (some material can easily be used for "filler" on cable).

At the same time that ICAP is marketing and distributing the work of independent producers, it is firmly committed to the artist. Legitimized, in a sense, by its nonprofit status in a field where making money is not only the primary but often the only goal, ICAP negotiates for fair rates for its artists and tries constantly to set new ones. Additionally, ICAP provides each artist with a contract that gives the organization the right to represent the work, and provides another contract each time a sale is made, indicating what the rate is, how many times the work will be shown, and where it will be shown, at least in the domestic marketplace.[37]

A marketing tool used by organizations to stimulate audience attendance at performing arts events has been the ticket voucher program. A ticket voucher is, in essence, a chit, a piece of paper that, like a food stamp is redeemable for goods. The goods, in this case, are usually a performance event. Pioneered by the Theatre Development Fund in New York in 1972, the voucher system spread to a number of cities across the country and then changed, either to accommodate a broader constituency, or to serve different needs in the arts community.

The original TDF ticket voucher was sold in a packet or set of five for 50¢ a voucher, or $2.50 a set. The price, which was set so low that the vouchers often remained unused, is now up to $2.50 per voucher and $12 for a set of five. Vouchers are available for sale to teachers, the elderly, labor union members, the handicapped, and low-income and social service clients. Presentation of a voucher at any theatre participating in the program (the list of Off Off Broadway theatres was extensive) gained entry for the voucher holder and subsidy from TDF for the participating theatre. Thus, the audience member and the theatre were subsidized simultaneously while the "fringe audience" was being developed. The extensive listing of theatres eventually became a publication of monthly performing arts events, and the theatre ticket voucher became a performing arts voucher, usable at hundreds of theatre, dance, and music events. A system of information as well as sub-

---

[37]Independent Cinema Artists and Producers Organization, Publicity Material, September 1981.

sidy was created with the purpose of "pump priming" on both performing arts attendance and economics.[38] But the voucher system, a scheme that may have appeared to many groups at its inception as a kind of handout, is in fact very competitive:

> It makes groups compete for audiences, and also the evidence of the competition is shown up afterwards in the financial reports in a way which is really nakedly capitalistic. It may reflect their ability to promote themselves, or to get good reviews, or just to use a system well . . . it has been an approach . . . to reduce to a very reasonable and cost efficient system the problem of developing audiences for relatively small entities that could not possibly afford outreach programs of their own and who, if all of them were to duplicate the set-up for themselves, would do so at a cost that would be many many times that of the collective system.[39]

The "above-ground" version of the voucher program is the half-price day-of-performance ticket booths run by TDF and labelled TKTS in Duffy Square and at the World Trade Center in Manhattan, on Fulton Street in Brooklyn, and for non-theatre events, in Bryant Park.

Prerequisites for such a voucher program in other cities include a "volume of capacity," and a fairly large number of professional organizations as well as a "marketing opportunity."[40] Obviously, collaboration among a number of those professional organizations will strengthen the program, as well as their involvement from its inception.

In 1979–80, Arts/Boston began a ticket voucher program that represented both commercial and non-commercial arts events in Boston; this program quickly turned into another and newer activity, Arts/Mail. A direct mail program with a good rate of return (averaging 10 percent as opposed to the normal 2 percent rate), Arts/Mail is a good example of a program whose original form needed revision.

With the aid of the Rouse Corporation, developer of the area around Faneuil Hall, Arts/Boston created the BOSTIX booth in the Quincy market—a kiosk that provided the only retail advertising space in the market area. Advertising space is sold to commercial and non-commercial arts groups and user fees are paid by producing orga-

---

[38]Vincent Marron and Hugh Southern, "Ticket Voucher Systems," *ACUCAA Bulletin,* Supplement, no. 79, May 1980 (Madison, Wis.: Association of College, University and Community Arts Administrators, 1980), p. 2.

[39]Ibid.

[40]Ibid., p. 3.

nizations that make tickets and information available at the booth. A service charge on the half-price day-of-performance tickets sold at the booth helps to meet operating expenses.

Arts/Boston has gone far beyond ticket programs for performing arts events. Currently, it is developing a "Harbor Pass," a collaborative promotional scheme for eight museums along the Harborwalk. The "Mass Pass," a destination promotion for Trailways Bus Services, was developed with the Department of Commerce and Development. The Arts/Pass is a promotional scheme to build audience awareness and attendance for museums and historical sites.[41]

Of course, discussion of any organization and its beginnings requires some knowledge of the climate in which it is created. Although the models provided here are not in-depth portraits, they are reflections of a certain time and place and a certain arts environment. When the Twin Cities Metropolitan Arts Alliance began as a membership organization in 1974, it had as a major interest the aid and support of individual artists. At that time, however, funding sources in the Minneapolis-St. Paul area were not very interested in individual artist-support programs. The Alliance, which served over 800 individuals, organizations, and friends of the arts could not meet expenses through the required dues or through grant monies, and in 1977 the focus of the organization changed. (It is interesting to note how the climate of the Twin Cities changed within just a few years to embrace individual artist support through groups like the Minneapolis Playwrights' Center, The Loft, Minnesota Independent Choreographers Association, and the Composers' Forum.[42])

By late 1977, the Alliance's commitment to artists services programs was abandoned and activities centering around audience development and marketing took its place. The MAT Voucher Program, begun in 1975, was continued (like TDF, sets of five vouchers are sold to targeted populations). Also continued was the Performing Arts Calendar (later known as the Metropolitan Arts Guide, or MAG) which provided a listing of performing arts events to voucher users thereby creating greater exposure for arts groups. While major public funding for the voucher program ended in 1981, almost 98 percent of its funding came from private local services (which may be one reason that it is one of the few arts voucher programs still in existence). Still,

[41]Arts/Boston promotional material, 1982.

[42]See the grant proposal from the Playwrights' Center in Chapter II for more information.

the lack of major funding has encouraged the Alliance to explore ways to redesign the program into a broader marketing service that will allow arts groups to fill seats that would remain unsold with paying customers. The Alliance is currently exploring cooperative mailing lists, discounted admission for groups, tourists and visitors, and a half-price or central ticket outlet service comparable to TKTS in New York and BOSTIX in Boston.

One self-sustaining cooperative activity that has been highly successful is the Alliance's Arts Action Kiosk Service which places tickets and membership information "in highly-visible locations while, at the same time, eliminating the costs associated with individual efforts at maintaining separate kiosks or racks/display units."[43] Eleven originating institutions use this service on a year-round basis including: Guthrie Theatre, Walker Art Center, Hennepin Center for the Arts, Northrop Auditorium, University Theatre (Rarig Center), Orchestra Hall, O'Shaughnessy Auditorium, Minneapolis Institute of Arts, Children's Theatre Company, and one rotating location. Libraries, hotels, and shopping malls have expressed an interest in this particular program, and some future alliances might be possible on a limited-time, low-fee basis.

With all this planning, an economic impact study conducted by the Alliance for the National Endowment for the Arts allowed it to measure the arts audience in the area; the data from this study can now be used in comparison with MAT Voucher users to develop new audiences.[44]

Two programs that essentially "failed" at Performing Arts Services in San Francisco[45] illustrate some of the pitfalls involved in joint efforts. A study was conducted to determine whether eight local arts organizations—ranging in size from the San Francisco Ballet to small emerging groups—should share computer services. The study showed that the highest degree of compatibility among these companies was in the area of list-maintenance for marketing, membership and fund-raising purposes. The question of list "ownership" was not at issue—each list "was to be maintained with its own integrity, but

---

[43]Twin Cities Metropolitan Arts Alliance, Grant Proposal, for period 9/1/1981 to 8/31/1983.

[44]Much of the information on the Twin Cities Metropolitan Arts Alliance was provided by a personal letter from William G. Driver, Managing Director, 12 May 1982.

[45]Not to be confused with the New York City cluster management group of the same name.

also with the ability to merge/purge between lists only upon consent of the 'owners.' "[46] The smaller groups were, however, threatened by start-up and maintenance costs and the large groups used the issue of scheduling restrictions to refuse participation.

In January 1980, PAS attempted to serve its membership with a group sales service. A bulletin was published promoting performing arts events in the San Francisco area and sent to 800 clubs and corporations. The intention of the service was to familiarize people with the broad range of performance events. After the initial mailing and some telephone follow-up, PAS was surprised to learn that customers, particularly repeat customers, tended to choose the same kinds of events over and over again, and that the events they chose were the well-known, the tried, and the tested. Causes for this were due to two factors: rapid turnover in personnel in the clubs and corporations so that no long-term linkages could be formed, and the search by the club or corporation for events with mass appeal. Neither potential income nor the services of a broad membership seemed to justify the existence of such a service, so the group sales effort was disbanded.

The problems of Performing Arts Services provide good material for the extreme rationales expressed by people who decry cooperative efforts in the arts. The danger, many say, is that an organization—particularly if it is small—expends too much energy with too little result, and that the effort spent doing things jointly might be better spent cultivating one's own garden. The nay-sayers at the opposite extreme vow that cooperative efforts do not go far enough, and that a combination of factors, including individual artistic and managerial personalities, programming needs and decisions, and protectiveness of one's products and strategies work to prevent true collaboration. Of course, informal cooperation goes on all the time, but the increase in the formal commitments that companies are making gives them new vulnerability. Perhaps the most important aspect of this commitment, whether in marketing, co-production, joint fund-raising or networks, is that artists and managers of small and emerging companies are beginning to make things happen, instead of letting them happen. Perhaps the recent economic setbacks have made them avoid an "on the dole" mentality. While cooperative efforts are not for every arts group, they may provide some with certain solutions to financial distress.

---

[46]Larry Campbell, Director of PAS, Personal letter, 13 May 1982.

CHAPTER FIVE

ARTS MONEY & THE NEW TECHNOLOGY

THE ART OF TELEVISION

While some areas of the new technology have been more responsive than others to arts programming, it is cable television that most recently has captured the hopes of many artists and institutions. They hope for a partnership that allows money for survival, exposure for their work, and the creation of a quality product in a medium that many find new and challenging. While transmission mechanisms include "over the air" network and public television, cable, satellite and microwave transmission, transmission through telephone wires, and transmission by videocassette and videodisc, many of the issues involved in the "technology revolution" are so current that material runs the risk of being outdated almost as it is written. Therefore, although issues addressed here must be seen in the context of their time, some of them encompass larger questions of aesthetics, artistic control, relationships between the medium and the viewer, and motivations behind marriages between television and art.

In 1976 Richard Adler succinctly addressed the central challenge of television as it relates to the arts and humanities:

> That challenge is to provide programming of humanistic value, programming that will engage not only the attention but the mind—and even the spirit—of its audience. It may be that the development of cable gives us a second, and perhaps the last chance to determine whether television will be used not merely to provide diversion or immediate information but to teach, to inspire, to enhance the quality of American life.[1]

Most people involved in the cable industry would probably agree that artistically, aesthetically, and humanistically, television has not yet met Adler's challenge, even though technological capabilities are

---

[1]Richard Adler, "The Humanistic Claim on Cable," in *The Electronic Box Office*, ed. Richard Adler and Walter S. Baer (New York: Praeger, 1980), p. 2.

221

rapidly developing. Some major questions arise in response to this immediate failure. Is the challenge remaining unmet because of the artistic
programming, or because of the translation of that programming to electronic technology? Would more money at the artistic end guarantee a better product? If so, would that product be more saleable and profitable for
the network that buys it? Is it the nature of the medium itself that makes
attracting large audiences for arts programming impossible? And what
about the "business" of putting the arts on television—how does one
reconcile commercial, money-making practices and standards with
groups who "do not see themselves as engaged in serving a market, but
in propagating a cultural tradition"?[2]

Television, as Twyla Tharp so aptly points out, is about "the rectangle and the dollar," and that rectangle has been described as a
frame, a window, a mirror, a trap, and a coffin.[3] At present, it provides the viewer with a set of electronically generated images—a
series of dots on a screen that cannot reproduce fine detail, intricacies
of light or shade, lateral space, depth, or texture. Even with programs
that are audio-simulcast, sound and tone cannot be perfectly reproduced. Besides the box itself, television places the camera between the
viewer and the subject, allowing it to intervene in the cultural space.
In addition, it is usually viewed in a room where other activities may
constantly distract the viewer. Martin Mayer contends that although
the only activities not excluded by television watching are "eating and
knitting . . . television pictures do not absorb the peripheral vision."[4]
Others describe television as "visual radio," claiming that people do
many other things while the television is on and tend to listen to it
rather than watch it. Some call it a

> home appliance; its space is the space of everyday life. People can afford
> to watch the tube seven or eight hours a day because they can do so many
> other things simultaneously—do household chores, read magazines, eat
> and drink, make telephone calls, do homework.[5]

---

[2]Richard A. Posner, "The Probably Effects of Pay Cable Television on Culture
and the Arts," in The Electronic Box Office, ed. Richard Adler and Walter S.
Baer (New York: Praeger, 1976), p. 82.

[3]Volunteer Lawyers for the Arts Conference: "Cable Production: What Every
Arts Organization Needs to Know," New York University, New York, 20–21
May 1982. Quote attributed to Ms. Tharp by Rhoda Grauer, Director of Me-
dia Development, American Ballet Theatre.

[4]Adler, p. 4.

[5]Robin White, "Great Expectations: Artists TV Guide," Artforum, Summer
1982, p. 43.

In its relay or translation function, television transmits an event either live at the exact moment it occurs or at a later time in the form of edited film or videotape.[6] Even in its live, unedited relay function, television cannot replicate the live experience, although it can attempt to generate a kind of you-are-there excitement particularly through the presence of a live audience. Joseph Papp's live 1981 performance of Elizabeth Swados's *The Haggadah* on PBS-TV was an effort to capitalize on the energy of the live performance. When Home Box Office shot the play *Vanities*, it spent $400,000 setting up a new production in the Westwood Theatre in Los Angeles so that the experience of a live audience could be captured.

In straining to recreate the live event, the point of view and intimacy of the players are often lost:

> In Showtime's production of *The Gin Game*, for example, the interaction between Hume Cronyn and Jessica Tandy, who play a couple condemned to life in an old-age home, is lost as the camera futilely attempts to capture the feeling of the actual stage piece.[7]

Besides, there are certain occupational hazards in shooting "live." Since curtain time equals television time, there is no such thing as running over even by a few seconds. (Rumor has it that intermissions of more than one televised production have found harried producers telling orchestra conductors to play the last few movements a little faster.) What is gained in spontaneity may be lost through mistakes—an actor walks out of camera range or a camera focuses incorrectly—that cannot be corrected later.

Finally, there are real cultural objections to what is being shown on television. The objectors complain that great theatre, great music, and great dance are nowhere to be found and that producers should not attempt to put events on television that they couldn't sell tickets to in a live theatre. In the visual arts, the problem is even more complex since "a kind of American pragmatism insists the image on the screen is inferior to the painting hanging on the wall *because it isn't the painting.*"[8]

There are, of course, certain things that television can do quite

---

[6]On some occasions, the "live" event is shown in its unedited form but at a later date.

[7]Bob Brewin, "Spectrum Wars!," *The Village Voice*, 22 June 1982, p. 74.

[8]"Viewpoint: Brian O'Doherty," *The Cultural Post*, May/June 1981, p. 11.

well, things that begin to turn the product into a television experience. It focuses the viewer's attention immediately. It allows for a kind of intimacy and scrutiny by the viewer, important in scenes reflecting character motivation, and physical and vocal technique. It provides close-up shots of things the viewer could not see at the live event—the intricate bowing of the first violinist, the hands of the pianist on the keys. In adapting a performance for television, new levels of interpretation may be opened up:

> Royal Shakespeare Company director Trevor Nunn staged CBS' presentation of *The Three Sisters* for the TV camera, and created shots that eventually looked like photographs. Because of this, the action seemed to exist in the present and in retrospect at the same time, and adapting for the camera resulted in a conception that further illuminated Chekhov's interest in perception over time.[9]

At certain times, television allows the viewer to see the total picture at one time in a way he or she might not see it live—as if viewing a football game from a prime seat. And television has the capability of recording a singular event for posterity—what finally convinced Vladimir Horowitz to appear on television was a question raised by producer Roger Englander: "I asked him what he would give to see Franz Liszt play the piano."[10] Beyond this, some agree with Brian O'Doherty, Director of the Media Arts Program at the National Endowment for the Arts, that "media are the great 20th century art. . . . In our society, to be visible is to exist. I am televised, therefore I am."[11]

Television cannot create "atmosphere" the way a live event does, something that depends on a number of live bodies together in one space, and it cannot create the interaction between the audience and performer that gives a performance resonance. In fact, television frequently seems antithetical to art. Freelance director Kirk Browning says, "Translation is not an art form; it's a craft. Television is not an art form."[12] M. Edgar Rosenblum, Executive Director of the Long Wharf Theatre in New Haven, says, "Opera and theatre do not re-

---

[9]Brewin, pp. 74–75.

[10]Kirsten Beck, ed., Conference Proceedings: *Cable Television and the Performing Arts*, School of the Arts, New York University (New York: 5–7 June 1981), p. 45.

[11]"Viewpoint: Brian O'Doherty," p. 12.

[12]Quoted in Beck, p. 40.

main opera and theatre when they are transferred; they become television."[13]

Television is fast, full of movement and sound, and searches to invade everyone's living room. It often replaces emotional activity with physical activity as it tries to do too much, to put too many images on the screen. It is flat, two-dimensional, it distorts color and defies depth. Art, on the other hand, frequently requires time. It is often slow, silent, even static or without movement. It aspires, at times, to the unusual, the rare, even the unique. It has depth and dimension, color and shape. And the audience cannot turn it off. If art is an experience, television is a picture of that experience in which the viewer has more authority than the medium:

> You can look at it, turn away from it, turn it off, turn to another channel. The psychology of the medium is so diabolical, and it is so hard to get anybody to care about what's on television. . . . Television hasn't even got a space of its own. It doesn't exist in any performance space. It has no aura at all.[14]

Material that is created specifically for television comes closer to solving certain problems inherent in the medium. Twyla Tharp's *Making Television Dance* (1977) was a breakthrough production incorporating such film and video techniques as stop-action, instant replay, and reverse action into a total dance experience. Not quite a documentary, nor a standard performance, *Making Television Dance* was clearly a work created both for and with television. Although Tharp is perhaps the most visible example, and one acceptable to the networks, a number of artists are eager to work with the medium of television, but not in traditional ways.

> Artists are learning how to use it [television] to express their ideas and discovering which ones are allowed and can best be communicated on TV, so that they can develop new visual images which will convey their information to an ever-expanding audience.[15]

In 1976 Kas Kalba described the differences, as he viewed them, between conventional television and video:

---

[13]Ibid., p. 56.
[14]Ibid., p. 49.
[15]Robin White, p. 41.

In conventional television, the underlying aesthetic structure of the medium—the mass audience, the copyright obligations, the set in the living room, the professional standards, etc.—is so taken for granted that the entire locus of development is on programming. Small variations in style or content keep the TV seasons flowing. In video, on the other hand, the emphasis is on re-inventing this underlying structure and consequently, the introduction of new aesthetic components, roles or relationships and the abandonment of prevailing ones is as important as the creation of individual videotapes.[16]

Kalba goes on to say that it is not only the technology that has made aesthetic innovation possible, but the imaginations of the artists who use video and all its components. He describes various kinds of experimental video activity including conceptual video, video as an element of live theatre and dance, the creation of graphic designs through the blending of images using keying and chroma-keying, image manipulation, negative color, and the use of multiple channels as well as multiple screens.

The more examples Kalba gives, the farther away the medium seems from the interests of cable television. Although certain video works using many of the techniques cited above are being used as "filler" for certain cable networks, the ways in which video artists are interested in extending and redefining the medium of television seem to have little interest for the distributors of cable programs. The relationship seems a little like the attitude of a midtown-Manhattan art gallery that sells Old Master paintings about the work of conceptual artists—questions of attractiveness, taste, and saleability do not even enter the picture. The work simply has no relationship to the commercial institution.

Many artists are learning about television to protect themselves from exploitation and to ensure artistic control of their products. Some television people feel artists are not entitled to such control without at least a basic knowledge of the medium and its requirements: no matter where the product originated, artistic control has to be earned. Others follow the kinds of emphases laid down by Kalba in 1976. Choreographer David Gordon feels, "We can reinvent the relationship of the work to the box if someone is willing to abandon the old rules."[17] The old rules include what Lee Breuer calls the "objectifi-

---

[16]Kas Kalba, "The Video Implosion: Models for Reinventing Television," in *The Electronic Box Office*, ed. Richard Adler and Walter S. Baer (New York: Praeger, 1976), p. 94.

[17]Volunteer Lawyers for the Arts Conference, 20–21 May 1982.

cation of performance on video," or just that "Live From . . ." experience that has set one precedent for cultural programming on television. Breuer, founder and co-artistic director of the New York-based avant-garde theatre group, Mabou Mines, is interested in things that are "vitally video" and that can be explored fully by artists. In a current project all technology—sound equipment, special effects generators, and cameras—is being run by artists, while technicians are used to make repairs when the equipment breaks down. Breuer also uses the camera as an actor and uses live imagery over pre-recorded tape.[18]

Media centers across the country have film and video artists whose interests are in the uses of the medium itself, but to whom broadcast is also a necessary component of the artistic process.[19] These artists will find it difficult in the current market to attract the financing and sponsorship that will allow them to show their works over any system, and the "technology revolution" that promises exposure if not financial reward to arts institutions has largely ignored these artists. As a former CBS Cable executive is reported to have stated, "If it isn't Mozart or Puccini, we're not interested." Nevertheless, for those truly interested in the fate of television as a potential art form—and it is clear from the quality of work being shown that new explorations of that form are needed—such explorations should not be dismissed.

But before the new technology, there was the "old technology" which should provide certain lessons for those involved in cable television. In terms of programming, cable is frequently being compared to radio which is programmed "vertically." "Vertical programming establishes a certain expectation about the nature of the station's programs."[20] Cable will have to do the same by creating channels that can be distinguished from each other and that have a differential advantage. Others liken the cable format to a magazine format and in fact at least one cable service is programming an arts magazine. But the most obvious precedent is commercial television.

The history of commercial television has been one where programs were determined at the very beginning by viewer interests, and afterwards, by the advertisers who supported those programs. In the late

---

[18]Ibid.

[19]Not all media artists view broadcast as a necessary component to their work. At a conference in June 1981 of the Media Alliance of New York State, broadcast was only one of several options discussed. Some of the others included home video, museums, and galleries.

[20]Quoted in Beck, p. 2.

1940s and 1950s, programming was dictated by a small elite of upper middle class viewers—the only ones who could afford to purchase a television set. Between 1947 and 1960 commercial television offered over 650 plays through its Kraft Television Theatre, plus more theatrical fare through Playhouse 90, Hollywood Television Theatre, Hallmark Hall of Fame, and Omnibus which also offered opera, ballet, and symphony programs. The Bell Telephone Hour, Kraft Music Hall, and the Ed Sullivan Show showed ballet performances. In 1950, Ballet Theatre's production of *Giselle* was seen and in 1955 Margot Fonteyn appeared in *Sleeping Beauty*. Orchestral and operatic events were also offered, one of the most notable being Gian Carlo Menotti's *Amahl and the Night Visitors* which was commissioned by NBC and shown every year at Christmastime.[21]

After 1960, while a certain number of single art events continued to be broadcast, television's focus turned toward variety entertainment. One of the reasons for the decline in arts programming had to do with the changing role of the advertiser. In the early days of television, the advertiser was essentially a sponsor. One recalls Philco Playhouse, Goodyear Playhouse, and Ford Television Theatre. Inherent in sponsor advertising was the inducement of the "gratitude factor"—people would buy the sponsor's product to show their appreciation to the sponsor for presenting the show.[22] With the decrease in the price of television sets and a more affluent post-war population, the viewing audience enlarged tremendously. The advertiser's message was now delivered in a much more direct way, as programming tried to "attract and hold a large portion of the entire American population to survive."[23] Today, 98 percent of American homes have at least one television set, close to 50 percent are estimated to have at least two sets, and the average number of television viewing hours per household is 47 hours per week.[24]

While commercial television became the great hypnotizer of the masses with its indistinguishable offerings of mostly light entertainment, public television tried to take up the cultural challenge. "An

---

[21]Tim Brook and Earle Maron, *The Complete Directory to Prime Time Network Shows, 1946–Present* (New York: Ballantine Books, 1979), Introduction.

[22]John Chappell and Laurie Salinitre, "The Performing Arts on Commercial Television." Paper presented at Arts Management Seminar, Columbia University, 1980.

[23]Adler, p. 7.

[24]White, p. 40.

uneasy relationship with governmental sponsors, confusion over its mission and intended audience, and, above all, chronic under-financing" contributed to the uneasy development of the only real alternative to commercial television until the new technology appeared.[25]

CABLE TELEVISION

Of all the new technology, the one that arts groups are most involved with at present is the oldest—cable television. Begun in the late 1940s to aid people in non-urban areas to obtain good television reception, CATV was a system which brought television signals to a community with coaxial cable. What began as a system of transmission quickly changed to a system of origination and then programming, as urban areas were penetrated and promises were made for "multiple channels, computer interface, and two-way communication."[26] Not only were people experimenting with the technology itself, but they were examining how to place the technology in the marketplace. Early systems of pay television in the 1950s and 1960s were Zenith's Phone-vision, Paramount's Telemeter International in Etobicoke, a suburb of Toronto, and NBC's Subscription Television (STV) in San Francisco and Los Angeles. While legal, financial, and political problems did not allow any of these systems to fully develop, the groundwork for present systems was laid.[27]

Today, close to 19 million subscribers view programs on two kinds of programming networks—basic cable and pay television. Basic cable provides basic reception, is advertiser supported, and offered free to viewers who take cable. Alpha Repertory Theatre Service (ARTS), the now defunct CBS Cable, and the USA Network are basic cable networks. Pay television charges viewers a monthly fee above and beyond the regular cable charge.[28] Home Box Office, Showtime, Bravo, the now defunct RCTV/The Entertainment Channel, and the Public

---

[25]Adler, p. 7.

[26]Red Burns, "Local Origination and Public Access: Community Information Systems," in *Cable Handbook*, ed. Mary Louise Hallowell (Washington, D.C.: Communications Press, 1975), p. 199.

[27]Martin Mayer, *About Television* (New York: Harper and Row, 1972), p. 351.

[28]Many homes receive their pay television programs not through cable wires but "over the air" from subscription TV (STV) stations. These stations transmit a scrambled signal to TV sets which are fitted with a special decoder.

Subscriber Network planned by PBS are all pay television networks.[29]

The oldest financially successful cable network to date is Home Box office, which began in 1972, turned its first profit in 1977, and by 1979 was the biggest money-maker of Time, Inc., topping profits from *Time* magazine.[30] In 1975, Time turned what was essentially a local operation into a national one by engaging RCA's Sitcom I satellite to transmit electromagnetic signals (carrying Home Box Office programming in this case) from "dishes" or "earth stations" to a satellite 23,300 miles above the equator.[31] (Before this time cable programming was transmitted through earthbound microwave distributors via a series of stations that transmitted signals sequentially.) The satellite received the signal and blinked it back to earth stations across the country. Cable systems equipped with "dishes" relayed the signals to a transmission center, and from there by coaxial cable wires, to subscribers' homes.[32] By 1979, there were eleven satellites, each equipped with a number of channels, or transponders, necessitating a rash of new programming.

While the early services, like Manhattan Cable and TelePrompTer in New York City, had between 10 and 30 channels, the number of possible cable channels is already speculated to be between 150 and 200. Of 83 transponders that will be used to carry cable programs in the next few years, 40 are owned by Warner-Amex Cable (a joint venture of Warner Communications, Inc. and American Express), Time, Inc., and Westinghouse Electric's subsidiary, Group W.[33] Among the cable services offered by these three giants are Time Inc.'s Home Box Office, Cinemax (a movie network), and USA Network (of which it owns a third); Westinghouse's Home Theatre Network ("G" rated movies), and Showtime (chief pay television rival to Home Box Office, Westinghouse owns half); and Warner Amex's Movie Channel (a pay television rival to HBO and Showtime), Nickelodeon (basic cable chil-

---

[29]Besides support through advertisers or viewers, financing is also possible through gifts and grants, and through direct support for cable operators who offer a certain amount of free programming to attract customers, but it is unlikely that cable will be financed in these other ways at this time.

[30]The only other cable network now in the black is Showtime.

[31]Tony Schwartz, "Where Cable TV Stands After FCC Deregulation," *The New York Times*, 21 August 1980.

[32]Susan Ferris, "Cable Television: A Primer," paper presented at Arts Management seminar, Columbia University, 1981.

[33]Brewin, p. 71.

dren's programming), and MTV, Music Television (basic cable) for an audience of 18 to 34-year olds.[34]

While satellite space is finite and satellite communication is an international issue, competition to normal basic and pay services has begun to develop. It includes those who distribute programs via microwave (MDS-multipoint distribution service), others who get programs for home or apartments by picking them up directly from a satellite (DBS-direct broadcast satellite), and still others who receive subscriber-selected graphic material or data over telephone lines or over the air (videotex).[35] The possibilities of scrambling signals and of outside electronic interference are a threat that the new technologies rarely mention, although intentional signal scrambling has been mentioned as a measure against piracy of products. The competition may develop a substantial edge if a bill passed by the Senate Commerce Committee gets through the Senate and the House. This bill seeks to strip municipalities of much of their power over cable broadcasting. Cable franchises have traditionally been the province of local governments (partly because the wires sometimes use city streets) and therefore have been politically useful in certain ways; the existing bill or one like it could overturn hundreds of existing franchises around the country.[36]

Although the cable services dealt with in this chapter are arts and culture-oriented, one-way systems, it should be noted that a commercial, interactive two-way system has been developed by Warner Amex Cable Communications. Its system, called Qube, has been operating for some years in Columbus, Ohio; other Qube systems have been discussed for Pittsburgh, Chicago, and Houston. While two-way interactive systems have been researched for two decades, Qube is the first fully commercial use of the technology marrying computers to two-way television.

A Qube user selects programs by punching buttons on a key pad that is connected by wire to the TV set. Charges are recorded automatically by

---

[34]Ibid.

[35]Certain large apartment houses like Co-op City in the Bronx are planning to band together to install their own $10,000 dish to receive satellite signals. This procedure is sometimes called a SMATZ.

[36]Ernest Holsendolph, "A Cable Bill Alarms Municipalities," *The New York Times*, 26 July 1982, p. C15.

the Qube central computer, which scans home terminals every six seconds to find out who's watching what.[37]

Arts groups have not yet explored the use of this system in any depth, although the system has been studied since the early 1970s by people interested in the arts. One economically compelling service that the two-way system experimented with is a pay-per-view channel in which a viewer pays a set amount for a specific television program or event. Profits from such an event could run into the millions of dollars for a single night.[38]

CABLE SERVICES

Although it is predicted that the entire country will be "wired for cable" before the end of the century, certain locations have access only to certain systems and some to no systems at all. One of the most publicized battles was the determination of cable franchises for the four boroughs of New York outside Manhattan. Since "where you live is what you get,"[39] cable operators have sometimes been accused of being monopolists whose only motive for incentive is profit.

Although one cannot choose the cable system, one can frequently choose among a wide variety of network services. At present, over half a dozen of those services deal in arts and cultural programming. Numbers of cablecast hours and days differ from service to service and are constantly being expanded or changed. At this writing, most programs remain commercial free, although there is constant discussion regarding the addition of commercials to cable television. Some companies prefer the sponsor role of the early days of commercial broadcast television, but many express a desire for a several-minute slot at the beginning or end of a program in which to sell their products through the development of a story or theme.[40] This informa-

---

[37]John B. Ford, *New Programs from New Outlets* (New York: Aspen Institute for Humanistic Studies, 1979), p. 16.

[38]Other two-way interactive systems now being developed include videotex— CBS, Inc. and American Telephone and Telegraph are testing consumers with this home information system as is Time, Inc.—and videodiscs.

[39]Jack Egan, "Will Cable Manhattan Keep Up With the Sticks?" *New York Magazine*, 28 September 1981, p. 17.

[40]The commercial television network in Italy makes use of this approach in its "Carousel" format.

tional advertising format has been called "propaganda masquerading as information" by some of its detractors.[41]

Basic advertiser-supported programming services automatically go to customers who sign up for a cable hook-up. They are charged a basic monthly fee of between eight and ten dollars. Those that offer arts and cultural programs include Alpha Repertory Television Service (ARTS), and the USA Network.*

Pay services charge between eight and twelve dollars over and above the basic monthly fee. Pay services offering programs on art and culture include Home Box Office, Showtime, Bravo, and the proposed Public Subscriber Network of the Public Broadcasting System.

BASIC CABLE SERVICES   ARTS and the former CBS Cable only recently entered the cable marketplace since major commercial networks were prohibited by law from offering cable services. Programs have been offered free of charge to subscribers and to cable systems.

ARTS is sponsored by ABC Video Enterprises and Warner Amex Satellite Entertainment Corporation. It began in April 1981 as the "first nightly cable television service devoted solely to the performing and visual arts."[42] It counts its potential audience at 7 million viewers as of Spring 1982 and narrowly targets its current audience who are assumed to be "arts loving" already.[43] Attempting a balance between the new and the traditional, ARTS acquired a lot of its early productions from abroad for reasons of availability and cost, but recently it

---

[41]Sandra Salmans, "Will Cable TV Be Invaded by Commercials?" *The New York Times*, 26 June 1981, sec. 2, p. 25.

*As an illustration of the constant changes in the cable industry, it should be noted that as of this writing CBS Cable and RCTV/The Entertainment Channel closed down at the end of 1982 and early 1983, respectively. While possibilities exist for specific products of CBS Cable to be bought by other entities and for an advertiser-supported service to replace the Entertainment Channel, this was a serious blow to many arts institutions. Nevertheless, CBS' activities in other areas of transmission (discussed throughout this chapter) should indicate the wealth of technological systems becoming available in the 1980s.

[42]Ronn Smith, "ABC Arts," *Theatre Crafts* 15 (October 1981), p. 23. The marketing material of most cable companies include this kind of "first" information—first to tape a live performance, first to negotiate with a particular union, first daytime service for the arts, etc.

[43]Liz Oliver, Manager of Program Acquisitions and Development, ABC Video Enterprises at Volunteer Lawyers for the Arts Conference, 20–21 May 1982.

has sought joint ventures with independent producers. Currently involved with several theatre companies, ARTS adapts dramatic fare for television and shoots it as TV drama. It has a small in-house production staff whose basic production function is the creation of ten-minute filler or promotional spots called "Arts Minutes," which have included profiles on Jean Renoir, Edgar Degas, and Henri de Toulouse-Lautrec.

CBS Cable had what many consider to be the best creative team in the cable industry, including Jack Willis, Vice President of Programming, who is known for such series as *The Great American Dream Machine* and *The 51st State*, Merrill Brockway, director and producer of *Camera Three* and *Dance in America*, Roger Englander, Senior Producer of Music, responsible for *Vladimir Horowitz at Carnegie Hall*, and the renowned *Omnibus* and *The Bell Telephone Hour*, and Stephanie Sills, former director of dramatic development at Twentieth Century Fox Television and a former Broadway producer.[44]

With a potential audience of several million, CBS Cable produced dance programs on Twyla Tharp, Ken Rinker, and May O'Donnell, as well as theatre pieces including David Storey's *Early Days* with Ralph Richardson, Pat Carroll in *Gertrude Stein, Gertrude Stein, Gertrude Stein*, Athol Fugard's Tony award-winning *Sizwe Banzi is Dead*, Robert Patrick's *Kennedy's Children*, and OyamO's *The Resurrection of Lady Bright*. Between 50 and 60 percent of CBS Cable's production was in-house, a partial result of a 1970 financial interest ruling by the Federal Communications Commission which sought to assist independent producers by limiting certain rights of the three major commercial networks.[45] The cost of original programming was estimated at $165,500 an hour for 1982, increasing at an annual rate of 7 percent.[46] Such costs often dictated certain artistic prerogatives—dramas with few characters, less lavish productions—and contributed to its unfortunate demise.

The USA Network, supposedly the second most popular basic cable network in the country, offers mixed programming—sports, women's and children's programs, and culture on the weekends. Owned by Time, Inc., MCA, and Paramount, it offers "The English

---

[44]Ronn Smith, "CBS Cable," *Theatre Crafts* 15 (October 1981), p. 22.

[45]Workshop with David Johnson, Director of Business Affairs, Home Box Office at Volunteer Lawyers for the Arts Conference, 20–21 May 1982.

[46]Irwin M. Stelzer and Geraldine Alpert, "Will Cable Save the Arts?" (New York: National Economic Research Associates, 1982), p. 13.

Channel,'' a culturally oriented series produced exclusively for cable TV.[47]

PAY TELEVISION SERVICES Home Box Office, now ten years old, has over 9 million subscribers through 3600 affiliated cable systems in all 50 states, Puerto Rico and the U.S. Virgin Islands. Sixty percent of its offerings are feature films. It also offers sports events, family programming, the first exclusive children's series, as well as 80 original special programs a year which are entertainment-oriented with a broad appeal including stand-up comedy, nightclub acts, and rock concerts. If one of cable television's greatest assets is ''narrowcasting''—targeting programs for a specific rather than a mass audience—Home Box Office has stayed on the track of its commercial predecessors and programmed services that appeal to the broad mass audience. Nevertheless, its financial success has prompted HBO to begin to narrowcast in certain areas. One of these areas is theatre.

Former Broadway and Off Broadway producer Arthur Whitelaw is responsible for developing theatrical properties for HBO. In Spring 1981, HBO mounted and shot Jack Heifner's comedy *Vanities* in a Los Angeles theatre with a live audience and Hollywood stars in the major roles. Plans through 1982 include shooting other recognized plays with well-known actors—*Barefoot in the Park* with Richard Thomas, *Sherlock Holmes, Plaza Suite,* and *Wait Until Dark* with Stacy Keach and Katherine Ross. While all of these offerings have already been made into movies, they were chosen because they were familiar to audiences and because the production rights were easily obtainable. Besides, the light fare is a partial inducement for a new audience based on the theory that heavier drama can be shown when that audience has been developed. One of the most interesting developments in terms of future work is HBO's development deal with the Manhattan-based Off-Off-Broadway theatre, Playwrights Horizons, which is being used to scout new plays for HBO.

Showtime, which began in Northern California in 1976, now has 2.9 million subscribers. It has presented a large number of theatrical offerings in its Broadway on Showtime series. Licensing Broadway hits or revivals with name actors usually over an 18-month period, Showtime has shot *Eubie!, Look Back in Anger, The Gin Game, The Amer-*

[47]Brewin, p. 71.

ican Dance Machine at the Brooklyn Academy of Music, *Hughie* at the Hyde Park Theatre Festival in New York State, *The Passion of Dracula, Little Johnny Jones* at the Goodspeed Playhouse in Connecticut, and *Cheaters* at the Fisher Theatre in Detroit. Some were taped before a live audience, others had only segments taped before an audience, and others were taped as teleplays in television studios and rehearsed there beforehand. Showtime has recently joined Home Box Office as a pay service running in the black.

Bravo, a division of the Rainbow Programming Service, is a pay service devoted solely to the arts and culture. It has transmitted a great many regional and nonmajor performing groups including the Aspen Festival Orchestra, the American Symphony Orchestra conducted by Leonard Bernstein, the Saint Louis Symphony, the Baltimore Symphony, the Houston Symphony, Ballet West, and the Indiana University Opera Theatre performing "The Greek Passion." Begun in December 1980, Bravo was the first television service to produce a "weekly, hard news cultural newscast."[48] An hour-long "video magazine" devotes part of its subject matter to personalities and topics in the arts, and Bravo hopes to achieve "direct mail contact with every viewer" to effectuate programming that is mandated by a carefully defined subscriber audience.[49]

RCTV/The Entertainment Channel was a joint venture of RCA Corporation and Rockefeller Center, Inc. with a potential availability to 3 million cable homes. In a quick blow to public television, RCTV arranged to have an exclusive "window" on selected materials from the British Broadcasting Corporation for between one and three years, after which time the material could be sold to commercial or public television. Thirty percent of its programming was to come from this source.[50] Included in the other 70 percent were classic American and foreign films, original series, and Broadway shows (a new production was slated for each month), some of which were negotiated with Broadway producer James Nederlander through his RKO Nederlander Productions. These include *Sweeney Todd, Emlyn Williams as Charles Dickens, I Do, I Do, The Canterbury Tales,* and *Lena Horne: The*

---

[48]Ronn Smith, "RCTV Cable," *Theatre Crafts,* p. 22.

[49]Erica Gruen and Marc Lustgarten, "The Electronic Concert Hall," *American Arts,* 12 (March 1981), p. 15.

[50]Smith, *Theatre Crafts,* p. 22.

Lady and Her Music. Also acquired from other sources were *Pippin, Piaf, Candida, The Drunkard,* and *A Christmas Carol.*[51]

A cultural network under discussion and under fire is the Public Subscriber Network proposed by the Public Broadcasting Service. With the intention of broadcasting educational courses and cultural events and being partially funded by public television stations and cultural groups, the service hopes to garner additional income from subscribers, advertisers, and ancillary services. Fear of competition for programming funds between PSN and PBS, recent staff cutbacks, the overall economic dilemma of public television and competition between such a service and its commercial counterparts may serve to defeat such a plan. Additionally, reports that PBS may use already licensed material on PSN before broadcasting it over PBS may create a certain rancor toward the service.[52]

AUDIENCES

It has become apparent to most people involved in the cable industry that there is no room for half a dozen cultural channels. It is becoming increasingly clear that basic cable—free TV—will give way to pay television, even pay-per-view television, and that probably one or at most two cultural cable television services will remain. Just for the financial record it should be noted that Home Box Office took six years to break even and spent $30 million doing it.[53]

Perhaps the most important information to be gathered in determining which services survive is data on audiences, and cable is no stranger to the same ratings that measure commercial television. In 1980, a group of cable concerns hired the famous firm of A. C. Nielsen to create a rating method for cable audiences. By June 1983, a Nielsen survey had determined that 31.7 million homes have cable reception, an increase of 4.3 million over the previous year,[54] but regular ratings have not yet been fully developed. More sophisticated measures un-

---

[51]C. Gerald Fraser, "New Cable Signs Stage Shows," *The New York Times,* 13 January 1982, sec. C, p. 24.

[52]Stelzer and Alpert, pp. 9–10.

[53]Peter Bernstein, "The Race to Feed Cable TV's Maw," *Fortune,* 4 May 1981, p. 308.

[54]Sally Bedell Smith, "Reporter's Notebook: Cable Meeting," *The New York Times,* 18 June 1983, p. 48.

doubtedly will follow, but there is an inherent difficulty in using the
Nielsen rating system especially as it applies to cable. Nielsen surveys
measure the number of viewing households, but not the value of specific programs to the viewers—except to the extent that turning the set
to a specific channel is a measure of value. In pay television, the value
of programming, or the measure of intensity of viewer preference, can
partially be measured by the fees paid. Still, "the full range and intensity of consumer preferences" cannot be truly reflected since, once
again, a viewer's preferences are shown by his or her payment of a fee
for an entire channel of programs.[55] The only real way to measure
viewer preference accurately is in a pay-per-program capacity, such as
those now offered through the Qube system, Subscription Television
(STV) like SelecTV of Los Angeles, and the videocassette and videodisc which actually allow individual products to be sold or rented.[56]

Additional difficulties ensue from commercial network research
which should serve as warning to those representing artistic interests
in the cable television market:

> Hollywood producers complain of being hostages to the numbers yielded
> by network research, on the strength of which networks add and delete
> characters, alter plot lines or discourage bold ideas. Performers are sub-
> jected to 'Q Ratings'—a recognition quotient that puts new talent at a dis-
> advantage. Pilots are presented at Preview House, where audience
> members turn dials to register their reactions. These and other research
> tools, together with the Nielsen ratings have brought the network busi-
> ness to a fever pitch of competition, truncating the lives of most series,
> confusing viewers with abrupt cancellations and replacements and driv-
> ing up costs tremendously.[57]

The cable services themselves have begun to amass some rudimen-
tary demographic information on their subscribers. They have at least
a general idea of who their audience is. They know, first, that the television audience is not a captive one. Its attention must be attracted
and kept. It is also not necessarily the same audience that attends live
events. Arthur Whitelaw, Director of Theatre Development for Home
Box Office, describes HBO subscribers in the following way:

> The typical HBO subscriber is rural, between 18 and 35, lives in a home
> with three children, is a college graduate, and, based on economics alone,

---

[55]Ford, pp. 13-17.

[56]Ibid.

[57]Aspen Institute, p. 21.

does not go to theatre or movies and does not buy books. The HBO subscriber watches television. He grew up with television and that is what he
does for recreation.[58]

Showtime's subscribers are "high school-educated, have incomes
of $15,000 and up, and the median age is 34."[59] The subscriber family
is "usually blue collar, with two paychecks."[60] Showtime viewers are
among the heaviest of all television, watching approximately 12 percent more often than they did before pay television.[61] An audience
profile conducted by Showtime indicated that television is the main
entertainment of its typical subscriber and a "sample of 1500 subscribers revealed that among 11 categories of desired programming, at the
top were Broadway and off-Broadway shows and Las Vegas-style
acts—that is, programs with a perceived ticket value.[62]

The audience for CBS Cable was referred to by Vice President of
Programming and Development Jack Willis as "an upscale audience."[63] Liz Oliver of ABC Video Enterprises (a parent company of
ARTS) describes their audience as light television viewers between 25
and 45 years of age who watch television more than twice a week for
special events, many of whom are opera fanatics. The ratio of male to
female viewers is fairly even, as against viewers of the Public Broadcasting System whom she defines as primarily female and over 55.[64]

Many of these rough audience profiles, sketchy as they are, are descriptive of mainly rural audiences. As urban franchises for cable are
awarded, these profiles are beginning to change. Projections for 1986
give the following information:

- Approximately 85 million homes in the U.S. will have television
  sets.
- Approximately 55 million homes will be passed by cable.

---

[58]Beck, p. 23.

[59]Ibid., p. 25.

[60]Aspen Institute, p. 22.

[61]Ibid., pp. 15–16.

[62]Ibid., p. 22.

[63]Beck, p. 29.

[64]Volunteer Lawyers for the Arts Conference, Discussion Group, 20 May
1982.

- Approximately 30 million will subscribe to cable.
- There will be approximately 30 million pay subscribers.[65]

In addition to these projections about cable are estimates about Subscription Television (STV), Multi-point Distribution Service (MDS)—both expected to fade eventually as competitors—and Direct Broadcast Satellite (DBS), expected to reach between 10 and 20 million homes not serviced by cable.[66]

The possibility of reaching such a tremendous number of people has not gone unnoticed by artists or arts institutions. Institutions are well aware of the exposure they can generate through a television broadcast, and the boost such a broadcast can give to their normal fund-raising activities. Artists, perhaps for the first time, are beginning to address their audience in television terms. Pioneer video artist Nam June Paik learned, after ten years of working with the Public Broadcasting System,

> that you must target your audience. When you're an artist you're not supposed to think about those things. Artists are taught, we are trained, only to talk, never to listen. This is the whole avant-garde movement since Picasso. . . . Yet suddenly you are confronted with a situation of making television programs for an undefined, individual, and unlimited audience.[67]

Artists who choose to try to reach the prime time mass audience may have to make certain compromises.

> If the goal is prime time, the parameters of that mentality must be understood—for example, how network TV censors itself by dictating the kinds of situation[s] that are acceptable to show and the points of view and interests which must be served in their programs. It is essential to consider how much the demand for 'entertainment value' may destroy the artist's initial conception.[68]

Artists and institutions that understand such restrictions must also understand that those currently involved in the cable industry are in-

---

[65]Beck, p. 6. "Subscribers" in this instance are counted according to the service to which they subscribe—one person, therefore, can represent a number of subscription services.

[66]Ibid., pp. 6–7.

[67]White, p. 44.

[68]Ibid., p. 47.

terested first, foremost, and perhaps exclusively, in making a profit. Whatever makes the biggest profit for the least investment will serve their needs. This means that the nourishment and nurturing of creative talent to create a kind of television that departs radically from the norm of mediocrity will not be forthcoming in the near future. Certainly the hiring of a staff of creative people to produce a series of quality shows that occurred in the early 1950s on commercial television has not happened since.

Some feel that cable is the "medium of plenty" in its multiplicity of outlets and that cultural programming should carve out a territory from the beginning so that audiences will view it as an essential component to the technology itself. Others feel that culture is one of the few kinds of programming that does not threaten commercial network affiliates who may not look kindly on their parent organizations creating ventures in direct competition with them.[69]

A lot rests on the audience or market for the work itself. And it should be remembered that this audience, as described by the services themselves, did not grow up with a traditional grounding in the arts. For many of them, the visual media are more real than the live event since they have been exposed to television, radio, film, records, and tape. For them, an experience is framed by the box, not the proscenium. Artists and institutions seeking to translate material to cable television have more than a new technology to deal with, they have a whole new audience to reach, to capture, to convert.

But what of the "other audience" for arts and culture on television, the one that some call the "elitist audience," the ones for whom television is not their main form of entertainment? According to recent survey research, "the likely audience for cultural programming uses other media heavily, watches television selectively, and accounts for only about 16–17 percent of all viewers. Its members already have many other leisure-time options—and money to spend on them."[70]

Elitists do not question whether or not cultural programming should be included on television: they assume that it should.

> For the elitist, the issue is clear-cut. Cultural programming is a necessary component of a civilized society: It furthers the artistic and social life of the

---

[69]Leland L. Johnson, *Cable Television and the Question of Protecting Local Broadcasting* (Santa Monica, California: Rand Corporation, 1970), 5–595–MF, p. 21.

[70]Aspen Institute, p. 45.

community. High-quality programming can improve the tastes of viewers by leading them to new artistic and cultural experiences. It may also, by setting an example and cultivating the market, improve the quality of commercial fare.[71]

Nevertheless, no matter how worthy the ideals, the 16–17 percent figure that represents cultural viewers will not take precedence over the percentage of viewers who represent the profiles of Home Box Office, Showtime, and the other cable networks.

In addition, while the potential audience for cable television numbers is in the millions, few cable services can claim those numbers now. One economic theory holds that the mass media have suffered from the same "cost disease" that has produced larger and larger deficits for performing arts institutions. While the switch from live performance to broadcast is most certainly the best example of productivity growth in the arts in the twentieth century—a single televised performance by a regional theatre, for example, can suddenly find its audience of 2500 transformed into one of 2 1/2 million—some claim that the one-time increase in audience is not enough. What is needed is an increase with each performance, one that may be gradual, but continuous.

While the initial burst of audience growth is likely to give a boost to the arts, it must be remembered that a high percentage of total broadcast activity in the arts is in performance costs. Performance costs will continue to rise as the price of human talent rises and there is really no cost-efficient way to eliminate such costs—one cannot ask the orchestra to "double up" on instruments, or to play Beethoven's Fifth Symphony "a little faster." At the same time that performance costs are rising, cost-saving expenses are extinguishing themselves—the actual cost of showing a film or videotape an additional number of times (exclusive of performance fees and creative costs) is a fraction of the original production cost.[72]

Another argument runs this way: if, after 25 years of "dedicated hoopla" through national, regional, and local arts activities, audiences are still not sufficient for our arts institutions, it is unlikely that they will necessarily appear for the arts on television. The capacity for

---

[71]Ibid., p. 46.

[72]General discussion on these points with economist William Baumol at Columbia University's School of the Arts, 17 February 1982.

turning "five thousand dollars worth of gate receipts into ten thousand dollars worth of expenses" may simply translate the deficits of live arts organizations into another medium.[73]

The economics of television coupled with the desirability of arts programming may require eventual subsidy for arts and cultural programming under the same rationale that our arts institutions are frequently funded, that they are social and public goods, things that are valuable beyond their economic worth.[74] Should such subsidy occur, the arts on television may be one step removed from the pressures of the commercial marketplace. Already impervious to critical reviews as a measure of success, the arts cablecast, if subsidized, runs the risk of ignoring consumer preferences as well. At the same time, it may provide more room for experimental work just as in many of our subsidized performing institutions.

Perhaps our most vivid precedent is public television, where "non-economic programming" is supported, but where economic constraints have resulted in less and less original arts programming and a plethora of foreign material.[75] In desperate need for new funding sources, public television is beginning to place its emphasis on membership, a strategy John Goberman, Director of Media Development for Lincoln Center, calls "pay television by guilt."[76]

COSTS: THE ECONOMIC REALITY

While the marketplace has yet to determine what kinds of programming are economically viable for cable television, it is imperative that arts groups that are considering entry into this marketplace familiarize themselves with the actual costs of production and with the realities of financial return on their artistic investment. The dreams for money to erase the continually increasing deficits of arts organizations are, in the short run at least, exactly that—dreams. A 1982 study by the National Economic Research Associates estimates the potential earnings

---

[73]David Earle, "The Video Boom: Does It Mean Big Money for the Arts?" *American Arts*, 11 (September 1980), p. 20.

[74]Aspen Institute, p. 46.

[75]Ibid., p. 47.

[76]NYC Commission for Cultural Affairs, "Self Help: Earned Income Opportunities for Cultural Organizations," Conference Proceedings, 26 January 1982, p. 28.

to all performing companies from cultural cable networks at $16.8 million in 1990—in 1980 the budget for the National Endowment for the Arts was $154.4 million.[77] The "big bucks fantasy" of the small arts group turning overnight into a financially solvent operation through a deal with cable television has begun to give way to a longer-range strategy. Exposure, publicity, the use of cable broadcast as a platform for future fund-raising on a regional or even a national scale, and the careful consideration of matters of product control, ancillary rights, and other markets like videocassette and videodisc have replaced the expectation for large and immediate financial rewards.

There are precedents in public television like the Boston Symphony Orchestra's "Evening at Symphony" that provide just enough added revenue and national exposure to give hope to groups confronting the new technology for the first time. Nevertheless, the new wave of performing arts television is not yet a decade old. As soon as television learned to maximize its profits in the early 1960s, the arts began to disappear from commercial television. It was not until the first telecast of *Live from Lincoln Center* in 1976 that public television gave the arts a new foothold. Had the board of Lincoln Center been a little less conservative, they might have listened to a young cellist turned arts manager named John Goberman who for two years researched the possibilities for the performing arts on television that led to that live telecast. Goberman also suggested very early on putting a satellite dish on the roof of Lincoln Center so that the complex could begin a cable network of its own. When transponders, or channels, were cheap, and the field wide open, Lincoln Center could have been the first on the block to develop an arts network. A conservative board vetoed the idea and just a few years later, in 1981, a seven-year lease for one transponder, payable in advance, was sold for approximately $14 million.[78] The role of the board of a nonprofit arts institution entering the new technologies should not be overlooked. An arts organization that plans to act as its own producer, as Lincoln Center does, had best make sure of the board's willingness to make up costs and liabilities incurred for any number of emergency situations, including going over budget.

Since that first *Live From Lincoln Center* broadcast, costs have risen

---

[77]Steltzer and Alpert, Report Highlights.

[78]Class discussion with Richard Baker, Associate Director of Media Development and freelance producer, *Live From Lincoln Center*, Columbia University, School of the Arts, 23 November 1981.

dramatically. Most cable companies acquire more than they originate because of such costs. Much work in the symphonic and operatic fields is obtained from Europe where it is cheaper and often adds a "touch of class" to the presenting network. The reverse pattern is true with some American works, most notably modern dance and some of the larger musical events like Lincoln Center's special evening with Joan Sutherland, Marilyn Horne, and Luciano Pavarotti. A program acquired from another source is not only cheaper than producing original material, but it "needs less promotion, and is a safer way to guarantee an audience."[79]

Production costs for original arts programming on cable television run from $100,000 to $400,000 and up per production.[80] Lincoln Center raises $2 million a year to produce *Live From Lincoln Center*. Each show costs between $200,000 and $300,000 and each time a constituent company is broadcast it receives a $35,000 fee.[81] A recent Twyla Tharp piece cost CBS Cable $300,000 to produce. Michael Bronson, Media Department Director of the Metropolitan Opera, quotes rough costs for 1982–83 *Live From the Met* programs:

> . . . the average cost is roughly $400,000 to get on the air including the cost of transmission for the radio simulcast. Above the line costs range from $120,000 to $150,000. This includes fees to company, stage hands, and other technical personnel. We don't make any money; we cover our administrative costs. We do, however, own it totally, so whatever other opportunities exist for those properties come back to us. We have netted $100,000 to $200,000 each of the last two years on that.[82]

Although these figures can give arts groups an idea of the general range of costs, they are unrealistic for several reasons. First, costs depend on who is producing the particular film or tape. Institutions generally have the capability of raising money to cover such projects.

---

[79]Aspen Institute, p. 7.

[80]Obviously, these are average figures. Works of independent producers may sometimes be a bit lower; special events may go much higher. One Dance in America program for public television was reputed to cost $800,000 since the choreographer insisted on going abroad to record a live foreign orchestra, instead of using pre-recorded music.

[81]The constituent companies of Lincoln Center that participate in *Live From Lincoln Center* are the New York Philharmonic Orchestra, The New York City Opera, the New York City Ballet, and the American Ballet Theatre. The Metropolitan Opera produces its own *Live From the Met*.

[82]Beck, p. 51.

While the larger ones have separate media departments, they are often mandated not to compete for funds with the ongoing programs of the institution. For the independent producer, network costs do not necessarily equal actual costs, since the independent does not usually have access to all the in-house facilities and services of a large institution. Second, costs depend on how the production is shot. Videotape is cheaper than film. "Live" performances are cheaper than edited ones and cheaper than productions shot in a studio. Third, costs depend on the property and the art form—a six-character, one set light comedy by Neil Simon will probably have lower original production costs than a production of *Aida*. The first might be shot in a studio, the second probably not. Fourth, costs depend on a number of "rights." One of the deciding factors in a great deal of cable programming is the availability of the rights to produce or show it. Works in the public domain are particularly in favor since they require no payments to the author (and no opinion from the author, either). In some productions, the Broadway musical, for example, the rights may be owned by several people—author, producer, composer, lyricist. The first cost the cable service is interested in is the cost of those rights.

Once the rights to the property are obtained, aesthetic and financial considerations begin to merge. Frequently, independent producers bring the finished product to the networks and the creative part of the work is a fait accompli. But for many arts institutions, either the live production is seen onstage as the prototype of the televised product, or an idea is brought in and a development deal is established to develop a shooting outline. Sometimes, the cable network puts up money to develop the idea or turn it into a co-production with another entity. In all cases, the network tries to obtain and retain as much control as possible.

Aesthetic demands mean money, especially when artistic personnel are battling to get the best out of the new technology. Arthur Whitelaw explains the conflict in terms of theatre:

> The problem is finding a way to bridge those two worlds, theatre and television, in a way that works on television. There are still a lot of problems when one medium is taped for another, but once they are solved, there's going to be a new art form.[83]

It should be noted that, in certain art forms, technology has begun to serve an ongoing function for recording and sometimes for creative

---

[83]Smith, *Theatre Crafts*, p. 43.

purposes as well. George Balanchine, Alvin Ailey, and Martha Graham have used videotape for recording and study. Twyla Tharp, Gerald Arpino, and Merce Cunningham use videotaped rehearsals to choreograph future work.

One of the most responsible and most respected artists working in cable is Twyla Tharp, who not only negotiated a precedent-setting deal with CBS Cable, but made her own scratch tapes of the dances to be shot prior to shooting. These scratch tapes allowed her to pre-design and choreograph the shots themselves before incurring television studio costs. The procedure, which Tharp calls putting the show together "through the camera, not in the cutting room," cost Tharp money, but it also provided an aesthetically finer product.[84]

In producing *Baker's Dozen, Short Stories,* and *Bach Duet,* Tharp insisted that she be the director. Producer Merrill Brockway who had worked with her in public television and had recommended her to CBS Cable, agreed. CBS Cable's financial investment of $300,000 might normally have given it total control over the production. Tharp argued that all the pre-production costs—choreography, having the dances, dancers, costumes, and other elements "ready" and pre-tested on live audiences, extra rehearsal time, lighting design, even dancing shoes—equaled at least $300,000. She fought for co-production status. Due to one interpretation of FCC rulings co-production was not possible, but instead the production was presented by CBS Cable in association with the Twyla Tharp Dance Foundation. Although CBS Cable does own the rights to the material, the Tharp Foundation has reversionary rights after a certain period of time.[85]

This example of negotiation is exceedingly important in a field where the rule is for the artist and company to gain exposure and some initial fee, and the network to reap profits forever after. Although the total control desired by Tharp was not possible, strides were made so that at least a shared production was possible. Directors and choreographers used to having total control over their companies find such negotiations extremely difficult. Playwrights whose works are adapted from the stage to the small screen have difficulty relinquishing their authority, too. Playwright/director Jay Broad tells of the time his play, *Conflict of Interest,* was being taped for Showtime. His

[84]Holly Brubach, " 'Counter to the World at Large,' " *American Arts,* 12 (May 1981), p. 17.

[85]Conversation with Barbara Hauptman, Manager of Operations, Theatre Development Fund and former manager of the Tharp company, 16 November 1981. See discussion of reversionary rights later in this chapter.

experience illustrates the conflict many artists feel when aesthetic interests are pitted against financial ones:

> I was in the booth as the time was getting tighter and tighter, when the director said, 'We have to shoot that shot over,' and the producer said, 'No, we'll just have to go with it. We don't have time.' This had happened 10 or 12 times that day, so I said 'No, listen, if we can't do the thing right, let's just stop the production. Everyone just stop!' And, because someone in the booth had said 'stop,' everyone backed away from the controls. The producer said, quite rightfully, 'This man does not have the right to stop this production.' And she was absolutely right, so everyone went back to the controls. I finally thought to myself, the only way I can stop this is by throwing myself across the monitors, so they won't be able to see to continue. And at that point, I said to myself, 'That's insane!' so I left, and they went on. This is not critical of them, as it all turned out pretty well, but just to say you must understand clearly who is in control. If you cannot retain control, don't invest your soul in the project.[86]

Lee Breuer, associate artistic director of the experimental theatre group, Mabou Mines, says something similar, "If you give up artistic control, give it all up, take the bucks and run. And if you don't, you might as well keep it all and lose your shirt."[87]

For independent producers, making and bringing in the finished product is probably the least cost-effective way they can operate, but unless have established reputations, it may be the only way the networks will deal with them. People often discourage independents from developing properties on their own, since they run the risk of creating material that cannot be broadcast. Financing can sometimes be obtained by early association with a network or with a videodisc or videocassette distributor. The distributor's involvement from the start gives a greater assurance of distribution of the product. Institutions, of course, raise money as part of their annual or even a separate budget, to cover the costs of media production and broadcast. Independents, depending on how they are organized, might do the same thing and frequently independent producers can take an investment tax credit equalling a certain percentage of the direct U.S. production cost.[88]

Because of the tremendous expense involved in the production of

---

[86]Beck, p. 56.

[87]Volunteer Lawyers for the Arts Conference, 20–21 May 1982.

[88]Ibid.

original programming, costs are often shared. Local stations tend to produce low-budget programs in order to meet FCC licensing requirements, but co-owned stations like Group W and Metromedia and separate stations that pool programming funds like those in public television can afford to be a bit more ambitious. The larger multi-system cable operators like those that own Showtime and Home Box Office can finance programs "for which they can guarantee a local outlet."[89] Cooperatively funded syndication is another cost-sharing method and the pay television networks now support a small volume of original programming for relatively low cost. The trend toward such programming may be encouraged with the growth of multi-pay cable systems where one system offers several full-channel pay services.[90]

Another financial option is co-production. In co-production there is an "advance plan for exhibition in more than one outlet or market"; each exhibitor contributes a certain amount of up-front pre-production financing even though the production itself may be controlled by a single entity.[91] A co-production might be financed by a pay cable network, public television and a videodisc firm.

Determining a budget is something the independent producer or the arts institution often does with the cable network, although it is wise to get the advice of an outside expert to familiarize oneself with costs and going rates before approaching a network. Frequently, as much as one-third of the budget is for "above the line" costs—rights, fees to talent, and support staff directly involved in the production, the TV producer and director, and consultants. "Below the line" costs include payment for studio space, sets, lights, costumes, production personnel, makeup, graphics, and post-production editing. In addition, sometimes "recognition fees" are paid—for example, a fee to a famous lighting designer who designed the original production even though the production is re-lit for television. Sometimes the company gets a fee for items like sets and costumes that are used in the TV production.[92]

In balancing creative needs with what the cable producer can or will afford, the budget needs to consider such items as number of cameras, special lighting, film or videotape (if the production remains

---

[89]Aspen Institute, p. 9.

[90]Ibid., pp. 9–11.

[91]Ibid., pp. 11–12.

[92]Volunteer Lawyers for the Arts Conference, 20–21 May 1982.

edited or unedited, shot in a studio, shot on a proscenium stage), the producer's profit, and the payments and fees for union members. Additionally, independent producers and small arts organizations need to be aware of a common payment procedure: one-third of the total negotiated fee is delivered upon signing the contract, one-third when a rough-cut is delivered, and one-third upon delivery of the final product. In the larger cable companies, it may take between 60 and 90 days to process the payment; for small arts organizations with a cash flow problem this can be devastating.[93]

Some pointers on budgeting are offered by Stuart Rekant, Vice President of Business Affairs for Home Box Office:

> A number of problems may arise in budgeting. Lighting is often underestimated in terms of both cost and need. Often the number of rehearsal days needed is underestimated. People sometimes do not allow for the time required to re-block and rehearse for a taping. A show may work well on stage, but may be too long for television. Always secure an agreement with the author that the show can be cut to a desired length for television. If the show is cut, bridging techniques may be required and they will cost additional money, so make budgetary allowances for this as well as the cutting itself. If the show is being taped with an audience, who gets the gate? Is there a gate, or is it an invited audience? What kind of look do you want your audience to have? . . . All of these issues need to be considered in your production plans.[94]

As in many areas of agreement in the commercial sector, almost everything is negotiable and depends on what kind of deal is made.

MAKING DEALS

BROKERS AND REPRESENTATIVES   While the quality and desirability of the artistic product are of course important, many artists and institutions find it difficult to negotiate terms with cable companies no matter how worthy they think their product is. A group of brokers or middlemen has emerged which represents both individuals and companies. Some of these brokers, like ELM Video Theatre, agree to represent an arts institution from its initial thoughts about cable through the distribution of the final product. A broker can present an

---

[93]Ibid.

[94]Beck, p. 53.

arts institution with the kinds of production options available, as well as the kinds of financing. He can research the backgrounds of any outside independents interested in co-producing, advise the arts institution on a step-by-step plan of action, work with a cable service and the arts institution to design the optimum "package" for television including stars, directors, and designers, and can make suggestions regarding ownership rights, artistic control, and potential union complications.

The number of brokers or "agents"—who, of course, receive either a percentage of the deal, a fee, or both for their services—has increased dramatically in the last several years. Some of these brokers are attorneys. Since cable negotiations are still so new it is frequently a handful of attorneys that are most familiar with recent rulings about copyright, ownership, ancillary and other rights which will determine the future remuneration for the arts institution. If an attorney is not acting as the broker for the arts institution from the beginning, it is wise to bring one into the negotiations when determining the above issues.

The hiring of such outside professionals may begin to make it clear to the arts institution that a certain amount of capital will have to be spent in order to achieve a production on television. This capital may be returned to the arts institution as cash—but probably not for a long time—or, it may be viewed as a long-range investment to free up other moneys in future, such as contributed funds from corporations and foundations, or from individuals who can now be reached nationally through a single televised performance.

Several of the larger arts institutions like the American Ballet Theatre and the Metropolitan Opera, have created separate departments for media development, but even they have limited resources and do not want to disrupt their normal activity too much. Additionally, many of them realize that it is important to have another agenda besides money. That agenda might include a desire for a visual record of an experience, particularly if it is a company's "signature piece," or a need for institutional exposure, plus a promotional tape to be used in fund-raising. Accompanying this motivational agenda, however, should be a distinct understanding of the kinds of rights available to the artist or the institution when making cable television deals.

RIGHTS   the first thing a cable network is interested in is who owns the rights to the property and how much it will cost the network to buy those rights. Legal documentation is required to verify ownership rights, which may belong to the company itself or may be divided among a number of different people—author, choreographer, composer, and even people to whom certain rights have been sold like the investors in the Broadway production of a show. In the visual arts, artwork that is filmed or videotaped may be subject to certain reproduction restrictions.

Usually, after a certain period of time, most rights revert to the authors of material,[95] but it is possible, for example, for an author to own some rights (stage rights) and not others (ancillary rights). In music, there are "grand rights" (for a "series of songs which are part of a whole dramatic work like *South Pacific*") and "small rights" (for a single song).[96] In the visual arts, such rights may belong to the institution or individual that owns the work—a museum, for example, or a private collector.

The cable network is only interested in dealing with the owner of the rights and it is possible that the owner may have no artistic interest, past, present, or future in the artistic product. This is a perfect illustration of the treatment in the United States of artworks as proerty which lack the moral and ethical rights of authorship they enjoy in some European countries. Cable networks are fond of dealing with works in the public domain since it is easier for them to buy the rights and to obtain control of the work. Still, some properties in the public domain in the United States are not in the public domain outside the country.

After the original pre-production rights are secured and negotiations with the cable network begin, post-production rights depend on who is financing the production. If the network is fully financing a production, it has what attorneys like to call a "possessory interest" and will try to secure all post-production rights. Nevertheless, steps can be built into a contract that arrange for payment to the arts institution after all production costs are recouped. Many different kinds of production arrangements are possible including the previously mentioned co-production, which may involve foreign as well as domestic entities.

In determining the appropriate balance between financial investment and rights, it is important for the artist or the arts institution to consider a number of points. How many uses are being made of this particular production and to how many markets will it be transmitted? What is the size of these markets and how many viewers will be

---

[95]"Authors" is used here comprehensively to mean the creator of the initial material.

[96]Beck, p. 36.

reached? Potential foreign and domestic markets include basic cable, pay cable (also known as pay television), Subscription Television (STV), Multi-Point Distribution Systems (MDS), Direct Broadcast Satellites (DBS), Optical Videodisc ("Laservision"), Capacitance Videodisc ("Selectavision"), VHS and Beta Tape Cassette, broadcast and secondary broadcast showings (UHF and VHF), separate sound-track records and audiotapes, non-theatrical showings (in-flight air-lines, closed circuit television, educational and instructional television), 16 millimeter film, derivative works, merchandise based on the product, and "future uses"—uses that have not yet been de-vised or exploited.[97] While foreign as well as domestic markets must be considered, foreign markets are often broken down into a number of geographic areas, each with different rates and negotiations.

An initial right to be determined is the one called sequence of play. Sequence of play means simply where the product is first seen and what follows after that first showing. Is it shown first on pay televi-sion, then on an airline, then on a videodisc, and finally on foreign free television? How many times can it be shown over a certain period—six times in one year? What about holding fees—the money paid during the period of time a production is held after the initial re-lease without being used? And what about exclusivity? Home Box Of-fice offers non-exclusive contracts during the contract period; ABC's ARTS does not.[98] CBS Cable reportedly made a deal for a Twyla Tharp production to play for 20 plays or two years, whichever came first, to recoup their investment and then agreed to pay Tharp a fee each time the production played after that.[99]

While negotiating sequence of play rights it is important that an arts group avoid a deal in which it would be competing with itself. Joseph Papp's televised version of *Much Ado About Nothing* hurt the box office for the live show. Pushing this self-competition to an ex-treme is a statement by Roger Englander, Senior Producer of Music at CBS Cable:

> . . . live is dead. The performance still has to exist, but have you ever con-sidered what it takes to actually go to a performance? It costs a lot: $50 at the Met if you want to get a good seat. You have to brave the crowds and

[97]New York State Council on the Arts, Film and Video Conference for Cul-tural Institutions, Cable and Pay TV Panel, Outline of Remarks by M. Scott Vayer, 1982.

[98]Volunteer Lawyers for the Arts Conference, 20–21 May 1982.

[99]Discussion with Barbara Hauptman, 16 November 1981.

possible muggings, and you have to dress, that is, wear a tie. I'd much rather stay at home and watch some television if it is well done.[100]

Conversely, some arts groups feel a televised performance will enhance their live work: the Paul Taylor Dance Company's spot on public television's Dance in America was aired in conjunction with their season at City Center in New York.

Another important right focuses on the amount of time the cable deal covers. Deals "in perpetuity" are to be avoided. Allowing a cable network control of a production for between three and five years— offering them a several year "window"—still leaves room for sale to other markets—motion picture, disc, cassette. Additionally, deals that require exclusivity from an organization over a number of years rather than for a specific product prevent the arts institution from maximizing its profit potential. It should be noted that the home-video market in Europe is more developed than in the United States where only about 3 percent of American homes have a Beta Tape recorder, VHS or cassette recorder, or a videodisc player. The home-video market is expected to succeed in this country particularly in areas where cable is unavailable. Once a production is made, transferring it to another medium is relatively simple so that discs and cassettes may carry essentially the same material as the cable networks. Individual discs and cassettes also provide the possibility for true measuring of consumer interest since the intensity of preference for individual programs is reflected in the purchase or rental of the individual disc or cassette. This measuring capability should allow more specific client-oriented programming.[101]

The videodisc is essentially a record that plays images, a "video record." Cheaper and with sharper quality than the videocassette, it is being treated more like a publishing item than a broadcast one as disc catalogs and marketing schemes are developed. Almost as it appeared on the market, a more sophisticated disc was developed called the optical laser disc. In the optical laser disc, a laser beam instead of a needle or stylus "plays the record." The hardware for optical laser technology is becoming more and more sophisticated. It will offer systems that get better and cheaper as time goes by and will allow interactive two-way programming as well as slow-motion, stop-action,

---

[100]Beck, p. 44.

[101]Volunteer Lawyers for the Arts Conference, 20–21 May 1982.

single-frame sequencing features, two-channel stereo, and a number of other features.[102]

What the disc lacks most particularly is the programming, or software, to accompany the hardware. At present, discs and cassettes will be playing the same kinds of specials and movies as each other and as cable, MDS, DBS, and STV. In an attempt to differentiate themselves from the competition, disc producers have begun to market the interactive disc as an educational tool. Among their potential clients are the Metropolitan Museum of Art, the Boston Museum of Fine Arts, the Chicago Museum of Science and Industry, and the Jerusalem Music Center. Museums see the disc as a complement or supplement to standing exhibits. Places like the Jerusalem Music Center might use a disc as a visual record for its hundreds of master classes now recorded on film and tape.[103] It is possible that videodiscs will be sold along with scarves and sculptural reproductions through the museum book store or gift shop. Even more possibilities present themselves with the hookup of the videodisc to the computer, which has happened in the research laboratories but is not yet in the marketplace. Such a combination might allow programming that is more personalized than other technologies and that offers both information and entertainment.

While certain factions in the arts and culture industry prefer certain kinds of technology—the movie industry favors the disc, for example, since it is extremely hard to make pirated copies of it—many potential purchasers are holding back until the hardware revolution calms down. Research in Japan and other countries puts new hardware on the market every year. At this writing, CBS has applied to the FCC for a direct broadcast satellite that uses high-definition television (HDTV), a system researched and developed by the Japanese for over a decade. In HDTV, the current 525 lines of vertical resolution jump to 1,125 lines per frame, accompanied by improvements in color rendition and wide screen aspect ratio. Many say this system equals the quality of 35 millimeter film.[104] Consumer confusion over the hardware alone creates a certain trepidation in buyers: afraid that they will purchase a machine that will be outdated, outmoded, or useless

---

[102]Michael Schrage, "Home Electronics: Images of the '80s," *New York Magazine*, 17 November 1980, pp. 46, 52–53.

[103]Ibid.

[104]R. B. Cohn, "ABCs of DBS," *Home Video*, May 1982, p. 48.

within a few years, they may buy nothing at all.[105] The lack of software reinforces such a choice.

REVERSIONARY RIGHTS   No matter what system an arts institution uses to disseminate its product through the new technology, the rights which are perhaps its most important are reversionary rights. These are the rights that state that after the time agreed to in the contract, the ownership of the work returns to the artist or the institution. This is one of the rights often called an "in-kind" right.[106] Since almost all cable companies are currently losing money and will therefore not make financial deals that promise the arts institution any immediate (or even long-range) cash remuneration, the arts institution can bargain for certain rights in place of money and in exchange for its product over a limited period of time. These reversionary rights allow the arts institution to seek other distribution outlets for its product.

ANCILLARY RIGHTS   The rights that allow for distribution after the initial outlet are called ancillary rights. Particularly with the constantly changing technology, it is important for arts institutions to plan for the reversionary and at least a percentage of the ancillary rights at the beginning of a negotiation. At the root of much union bargaining is the same hope and inclination that a product may have several different methods of exposure that will enable a number of participants to earn money a number of times for their original participation.

Even with a knowledge of all its rights, a quality product and a good relationship with a cable network, an arts institution has no real model on which to base its negotiation except for the experience of colleagues. No two contracts are alike and industry-wide standards are not yet set in all areas. Each contract depends on the "relative hunger and skill of the negotiators."[107]

In addition to the areas mentioned above, contracts for cable television may include such provisions as: length of the program, where and when the taping or shooting will occur, the number of complimentary seats offered the producer if a live audience is invited to the taping, how the opening and closing credits will read and who will produce them, rights to edit, cut, and dub a program for "time,

---

[105]Schrage, p. 52.

[106]Another "in-kind" right might be partial payment to the arts organization in goods instead of cash.

[107]Beck, p. 21.

broadcast standards and practices, advertising and foreign censor-ship," delivery and uses of promotional and photographic material by the producer, provisions for extraordinary expenses such as rehearsal and overtime costs, rewrites, special costumes and makeup, systems of accounting by both parties, liability insurance, and the producer's agreement to take responsibility for cable residual costs.[108] This last point provides an excellent illustration of the difficulties involved when an arts institution becomes its own producer for the new tech-nology. Each time a show is played, residual and pension and welfare payments must be paid to all the above-the-line personnel according to their union agreements—performers, designers, choreographers, stage directors, musicians, stagehands, and sometimes the company itself. Even if these people are no longer members of the arts institu-tion, they must be tracked down. The strain of this and other respon-sibilities on an institution whose main function is to appear "live" may be too much of a burden on an already deficit-ridden operation.

As important as any right for creating a product is the right to ter-minate its life in the event of contingencies over which the arts institu-tion has no control—death of the star, labor strikes, natural catas-trophes like hurricanes or blizzards that prevent production (called "Acts of God")—and the right to prevent its showing unless it is artis-tically sound. Rights of final review and final edit are difficult for an artist or arts institution to obtain unless a piece is so extraordinary that its worth goes beyond economic realities even for its producers (*Vladimir Horowitz at Carnegie Hall* would be a good example). Even more difficult are rights to take the work off the market at a certain time. Although reversionary rights can guarantee the return of a work to its "author," what if a choreographer, for example, changes his or her direction so radically that it is felt the earlier work, as represented by specific video performances running on pay television, no longer shows the artist to advantage? The ramifications of this kind of a "right" can be extremely far-reaching, since they impinge on the rights of others, particularly the performers who not only make sub-stantial contributions to the work itself but who stand to earn income in the form of residuals each time a sale is made or the televised prod-uct is shown.

UNIONS The unpredictable, difficult nature of union negotiations in the arts in this country as they relate to the new technology have

---

[108]Sample Production Contract, Volunteer Lawyers for the Arts Conference, 20–21 May 1982.

made acquisitions of European properties a frequent occurrence. Copyright laws in many European countries as well as cheaper union payments have contributed to the amount of European programming shown in American markets. While arts unions in the United States generally have reached no firm industry-wide agreements, some unions are more visible and more vocal than others and it is their representatives who are holding out for more than a token piece of the technology pie.

Sometimes provisions for industry-wide deals for public television programs with supplemental riders form the basis of agreements. Sometimes a contract is negotiated between a union and a particular employer like the Metropolitan Opera. For some time, managers of several of the largest American symphony orchestras and opera companies have met with the American Federation of Musicians to create an agreement for audiovisual material. At this writing no agreement has been reached so that these organizations cannot enter into videodisc and cassette agreements. Occasionally, a union negotiates a contract with a cable service, as the American Federation of Musicians did with Bravo.

The rules of the American Federation of Musicians which govern its members who work in non-standard (pay television) television cover a per-musician payment for symphony, opera, and dance musicians. They include provisions for re-use payments, sound track regulations, pension payments, foreign use, rehearsal conditions and payments, radio simulcasts, doubling (musicians who play more than one instrument), makeup, costumes, and music preparation services.[109]

Rights are frequently negotiated only for the first live broadcast or cablecast, requiring a return to the negotiating table for any further distribution arrangements. There are standards now being set up by each union that allow for payment for both the original broadcast or cablecast and residual payments. Some unions, like the Directors Guild of America, are setting up residual payments on a percentage of sales basis. For example, a producer pays the director 15 percent of his or her initial directorial fee for the first $18,000 worth of sales, another 10 percent for the next $20,000 worth of sales, and another 10 percent on the next $10,000 worth of sales. Producers that want the director to be paid off in one shot might offer 35 percent of the initial fee and no

---

[109]Non-Standard Television Agreement, American Federation of Musicians of the United States and Canada, May 1, 1980-May 31, 1982, New York City.

residuals.[110] Other unions, like the American Federation of Musicians, have set up residual payments on a regional basis. For example, a musician gets 20 percent of the original performance fee for a production shown in England, Scotland, Wales, Ireland and the Island of Cyprus, 10 percent of that fee for a production shown in all European countries excluding the above and including Iceland, and 5 percent each for three other categories including Japan and the Orient, Africa, and Latin and South America. If a producer instead wishes to compensate a musician once and once only, he or she can pay the musician 45 percent of the original performance fee.[111]

The Screen Actors' Guild (SAG) and the American Federation of Television and Radio Artists (AFTRA) use the National Code of Fair Practice for Network Television Broadcasting as their basis for negotiation, and add continual updates regarding rates and conditions for broadcasting, pay television, videodiscs, and videocassettes.

Since cable is a repeat medium, union artists realize the potential for payments which are made each time a work is shown. Although designers of sets, costumes, and lighting frequently feel that consultation and compensation for their original work is not at the level it should be, the labor strike of several performers' unions a few years ago included the issue of residual payments from the new technology. While producers are not receiving residuals, stagehands certainly are. The "talent" fighting for their fair share of the product know that the new technology offers possibilities for their work to be played over and over again because the programming simply cannot keep pace with the hardware. Martin Mayer's words from a decade ago still hold true, "All the English-language theatre worth preserving since *Gammer Gurton's Needle* would not fill 5 percent of the time the networks must program each year."[112]

LOCAL ORIGINATION AND PUBLIC ACCESS

Up until this time, cable television, which began as an answer to local and regional reception problems, has retained a commitment to local programming through public access or local origination. As recom-

---

[110]These figures are rough estimates.

[111]Non-Standard Television Agreement, American Federation of Musicians, pp. 10–11.

[112]Martin Mayer, *About Television* (New York: Harper and Row, 1972), p. 404.

mended by the Sloan Commission Report of 1970, public access channels have become part of the local cable franchises awarded in large
metropolitan areas.[113] Since the time on these channels is free and offered on a first-come, first-served basis, problems of administration
and coordination abound. While there is some censorship of material
which the local cable network regards as obscene, the democratic nature of access may mean a lack of judgment regarding the quality of
what is shown. This is not to say that network television airs quality
material simply because its system is autocratic, but that the goals of a
public access channel can allow work to be shown for reasons that
have nothing to do with art.

Manhattan's two franchised cable companies, Manhattan Cable
and TelePrompTer,[114] have provided two public access channels since
July 1971. At this writing there are at least six weekly programs pro-
duced by artists that show programs of artists: "Soho Television,"
"Communications Update," "Some New Faces," "Potato Wolf,"
"Anthology Film Archives," and "Andy Warhol's T.V."[115] "Soho
Television" shows artists' tapes and has been on cable weekly in New
York since 1978. It is currently at work on six programs called "The
Live Show" which will incorporate live and taped performances, interviews, narratives, and electronic animations. "Potato Wolf" is produced by an artists space called Collaborative Projects (Colab). Each
program costs approximately $90 and many of them, shot live, are ex-
perimental, original, and somewhat uncontrollable as to direction and
format.[116] The low-budget, low-profile nature of local origina-
tion/public access television acts in one sense as a liberating force for
artists, since it frees them "from the pressures of achieving visual
slickness and technical perfection."[117] But, at the same time, if the
work is successful it may aim toward exposure on pay television.

In its capacity as a transmitter or translator of institutional work,
the local cable company cannot usually afford to pay union salaries or
studio and other costs related to a network production. In addition,
limited money and staff as well as the mandate to respond to a variety

---

[113]Sloan Commission on Cable Communications, *On the Cable: The Television of
Abundance* (New York: McGraw Hill, 1971), p. 127.

[114]Group W, Westinghouse, which recently purchased TelePrompTer for $641
million, is now the third largest cable television system.

[115]White, p. 43.

[116]White, p. 45.

[117]Ibid., p. 44.

of community and ethnic concerns make local cable companies turn to arts groups that are not unionized, offering them exposure and a copy of the videotape for promotional or archival purposes.[118] Examples of such programming include Manhattan Cable's documentaries on Ballet Hispanico and on the history of jazz in Harlem, "Looking for the Pretty Notes," as well as its live call-in show with modern American artists and New York City's former Commissioner of Cultural Affairs, Henry Geldzahler.[119] One problem with local origination arts programming is cited by producer/director Merrill Brockway, using ballet as an example:

> . . . excellence is judged by the standards of the New York City Ballet. If the Milwaukee Ballet appears, it is immediately in competition with the New York City Ballet. Viewers do not separate and do not apologize for regions. They only understand quality.[120]

Obviously, the diversity of what can be programmed on public access television is great. In addition to the potential of having work shown, arts groups in certain areas may have access to production facilities, and production and editing equipment. Cable companies competing for franchises in New York's four boroughs outside Manhattan were fond of promising access and origination studios. Once programs are made, however, there is often a problem with regular scheduling—necessary for any group to develop its own audience—and with a listing of programs to be shown. Many newspapers refuse to list public access programming, and the chaotic scheduling problems of some cable companies produce inaccurate listings and disgruntled viewers. In this area, commercial cable companies also receive short shrift from nationally oriented publications that argue about the publication's responsibility to such a small audience. But commercial cable companies are at least printing their own monthly program guides.

Because of limited financial and technical resources and the competition for local programming, local arts programming often appears erratically. Now that urban areas are being wired for cable, the whole concept of local programming may change if major arts groups decide they can afford to be shown on public access television instead of com-

---

[118]Volunteer Lawyers for the Arts Conference, 20–21 May 1982.

[119]Ibid.

[120]NYC Commission for Cultural Affairs, p. 18.

mercial cable. (Perhaps public access television will then become a
stepping stone to commercial markets, a place to "try out" the material first.) One of the most frequently cited failures of public access
television was TelePrompTer's inability to transmit the New York City
Opera in 1972. In that year, the New York City Opera offered
TelePrompTer the right to live transmission of a season's performances. The price of $25,000 per performance, or $1 million for the
44-performance season, was low by broadcast standards. Yet it was
impossible for TelePrompTer to meet.[121]

Linking cable systems together in a geographic area to provide
jointly sponsored programming might provide more varied offerings
and a sharing of costs. Project Metrolink is a study determining the
feasibility of just such a scheme in New York State. It has also been
suggested that a nonprofit arts institution might provide certain "educational" services for a public access channel either for a fee or
through a subsidiary that allows the nonprofit organization part ownership.[122]

The involvement of basic cable networks with material that was
previously directed only at public access may also affect the audience
for local programming. USA Cable has been showing a program
called "Nightflight" which includes an eight-week series of 15-
minute segments called "The Video Artist." These segments are
shown after midnight on Saturdays.[122] In addition, the Public Broadcasting System's "Video Film Review" on WNET in New York since
1975, and "Artists' Showcase" on WGBH in Boston since 1977
(broadcast not cablecast media) have begun to blur distinctions between what is "appropriate" for public access, public television, and
other markets. This blurring of distinctions is all to the good as artists
begin to cross boundaries between experimental video and commercially marketable material.

While public access television clearly eschews profit as its main
motivation, its goals of community involvement and response to public interest will not necessarily provide quality products. The issue of
quality as it affects the arts product is eminently important not only as
a reflection of the worth of the endeavor but as a precedent for future
televised material. It seems that the arts, trying valiantly to understand and master at least the fundamentals of rapidly changing tech-

---

[121]Adler and Baer, p. 14.
[122]Discussion at Media Alliance of New York State Conference, June 1981.
[123]White, p. 43.

nology, are caught somewhere between commercial standards, where what plays is determined by the number of households, individual viewers or subscribers, and the standards of public access, where a completely democratic selection process allows productions of almost any artistic level to be shown.

The solution of an outlet where intelligent selectivity of product is balanced with an attempt toward quality that does not attempt to reflect commercial standards should already have been found in Public Television. It would be a disservice to try to explain in a paragraph the reasons for Public Television's failure in this area, but several factors have placed PBS in a curious limbo. Difficulties in funding and governance, discussion of the Public Subscriber Network (PSN), and the plethora of foreign programming which is frequently applauded for its foreignness rather than its actual quality are a few of the more salient complaints.[124]

Nevertheless, the strides made for arts groups through their affiliation with Public Television must not be overlooked. Nor should the support and exhibition of work by independent producers. These producers are finally, and only after long struggle, being recognized as resources instead of competitors by producing stations that now find it impossible to house full-time creative and technical staffs. Unfortunately, many of the people responsible for the guidance that shaped some of the better programming for public television have defected to the competition and are now hard at work for commercial cable companies, another blow to public television as it seeks to regain its balance in the broadcast marketplace.

FINAL PAYMENTS

Many involved in the business of the new technology predict that within the next decade only one or two arts television services will exist and these will be run as pay television systems. The continually changing hardware and transmission systems may tend to make cable television a fossil before its time. More than two-thirds of all cable systems have 12 or fewer channels available; although urban systems now under franchise will make 80-channel systems commonplace,

---

[124]Michael Rice, "Public Television: Issues of Purpose and Governance" (New York: Aspen Institute for Humanistic Studies, 1981), p. 22.

this will not happen for several years.[125] At this writing, CBS has requested approval from the Federal Communications Commission to establish "multichannel over-the-air pay television services in five of the nation's biggest media markets"—New York, Los Angeles, Chicago, Philadelphia, and St. Louis. Each of these cities has little cable penetration at this time. Should the CBS request be granted, the over-the-air systems could be established even before cable companies could wire and hook up an area.[126] Each system would be able to carry between 4 and 8 channels of programming and would be distributed through multipoint distribution systems (MDS).

While the change in methods of distribution may have little effect on the arts product, in some cases like videodiscs, the advances in the hardware itself will allow a radically different product to be created. Recent experiments with discs allow control over material through touch-sensitive screens and computerized chairs. Researchers envision an electronic candy store where the speed, color, and even the content of televised material will change almost as quickly as a thought enters the viewer's head.

Labor and related costs will continue to make production difficult but may "enhance the opportunity for entry by less experienced producers."[127] Joint financing will continue and will include a number of international sources. Resources will be pooled in certain areas to avoid duplicating costs and services. Joint marketing, special membership deals, and trading of subscriber lists between institutions and television systems may develop. It is possible, for example, to envision a marketing campaign that urges one to become a subscriber of a pay television service which includes a benefit membership/subscription to the New York City Ballet (and vice versa). Marketing itself will become a more sophisticated and probably more aggressive tool for selling the arts on television.

Outside experts in the form of lawyers, consultants, and independent producers will continue to try to stay on top of the most recent precedents for negotiations, contracts, rights, legislation, and issues. They will most certainly earn money from the new technology. Whether the arts groups themselves will is still an open question.

---

[125]Tony Schwartz, "The Cable-TV Scramble," *The New York Times*, 23 December 1981, sec. C, p. 8.

[126]Andrew Pollack, "CBS Requests Approval for 5 Pay-TV Systems," *The New York Times*, 4 August 1982, sec. D, p. 1.

[127]Aspen Institute, p. 54.

Should an arts group venture into the new technology? In one sense, such a proposition is like asking someone who has just heard of the Wright Brothers whether he will fly to Florida for the winter, or like asking the silent movie producers about the potential for talking pictures. Or perhaps, it is like asking people on radio what they thought of commercial television in the 1940s. In the late 1940s, television was really radio that could be seen as well as heard. As the technology improved and became more affordable for the everyday consumer, television developed on its own until, in 1982, 98 percent of American homes had at least one television set. What also developed after the 1940s, however, was the virtual extinction of arts and cultural programming in favor of the variety show, the situation comedy, the talk show, and a number of other standard offerings in which the names changed but the material remained essentially the same.

The warning should be clear: the technology itself is inevitable and its possibilities have barely been tapped. Clearer pictures, less "snow" and "confetti" (flickering colored specks), better color and audio reception are only the beginning. Already in existence are an "electronic palette" that allows a video artist to " 'paint' on video and produce work that seems to have been made by oils, watercolor, or pen and ink," and scenery created by laser light. Possibilities exist for a camera small enough to be sewn into a dancer's costume or rest on a conductor's podium, and for 3-dimensional holographic television.[128] But an arts group must decide whether venturing into the new technology is something its resources, its finances, its staff, board, and managers can afford, whether it can retain enough rights to make the effort worthwhile, what its motivations and expectations are, and what the costs and benefits are—in human as well as financial terms—to the institution and to the artists involved.

Beyond that there is the call to quality which no amount of democratic public access can achieve and no amount of profit motivation can quell. In the translation and the transmission of the arts to the world through technology it is hoped that quality will be of paramount importance. The words of E. B. White to the first Carnegie Commission on Educational Television provide a challenge worth heeding:

I think television should be the visual counterpart of the literary essay, should arouse our dreams, satisfy our hunger for beauty, take us on jour-

---

[128]Alexis Greene, "The Coming Impact of Technology on the Arts," *The New York Times*, 26 February 1978, sec. 2, pp. 1, 22.

neys, enable us to participate in events, present great drama and music, explore the sea and the sky and the woods and the hills. It should be our Lyceum, our Chatauqua, our Minsky's, and our Camelot.[129]

As exciting and interesting as some of the possibilities are for arts groups to earn income outside their normal fundraising activities, there is tremendous regret at leaving behind a group of sympathetic staff members at various public and private funding agencies who, in many ways and over many years, have nurtured, protected, and encouraged arts activity in this country. The community of small- to medium-sized arts groups found a listening ear among an even smaller group of people — many of whom came from the arts themselves — who made decisions about money in the *support* of art. In the 1980s, the marketplace has changed to one in which money is frequently given in *exchange* for art, and the freedom certain groups experienced seems threatened by measurements made in terms of cold hard cash. Trying to balance their artistic needs with their financial necessities, many groups are caught between becoming solvent by paying the piper who calls the tune or remaining poor but pure.

Since this book was written, more people are hooked in and hooked up to television than ever before. And although a number of the cable services offering the arts as a mainstay of their programming have disappeared, a September 1987 survey by *Consumer Reports* indicates that about 50% of all Americans subscribe to cable TV and that the national average of TV watching is up to 50-60 hours per week.[130]

What has changed is the potential for profit from cable, since a 1984 federal law deregulated local government control over cable prices, and cable companies are now able to charge whatever the market will bear. In areas where only one cable service operates, there is no immediate competition providing incentives to restrain prices. In the 14 cable systems regulated by the city of Los Angeles, the average basic monthly rate increased 78% from 1984 to 1988 from

---

[129] Aspen Institute, p. 59

[130] *Consumer Reports*, September 1987, pp. 547-555.

$9.30 to $16.54; Manhattan saw a 53% increase from $9.75 to $14.95, according to research by Paul Kagan Associates.[131]

HBO, still the biggest of the cable networks, and Showtime continue to focus on a staple of movies, with some concerts and comedy specials. Cinemax and Festival are relatively new siblings of HBO, narrow-casting the market even further to young adults and young people. Showtime's sibling is The Movie Channel, and American Movie Classics features old movies. Referred to as the more "highbrow" channels, Bravo and Arts and Entertainment show theater, opera, dance, music, foreign films, and "culture," A & E importing much of its fare from the British Broadcasting Corporation.

In terms of technology, a debate currently rages over Congressional prohibition of telephone companies owning cable companies. Should the ban be lifted, cable television might be piped into our homes via the telephone wires. Even if this does not occur, it is clear that television is currently the single most accessible medium to the average American household, possibly outdistancing the radio in the purchaser's mind. What former Federal Communications Commission chairman and guru Mark Fowler once called a "toaster with pictures" has drawn in audiences of "channel flippers." According to one report, more than half of the 85.9 million TV households now reached by cable or satellite dishes reflect this restlessness in selecting programs.[132]

Although the issues for arts groups have not changed, they have deepened in the last few years. The widespread and growing use of the video cassette recorder (VCR) raises important questions about copyright protection and piracy, both domestically and in international markets. The rapid sophistication of computer technology provides additional possibilities for the future. The options for arts groups to plug into technology (which will continue to be highly consumer-directed) are many. They range from promotional videos taking a creative lead from the rock-music cable network MTV, to collaborative programming among performing-arts groups, to behind-the-scenes tours of storage and archival areas, registries, and conservation laboratories of museums. One can imagine a time in the near future when subscriptions to live events will be offered through the combined technology of the television, the telephone,

---

[131]Geraldine Fabrikant, "In Free Reign of Cable TV, Fees Are Up," *New York Times*, December 11, 1988, pp. 1 and 46.

[132]Salley Bedell Smith, "New TV Technologies Alter Viewing Habits," *New York Times*, October 9, 1985, C22.

and the computer, where patrons choose the event, pick the exact seat location, and order and pay for their tickets, all from their living rooms.

Perhaps the area to which most attention should be paid is the potential of the technological media to reach the new and growing audiences which our changing demographics will make a reality by the year 2000. Hispanic broadcasters and narrow-casters are heavily invested in this area, particularly in states like California where populations already demand serious programming. Our arts institutions and groups might learn from the media and seek to cooperate with them. Will it be possible to offer a subscription that includes a certain amount of Hispanic cable programming, a certain number of Hispanic movies, and a certain number of *live* Hispanic arts events through a single package and with a single bill?

Finally, a singular and pre-eminent issue for arts organizations is the product itself. Television is the always hungry maw with never enough product to nourish it. Sometimes, from the point of view of the arts and culture, the medium itself seems to trivialize creative intentions, an idea aptly captured in the title of Neil Postman's book on the subject, *Amusing Ourselves to Death*. And the product, it must be noted, has a life of its own on television that it lacks as a live event.

One insidious danger for the arts is the tendency, because of television, for patrons, supporters, funders, and financiers to demand that the arts always reach a broad audience and bring in large numbers of consumers. This is what critic Samuel Lipman calls "Bohème in the Superdome," fostered by a mentality that only understands audiences in terms of the Dallas Cowboys.

The answer for arts and cultural groups to the question, "Is there life after television?" depends very much on the groups themselves. While it is not "old enough to have matched printing's output of junk," television certainly has the potential to do so.[133] It is the responsibility of the arts to address that problem, since television and technology have the potential to reach more people in one sitting than were entertained in the Roman coliseum. The challenge to keep one's balance in a world focused, as Twyla Tharp says, on the "rectangle and the dollar," is a formidable one.

---

[133]Neil Postman, *Amusing Ourselves to Death* (New York: Viking Penguin), 1985, p. 16.

BIBLIOGRAPHY

Aarons, Philip. President, New York City Public Development Corporation. Interview, 28 April 1981.

Adler, Richard, and Baer, Walter S., eds. *The Electronic Box Office: Humanities and Arts on the Cable.* New York: Praeger, 1976.

American Federation of Television and Radio Artists (AFTRA) 1976–1979 National Code of Fair Practice for Network Television Broadcasting plus Exhibit A and Pay TV Supplement. New York: American Federation of Television and Radio Artists, 1976–1979 and 1980.

and/or Reports. Seattle, Washington: and/or, March 1982.

Artech. 1981 Annual Report. Seattle, Washington.

Artists Equity Association of Northern California. *Artists live/work Space: Changing Public Policy.* San Francisco: Artists Equity of Northern California, 1981.

The Artists Foundation. *Artists' Space: A Study of the Development of Artists' Living and Working Space in Boston.* Boston: The Artists Foundation, 1981.

Arts/Boston. Promotional Material. 1982.

Aspen Institute for Humanistic Studies. *Expanding the Choices for Television Viewing.* New York: Aspen Institute, 1981.

Baer, Walter S. *Interactive Television: Prospects for Two-Way Services on Cable.* Santa Monica, Cal.: Rand Corporation, 1971.

Bakan, Joseph D., and Chandler, David L. *Access II: The Independent Producer's Handbook of Satellite Communications.* Washington, D.C.: National Endowment for the Arts, 1980.

Baker, Richard, Associate Director of Media Development. *Live From Lincoln Center.* Lecture, Columbia University, School of the Arts, 23 November 1981.

Ballet, Arthur, and Zesch, Lindy, eds. *The 1978 TCG Conference Report.* New York: Theatre Communications Group, 1978.

Baumol, William. Lecture, Columbia University, School of the Arts, 17 February 1982.

Bay Area Creative Reuse. Publicity Material. San Francisco, California. Winter 1982.

Beck, Kirsten, ed. Conference Proceedings, *Cable Television and the Performing Arts*. New York University, School of the Arts, 5-7 June 1981.

Belth, Stephen. "Cultural Networking." *American Arts* (November 1981): 10-11.

Bernstein, Peter. "The Race to Feed Cable TV's Maw." *Fortune*, 4 May 1981.

Bittker, Boris I., and Rahdert, George K. "The Exemption of Nonprofit Organizations from Federal Income Taxation." *The Yale Law Journal* 85 (January 1976): 301-58.

Brewin, Bob. "Spectrum Wars!" *Village Voice*, 22 June 1982, pp. 69-83.

Brook, Tim, and Maron, Earle. *The Complete Directory to Prime Time Network Shows, 1946-Present*. New York: Ballantine Books, 1979.

Brooks, Gene R. "Arts Amenities in Comprehensive Plans." In *The Arts and City Planning*, pp. 41-57. Edited by Robert Porter. New York: American Council for the Arts, 1980.

Brubach, Holly. " 'Counter to the World at Large.' " *American Arts* (May 1981): 16-19.

California Confederation of the Arts. Proposal Package. Los Angeles. 23 February 1981.

Campbell, Larry, Director, Performing Arts Services, San Francisco, California. Personal letter, 13 May 1982.

Caplin, Lee Evan. "Tax-Exempt Arts Activities With Commercial Potential," *Performing Arts Review*, 8, no. 4 (1978): 425-56.

Carnegie Corporation. *Keeping PACE With the New Television*. New York: Carnegie Corporation, 1980.

Carr, Robert. "In Your Best Interest." *American Arts* (September 1981): 14-15.

Chappell, John, and Salinitre, Laurie. "The Performing Arts on Commercial Television." Paper presented at Arts Management Seminar, Columbia University, 1980.

Clark, George. "Footlights Districts." *The Cultural Post*, January/February 1982, pp. 1-6.

Clotfelter, Charles T., and Salamon, Lester M. *The Federal Government and the Nonprofit Sector: The Impact of the 1981 Tax Act on Individual Charitable Giving*. Washington, D.C.: The Urban Institute, 1981.

Cohn, R. B. "ABCs of DBS." *Home Video*, May 1982.

Coleman, William. *Grants in the Humanities: A Scholar's Guide to Funding Sources*. New York: Neal-Schuman, 1980.

_____; Keller, David; and Pfeffer, Arthur. *A Casebook of Grant Proposals in the Humanities*. New York: Neal-Schuman, 1982.

Collection Decentralization Program, Solomon R. Guggenheim Museum. New York. Brochure. Spring 1982.

Conference Tapes, Media Alliance of New York State. Conference, June 1981.

Connors, Tracy D., ed.-in-chief. *The Nonprofit Organization Handbook*. New York: McGraw Hill, 1980.

Convisser, Martin. "The Arts and Transportation." In *The Arts and City Planning,* pp. 80-87. Edited by Robert Porter. New York: American Council for the Arts, 1980.

The Council of New York Law Associates, Volunteer Lawyers for the Arts, Community Law Offices. *The New York Not-For-Profit Organization Manual.* New York: Volunteer Lawyers for the Arts, 1978.

Crawford, Ted. Managing Director, Midwest Playwrights' Program, The Playwrights' Center, Minneapolis, Minnesota. Interview, 24 April 1982 by telephone.

Cultural Assistance Center. *Partners: A Practical Guide to Corporate Support of the Arts.* New York: Cultural Assistance Center, 1982.

Cultural Resources/Economic Development, Strengths and Limitations, a Roundtable. December 8, 1980: Final Report for the U.S. Department of Commerce. Washington, D.C.: The Brookings Institution, 1980.

"Culture: A 'Miracle' in Carolina." *U.S. News and World Reports,* 26 December 1977 - 2 January 1978, pp. 64-75.

Dance Theater Workshop, New York City. *Membership Kit 1980/81.*

_____, New York City. *Ten Year Report.* April 1, 1981.

Denver Children's Museum. Press Material. Fall 1981.

Donaldson, Lufkin, and Jenrette Securities Corporation. *Industry Viewpoint: Cable Television 1981.* New York: Donaldson, Lufkin, and Jenrette, 1981.

Driver, William G. Managing Director, Twin Cities Metropolitan Arts Alliance, Minneapolis-St. Paul, Minnesota. Personal letter, 12 May 1982.

Dunning, Jennifer. "Videotape—Almost Everyone's Using It." *The New York Times,* 3 February 1980, pp. 16-17.

Earle, David. "The Video Boom: Does It Mean Big Money for the Arts?" *American Arts* (September 1980): 20-21.

Easter, Leonard. Director of Legal Services, Volunteer Lawyers for the Arts, New York City. Interview, June 16, 1981.

The Economic Impact of the Arts, Conference at Cornell University, 1982. Abstracts.

Egan, Jack. "Will Cable Manhattan Keep Up With the Sticks?" *New York Magazine,* 28 September 1981, pp. 16, 18.

Elsen, Albert, and Merryman, John Henry. "Art Replicas: A Question of Ethics." *Art News,* 78 (February 1979): 61.

Fantel, Hans. "Getting High-Fidelity From Cable." *The New York Times,* 5 July 1981, p. 17.

Ferris, Susan. "Cable Television: A Primer." Paper presented at Arts Management Seminar, Columbia University, 1981.

Fichandler, Zelda. "The Long Revolution." In *1978 TCG Conference Report.* Edited by Arthur Ballet and Lindy Zesch. New York: Theatre Communications Group, 1978. pp. 10-24.

Focke, Anne. Director, and/or, Seattle, Washington. Interviews, 9 June 1981 and 23 May 1982 by telephone.

Ford, John B. *New Programs for New Outlets.* New York: Aspen Institute for Humanistic Studies, 1979.

42nd Street Theater Row. Publicity Packet. Spring 1982.

Gallery Association of New York State. *About the Gallery Association.* Harrison, New York: Gallery Association of New York State, 1980.

Gilbert, Julie Noel. "Tax Wise." *American Arts* (May 1981): 10–12.

Gladstone, Michael. Director, The Publishing Center for Cultural Resources, New York City. Interview, 12 May 1982.

Gottlicher, Ulrike. "Shared Opera Productions." Paper presented at Arts Management Seminar, Columbia University, 1981.

Gottlieb, Len. Boston Children's Museum. Personal letter. 8 February 1982.

Greater Philadelphia Cultural Alliance. Publicity Packet. Spring 1982.

Greene, Alexis. "The Coming Impact of Technology on the Arts." *The New York Times,* 26 February 1978.

Gruen, Erica, and Lustgarten, Marc. "The Electronic Concert Hall." *American Arts* 12 (March 1981): 14–15.

Hallowell, Mary Louise, ed. *Cable Handbook.* Washington, D.C.: Communications Press, 1975.

Hauptman, Barbara, Director of Operations, Theatre Development Fund. Interview, 16 November 1981.

Helman, Lillian. *An Organizational Manual for Chamber Ensemble.* New York: Chamber Music America, 1981.

Henn, Harry G., and Pfeifer, Michael George. "Nonprofit Groups: Factors Influencing Choice of Form." *Wake Forest Law Review,* 11 (June 1975): 181–217.

Holsendolph, Ernest. "A Cable Bill Alarms Municipalities." *The New York Times,* 26 July 1982, sec. C, p. 15.

_____ "Tougher Times for Cable TV." *The New York Times,* 11 July 1982, sec. 3, pp. 1, 24.

Independent Cinema Artists and Producers. Publicity Material, September 1981.

Internal Revenue Service. *Exempt Organizations Continuing Professional Education Technical Instruction Program for 1982.* Washington, D.C., 1982.

Internal Revenue Service Publications:

> #578 *Tax Information for Private Foundations and Foundation Managers* (October 1981)
>
> #557 *How to Apply for and Retain Exempt Status for Your Organization* (February 1980)
>
> #526 *Charitable Contributions* (November 1981)
>
> #598 *Tax on Unrelated Business Income of Exempt Organizations* (September 1981)
>
> #561 *Determining the Value of Donated Property* (November 1981)

Jeffri, Joan. *The Emerging Arts: Management, Survival, and Growth.* New York: Praeger, 1980.

Johnson, Leland L. *Cable Television and the Question of Protecting Local Broadcasting.* Santa Monica, California: Rand Corporation, 1970.

Joint Purchasing Corporation. *Index of Purchasing Agreements.* New York: April 1981.

Jones, Phil. Executive Director, Ithaca Video Project, Ithaca, New York. Interview, 20 July 1981.

"Kicking the Grantsmanship Habit." *News Monitor of Philanthropy* 11 (January 1981): 1, 16–18.

The Kitchen Center for Video, Music, Dance, and Performance, New York. Press Material. July 1981.

Lakelands Consortium in Support of the Arts, Oshkosh, Wisconsin. Publicity material. Spring 1982.

Lanegran, David. Workshop #1 Case Study: The Role of the Arts In Urban Economic Development: The Case of Landmark Center, St. Paul, Minnesota. Professor of Urban Geography, Macalaster College; President, Minnesota Landmarks. From Partners for Livable Places.

Leaming, Susan. "From Theater to Television: Three Approaches to Visual Translation." Masters Thesis, School of the Arts, Columbia University, 1981.

Levy, Lynn. "The Cooperative Orchestra." Paper presented at Arts Management Seminar, Columbia University, Spring 1981.

Lidell, Wendy. Assistant Director, Association of Independent Video and Filmmakers. Interview, 2 September 1981.

Little, Stuart W. *After the FACT, Conflict and Consensus: A Report on the First American Congress of Theatres.* New York: Arno, 1975.

Lowry, W. McNeil, ed. *The Performing Arts and American Society.* Englewood Cliffs, New Jersey: Prentice-Hall, 1978.

MacArthur, Mary. Executive Director, The Kitchen Center for Video, Music, Dance, and Performance, New York City. Interview, 8 May 1981.

Marlowe, Howard. "How to Affect Legislation Before It Affects You." *The Grantsmanship Center News,* January/February 1978, pp. 23–30, 47–54.

Marron, Vincent and Southern, Hugh. "Ticket Voucher Systems." *ACUCAA Bulletin,* Supplement, no. 79, May 1980. Madison, Wisconsin: Association of College, University, and Community Arts Administrators, 1980.

Marshall, Richard. Manager, Charlotte Opera, Charlotte, North Carolina. Interview, 14 January 1982 by telephone.

Materials for the Arts. Publicity Material. New York: Department of Cultural Affairs, 1981.

Mayer, Martin. *About Television.* New York: Harper and Row, 1972.

_____. *Cable and the Arts.* Report prepared for Sloan Commission on Cable Communications, New York, 1971.

McGovern, James J. "The Exemption Provisions of Subchapter F." *Tax Lawyer* 29 (Spring 1976): 523–48.

Media Alliance of New York State. Taped discussions from Conference. June 1981.

Metropolitan Cultural Alliance, Boston, Massachusetts. Publicity Packet. Spring 1982.

Meyer, Karl E. *The Art Museum: Power, Money, Ethics.* New York: William Morrow, 1979.

Mid-America Dance Network. Kansas City, Missouri. Publicity Material, 1980.

Miller, John. Chemical Bank, New York City. Interview, 20 November 1981.

Miller, Lisa Farber. "Creative Self-Sufficiency." Speech presented at the annual meeting of the Ohio Arts Council, 17 September 1981. (Photocopied.)

Mokwa, Michael P.; Dawson, William M.; Prieve, E. Arthur. *Marketing the Arts.* New York: Praeger, 1979.

Morgan, Kitty. Executive Director, Independent Cinema Artists and Producers, New York City. Interview, 2 September 1981.

Netzer, Dick. *The Subsidized Muse.* New York: Cambridge University Press, 1978.

New York City Commission for Cultural Affairs. *Self Help: Earned Income Opportunities for Cultural Organizations.* Conference Proceedings. New York: Department of Cultural Affairs, 26 January 1982.

Newsom, Barbara Y., and Silver, Adele Z., eds. *The Art Museum as Educator.* Los Angeles: University of California Press, 1978.

1976 Session Laws, chapter 902. Trusts. Cultural Resources Trusts. Article 13-E NYS Cultural Resources Act, July 27, 1976.

Non-Standard Television Agreement, American Federation of Musicians of the United States and Canada, May 1, 1980–May 31, 1982. New York: American Federation of Musicians, 1980.

O'Connor, John J. "High Quality on Premium Channels." *The New York Times,* 20 September 1981, p. 37.

O'Donnell, Thomas, and Gissen, Jay. "A Vaster Wasteland?" *Forbes,* 24 May 1982, pp. 109–116.

Oleck, Howard L. *Nonprofit Corporations, Organizations, and Associations,* 4th ed. Englewood Cliffs, New Jersey: Prentice-Hall, 1979. 3rd. ed. Englewood Cliffs, New Jersey: Prentice Hall, 1974.

Partners for Livable Places. *Economics of Amenity News,* 1 December 1980. Special Issue: The Economics of Amenity Program. Vol. 1, no. 4.

_____. *Economics of Amenity News,* May 1981 Vol. 2, No. 9.

_____. Press Material, Washington, D.C. January 1982.

Peck, Ben. Director, New York Cornet and Sacbut Ensemble, New York City. Interview, 10 March 1982.

Petrucelli, Alan W. "42nd Street Theater Row." *Showbill,* April 1982.

Pilot Project for Advancement of Early Music and Dance in New York City. Supporting Materials. Spring 1982.

Pittas, Michael J. "Planning for the Arts." In *The Arts and City Planning,* pp. 18–23. Edited by Robert Porter. New York: American Council for the Arts, 1980.

The Playwrights' Center, Minneapolis. Publicity Packet.

Plumstead Theatre Society v. Commissioner 74 T.C. 1324, 1980.

Pollack, Andrew. "CBS Requests Approval for 5 Pay-TV Systems." *The New York Times*, 4 August 1982, sec D. pp. 1, 6.

"Profile: The Theater Row Story." Press Kit. 42nd Street Development Corporation, January 1982.

A Quick Guide to Loans and Emergency Funds. New York: Center for Arts Information, 1982.

Reichard, Stephen. Livet/Reichard, New York City. Interview, 1 June 1981.

Report to the President, Presidential Task Force on the Arts and Humanities, Washington, D.C., October 1981.

Rice, John. Association of Independent Video and Filmmakers, New York City. Interview, 2 September 1981.

Rice, Michael. *Public Television: Issues of Purpose and Governance*. New York: Aspen Institute for Humanistic Studies, 1981.

Rifkind, Carol. "Cultural Tourism: A New Opportunity for the Industrial City?" *Environmental Comment*, January 1981, pp. 4–7.

Rosenbaum, Lee. "MoMA's Construction Project: Reflections on a Glass Tower." *Art News*, November 1977, pp. 12–16, 21–24.

_____. "A New Foundation for MoMA's Tower." *Art News*, February 1980, pp. 64–75.

Roud, Richard. *Cable Television and the Arts*. Report prepared for Sloan Commission on Cable Communications, New York, 1971.

Salmans, Sandra. "Will Cable TV Be Invaded By Commercials?" *The New York Times*, 26 June 1981, sec. 2, p. 25.

Sample Production Contract. Volunteer Lawyers for the Arts Conference: "Cable Production: What Every Arts Organization Should Know." New York University, 20–21 May 1982.

Schrage, Michael. "Home Electronics: Images of the 80's." *New York Magazine*, 17 November 1980, pp. 38–56.

Schwartz, Tony. "The Cable-TV Scramble." *The New York Times*, 23 December 1981, sec. C, p. 8.

_____. "Opportunities Knock for Performers and Producers." *The New York Times*, 5 July 1981, pp. 1, 22.

_____. "Where Cable TV Stands After FCC Deregulation." *The New York Times*, 21 August 1980.

Seattle Artists' Housing Handbook, Seattle Arts Commission, Seattle, Washington. April 1980.

Shanahan, James L. "Using the Arts in Economic Development Strategies." Cultural and Leisure Studies Unit, Center for Urban Studies, University of Akron.

Sheldon, Richard. Program Officer, The Ford Foundation, New York City. Interview, 2 June 1981.

Shillingburg, J. Edward. "Museums, Reproduction Sales and Taxes." Metropolitan Museum of Art Workshop at Asia House, New York, 5 February 1982.

Should You Incorporate? New York: The Council of New York Law Associates, 1977.

Shuler, Arlene. Executive Director, Volunteer Lawyers for the Arts, New York City. Interview, 16 June 1981.

Simril, Geoffrey S. "The Arts Edge," *American Arts,* (January 1982), pp. 18–21.

Sinclair, Stephen. "Arts Giving and Taxes." *The Cultural Post* 8 (May/June 1982).

Sloan Commission on Cable Communications. *On the Cable: The Television of Abundance.* New York: McGraw Hill, 1971.

Smith, C. Ray. "A Tour of Museum Mile." *Cooper Hewitt Newsletter,* 3 (Winter 1980): 1.

Smith, Craig. "The Pain of Cities." *Foundation News,* January/February 1982, pp. 9–13.

Smith, Helen C. "A Culture Boom Is City's Boon." *The Atlanta Constitution,* 14 December 1981, pp. 1-C, 5-C.

Smith, Ronn. *Theatre Crafts* Special Issue: Cable Television. "ABC arts," "CBS Cable," "RCTV Cable," "Home Box Office." 15 (October 1981).

Smith, Sally Bedell. "Reporter's Notebook: Cable Meeting." *New York Times,* 18 June 1983, p. 48.

Smith, Thomas S. Executive Director, Lakelands Consortium in Support of the Arts, Oshkosh, Wisconsin. Personal letter, 31 March 1928.

Snedcof, Harold. "San Francisco: Cultural Overkill?" *Federal Design Matters,* Fall 1981, p. 14.

Solomon R. Guggenheim Museum, New York. Press Release, 23 October 1981.

Southern Opera Conference. Publicity Packet. Spring 1982.

Stasio, Marilyn. "The Reprieve—for now—of Theater Row." *Newsday,* 30 August 1981, sec. III, pp. 1-2.

Stelzer, Irwin, and Alpert, Geraldine. "Will Cable Save the Arts?" New York: National Economic Research Associates, 1982.

Stone, John K. P. "A Tax Attorney Calls for Clarity." *Museum Stores Association* (Winter 1980), pp. 14–15, 38.

Sullivan, Linda. "Profile: The Cooper Hewitt Museum." Paper presented at Arts Management Seminar, Columbia University, Spring 1982.

Theatre Development Fund. *Annual Report.* 1979–80. New York: n.p., 1980.

Twin Cities Metropolitan Arts Alliance. Grant Proposal for period 9/1/81 to 8/31/83.

Ullberg, Alan D., and Ullberg, Patricia. *Museum Trusteeship.* Washington, D.C.: American Association of Museums, 1981.

Vayer, M. Scott. Outline of Remarks for Cable and Pay TV Panel, Film and Video Conference for Cultural Institutions, New York State Council on the Arts, 1982.

"Viewpoint: Brian O'Doherty." *The Cultural Post,* May/June 1981, pp. 10–12.

Volunteer Lawyers for the Arts Conference: "Cable Production: What Every Arts Organization Needs to Know." New York University, New York. 20–21 May 1982.

Weinlein, Craig W. "Federal Taxation of Not-for-Profit Arts Organizations: A Primer for Arts Managers." *Journal of Arts Management and Law* 12 (Summer 1982): 33–50.

White, David. Executive Director, Dance Theater Workshop, New York City. Interviews, 4 June 1981 and 13 May 1982 by telephone.

White, Robin. "Great Expectations: Artists' TV Guide." *Artforum,* Summer 1982, pp. 40–47.

White, Virginia. *Grants for the Arts.* New York: Plenum, 1980.

Wiener, Louise. "The Arts and Economic Development." In *The Arts and City Planning,* pp. 58–66. Edited by Robert Porter. New York: American Council for the Arts, 1980.

Winfrey, Cary. "Leading Consultant Foresees the 'Wired Society.' " *The New York Times,* 5 July 1981, pp. 1, 21.

INDEX

Joan Jeffri is director and founder of the Research Center for Arts and Culture and adjunct professor of arts administration at Columbia University. She is the author of *The Emerging Arts: Management, Survival, and Growth* (1980), editor of *Artisthelp: The Artist's Guide to Work-Related Human and Social Services* (1989), and an executive editor of the *Journal of Arts Management and Law*, where she has supervised special issues on public policy, labor relations, and social responsibility and the arts. Jeffri has taught and advised on arts administration on four continents. A former professional actress, she earned her B.F.A. cum laude at Boston University, and also studied at the Bristol Old Vic Theatre School, Columbia and Northwestern universities, and with Uta Hagen at the Herbert Berghof Studio.